Social Status and Cultur

How does cultural hierarchy relate to social hierarchy? Do the more advantaged consume 'high' culture, while the less advantaged consume popular culture? Or has cultural consumption in contemporary societies become individualised to such a degree that there is no longer any social basis for cultural consumption? Leading scholars from the UK, the USA, Chile, France, Hungary and the Netherlands systematically examine the social stratification of arts and culture. They evaluate the 'class–culture homology argument' of Pierre Bourdieu and Herbert Gans; the 'individualisation arguments' of Anthony Giddens, Ulrich Beck and Zygmunt Bauman; and the 'omnivore–univore argument' of Richard Peterson. They also demonstrate that, consistent with Max Weber's class–status distinction, cultural consumption, as a key element of lifestyle, is stratified primarily on the basis of social status rather than by social class.

TAK WING CHAN teaches sociology at the University of Oxford, where he is also a fellow and tutor of New College, and the Director of the Oxford Network for Social Inequality Research.

Social Status and Cultural Consumption

Edited by
TAK WING CHAN

CAMBRIDGE
UNIVERSITY PRESS

CAMBRIDGE UNIVERSITY PRESS
Cambridge, New York, Melbourne, Madrid, Cape Town,
Singapore, São Paulo, Delhi, Mexico City

Cambridge University Press
The Edinburgh Building, Cambridge CB2 8RU, UK

Published in the United States of America by Cambridge University Press, New York

www.cambridge.org
Information on this title: www.cambridge.org/9781107406988

First published 2010
First paperback edition 2012

A catalogue record for this publication is available from the British Library

Library of Congress Cataloguing in Publication Data
Social status and cultural consumption / edited by Tak Wing Chan.
    p.   cm.
Includes bibliographical references and index.
ISBN 978-0-521-19446-4
1. Consumption (Economics) – Social aspects.   2. Social status.
I. Chan, Tak Wing.   II. Title.

HC79.C6S63   2010
306.3 – dc22   2010001100

ISBN 978-0-521-19446-4 Hardback
ISBN 978-1-107-40698-8 Paperback

To my mother,
Wai Fong Poon

and

in fond memory of my father,
Chun Mou Chan
(1925–2007)

Contents

Figures

Tables

Contributors

ARTHUR S. ALDERSON is Professor of Sociology at Indiana University.

ERZSÉBET BUKODI is a research fellow at the Institute of Education, University of London.

TAK WING CHAN is a university lecturer in sociology, and a fellow and tutor of New College, University of Oxford.

PHILIPPE COULANGEON is Chargé de Recherche of the Centre National de la Recherche Scientifique, Paris.

JOHN H. GOLDTHORPE is an emeritus fellow of Nuffield College, University of Oxford.

ISAAC HEACOCK is a PhD candidate in sociology at Indiana University.

AZAMAT JUNISBAI is Assistant Professor of Sociology at Pitzer College.

GERBERT KRAAYKAMP is Professor of Sociology at Nijmegen University.

YANNICK LEMEL is Inspecteur Général of the Centre de Recherche en Économie et Statistique, Paris.

FLORENCIA TORCHE is Assistant Professor of Sociology at New York University.

WOUT ULTEE is Professor of Sociology at Nijmegen University.

KOEN VAN EIJCK is an associate professor in the Department of Arts and Cultural Studies of Erasmus University.

Acknowledgments

This book grew out of a research project that was jointly funded by the Economic and Social Research Council and the Arts and Humanities Research Council (RES-063-27-0200). At the stage of manuscript preparation, I have received further and very timely support from the Ludwig Family Foundation, via New College, Oxford. I am very grateful to these funding bodies, and to Professor Frank Trentmann, director of the Cultures of Consumption Research Programme, for their support, material and intellectual, over the past few years.

Many colleagues have read and commented on earlier drafts of this book, or have acted as discussants of our presentations at various meetings. They include Gunn Elisabeth Birkelund, Ann Bridgwood, Catherine Bunting, David Halle, Douglas Holt, Tally Katz-Gerro, Emily Keaney, Paul Lambert, Edward Laumann, Andrew Miles, Michèle Ollivier, Anni Oskala, Richard Peterson, Mike Savage, Sara Selwood, Kees van Rees, Alan Warde and Meir Yaish. Thank you all for your thoughtful comments. All remaining flaws of this book are, of course, mine alone.

At a more practical level, I am grateful to Adam Houlbrook for his skilful editing, to Jon Billam for his careful copy-editing, and to Brendan Halpin, Frank Holzwarth and Sehar Tahir for patient guidance through the intricacies of LaTeX.

Finally, almost all contributors of this book are long-standing members of the Research Committee 28 on Social Stratification and Mobility of the International Sociological Association. For many years, RC28 has been a most fruitful, stimulating and collegiate forum for students of social stratification. Many ideas of this book were first mooted and discussed at its meetings. As this collection is, in many ways, a collaborative RC28 endeavour, the royalties from the sale of this book will go to a travel fund of the research committee, in support of young scholars attending future RC28 meetings.

Tak Wing Chan

1 Social status and cultural consumption

TAK WING CHAN AND JOHN H. GOLDTHORPE

The research project on which this volume reports was conceived with two main aims in mind. The first and most immediate aim was to extend our knowledge of the social stratification of cultural consumption, and to do so in a cross-national perspective. In this regard, we obviously looked to build on previous research in this area, which has in fact been steadily growing in volume over recent decades. At the same time, though, it appeared to us that in certain respects this research was subject to limitations, especially in its treatment of social stratification, both conceptually and, in turn, operationally. As a result, the large potential that such research offers for increasing our more general understanding of the form of stratification of present-day societies was not being fully realised. The second aim of our project was therefore to bring research on the social stratification of cultural consumption into a somewhat closer relationship with mainstream stratification research, and in the hope that a better appreciation might thus be gained, on the one hand, of how social inequalities in cultural consumption actually arise and are sustained and, on the other hand, of what these inequalities reveal about the larger structures of social advantage and disadvantage of which they form part.[1]

In this introductory chapter, we first of all outline a number of arguments concerning the social stratification of cultural consumption that have emerged from previous research and theory, and seek to provide some evaluation of their present standing. We also pose, in each case, a number of questions that arise and call for further investigation. In the second section of the chapter, we turn to our criticisms of the treatment of social stratification in previous work, and introduce the alternative and, we believe, more conceptually and empirically adequate approach

[1] Most participants in the project have a background in social stratification research and a shared history of participation in the activities of the International Sociological Association Research Committee 28 on Social Stratification and Mobility.

that we wish to follow, and that turns on the Weberian distinction between *class* and *status*. This section thus indicates the motivation for the development of the status scales that are described in detail in Chapter 2. In the third section, we then take up a number of other methodological issues that relate to the kinds of data that have been typically exploited and the analytical techniques that have been typically applied in the course of the project, and also to our comparative ambitions and strategies. And finally, in the fourth section, we briefly introduce each of the national contributions that make up Chapters 3 to 8, and point out features of particular interest. Our assessment of the main empirical findings of the project and of their theoretical implications, as viewed in comparative perspective, we reserve for the concluding chapter of the volume.

1.1 Previous research and theoretical argument

Research by sociologists into the social stratification of cultural consumption has been in large part prompted by wide-ranging debates on cultural change that have been recurrent in Western societies in the course of the twentieth century. Central to these debates are concerns over the apparent divergence of 'highbrow' and 'lowbrow' culture, the growing importance of the mass media, and the rise of commercialised, 'mass' culture.[2] Sociologists have sought to intervene in two main ways. They have engaged in research to increase the body of empirical evidence on the nature and extent of differences in cultural tastes and consumption across social strata; and they have tried to provide some theoretical explanation and understanding of the interrelations that can thus be shown to exist between cultural and social hierarchies.

[2] Contributions to these debates – from widely differing socio-political standpoints – that had evident influence on sociologists include F. R. Leavis (1930), Q. Leavis (1932), Benjamin (1936), Horkheimer and Adorno (1972), Eliot (1948) and MacDonald (1957). It may be added here that in their work in the area in question sociologists have in the main followed authors such as the above in understanding 'culture' not in the wider anthropological sense of the term but rather in the narrower sense of, to quote a recent formulation by Gans (1999, p. 5), 'the practices, goods and ideas classified broadly under the arts (including literature, music, architecture and design etc., and the products of all other print media, electronic media, etc.) whether used for education and aesthetic and spiritual enlightenment or for entertainment and diversion'. We accept a similar understanding in this collection.

For example, in a relatively early but still often cited study, Herbert Gans (1974) presents a range of research findings in support of the view that 'highbrow', 'lowbrow' and also versions of 'middlebrow' cultural taste and consumption do in fact rather systematically map onto the 'socio-economic' stratification of American society. Culture, that is to say, has to be seen as stratified rather than 'massified'. And, correspondingly, Gans rejects more critical, 'elitist', accounts that would represent all other than highbrow culture as mass culture, and as the product simply of commercial greed and public ignorance. In his view, a number of 'taste cultures' have to be recognised, each of which embodies differing aesthetic values and standards that can be understood as having, so to speak, functional equivalence as responses to the differing wants and resources, material and symbolic, of individuals in socially more or less advantaged positions. Thus, in this perspective, all taste cultures are to be regarded as being, at least potentially, of equal worth and validity: that is, as being equally appropriate to the social contexts within which they are formed and expressed.

Gans's work can then be taken as providing one of the leading examples of what we would label as 'homology' arguments: that is, arguments to the effect that a close correspondence exists between social and cultural stratification, and one that is created and maintained by certain identifiable processes. Homology arguments, in one version or another, could in fact be regarded as representing the orthodoxy in the field for some twenty years or more after Gans wrote. And it may be noted that in a second, updated edition of his book, Gans (1999) reasserts its central theses with only rather minor modifications.

However, during the period in question, a new, far more ambitious and generally more influential form of the homology argument was elaborated in the work of Pierre Bourdieu (see esp. Bourdieu, 1984). For Bourdieu, the correspondence that prevails between social and cultural stratification is yet more strongly determined than that envisaged by Gans and has also a much larger significance. Social classes display different patterns of cultural taste and consumption – and also of distaste and aversion – as part of their characteristic lifestyles, along with closely related patterns of material consumption as, for example, in food and dress. The internal consistency or 'semantic unity' of these lifestyles, and likewise their sharp demarcation across classes, is the product and expression of the *habitus* of individual class members: that is, of the socially constituted 'system of dispositions' that they acquire in early life, that exerts a quite pervasive influence on their perceptions and practices, and that reflects the possibilities and exigencies that are created by particular 'class conditions'.[3]

Further, though, in Bourdieu's analysis, far more is here involved than cultural differentiation alone. The cultural field, he insists, no less than the economic field, is one in which class competition and conflict are always present. The 'dominant classes' of modern societies use their superior 'cultural capital', no less than their superior economic capital, in order to maintain their position of dominance. Differentiation inevitably serves as a means of underwriting hierarchy. More specifically, members of dominant classes seek to demonstrate and confirm the superiority of their own lifestyle over those of other classes by arrogating to it cultural forms that they can represent as 'canonical', 'legitimate' or otherwise 'distinguished' – while maintaining 'aesthetic distance' from other forms deemed to be inferior. Through such 'symbolic violence', as exerted, in particular, within the educational system but also more generally in public life, cultural capital can in fact be converted into economic capital, and cultural reproduction thus serves as a crucial component in social reproduction more generally.

Largely under the influence of Bourdieu, sociological thinking about the relationship of social and cultural stratification did then tend to be dominated by notions of homology at least up to the 1990s. At this time, though, Bourdieu's work began to attract a greater amount of sceptical commentary, especially American, and this can now be seen as opening the way for the more radical criticism and the alternative theoretical approaches that subsequently emerged.

One focus of scepticism was on the extent to which Bourdieu's analyses could be generalised from the French – or even perhaps from the Parisian – case.[4] Thus, several authors (e.g. Lamont and Lareau, 1988; Lamont, 1992; Halle, 1993; Erickson, 1996) observed that, at least in North America, members of higher social strata were not obviously distinguished by their refined aesthetic tastes and their levels

---

[3] The use of the term 'homology' to refer to this form of correspondence between social and cultural stratification would appear in fact to originate with Bourdieu (see e.g. Bourdieu, 1984, pp. 175–177).

[4] The surveys that provided most of the empirical material used by Bourdieu (1984) dated from the 1960s and were not based on samples of any well-defined population. Parisians were in fact heavily over-represented as compared to 'provincials' (as also were members of higher as compared to lower social strata).

of participation in high cultural activities; and that the nature and extent of their cultural consumption was often not regarded, either by themselves or by others, as playing any great part in the maintenance of their social superiority.

Further, though, there were doubts as to whether *in general* the pursuit of cultural exclusiveness could be regarded as a characteristic feature of the lifestyles of dominant classes. In the course of earlier debates on mass culture, researchers such as Wilensky (1964) had already produced evidence to show that participation in such culture – via TV, newspapers, magazines etc. – was in fact quite extensive across *all* strata of American society; and also that while the small minority who did effectively 'insulate' themselves from mass – or popular – culture tended to be of high status, they in no way constituted a dominant elite. They were, rather, a marginalised group, 'generally estranged from the major power centres in the United States' (Wilensky, 1964, p. 194; and for Great Britain, cf. Abrams, 1958). Thus, in the 1990s attention was drawn back to this work and at the same time to that of commentators such as Shils (1972) and Bell (1976), who, pre-Bourdieu, had been more concerned to stress the diversity than the uniformity of lifestyles and cultural orientations among higher social strata and, more generally, the lack – and perhaps the growing lack – of correspondence in modern societies between social and cultural hierarchies.

In this context, new approaches to the understanding of the interrelation of cultural consumption and social stratification were thus encouraged, and homology arguments became challenged by rival arguments of at least two main kinds.

The first of these we would label as 'individualisation' arguments. Such arguments have a rather close affinity with more general claims of the decay or even 'death' of social class that became common in the later twentieth century. Authors such as Beck (1992) or Giddens (1991) maintain that the societies of 'high' or 'late' modernity are characterised by an accelerating process of the 'individualisation of social inequality'. In many respects, these authors would accept that structures of inequality display a remarkable stability over time. None the less, they believe, class – and status – have declining influences on social action and, above all, on the formation of lifestyles and of the patterns of consumption, material and cultural, through which they are expressed. In these respects, class no longer provides an adequate 'context of orientation' and status-based social milieux 'lose their lustre' (Beck, 1992, pp. 88–89). Rather, rising standards of living, greater geographical and social mobility and exogamy, and a growing awareness of alternative social bases of identity – for example, gender, ethnicity or sexuality – all help to free individuals from class constraints and status preoccupations and allow them to develop their own lifestyles as a matter of personal choice and so as to give expression 'to a particular narrative of self-identity'. Indeed, not only do individuals increasingly choose their own lifestyles but they are increasingly *forced* to do so. They have no choice but to choose, and, moreover, since lifestyles are now followed 'reflexively', they are always open to revision and change 'in the light of the mobile nature of self-identity' (Giddens, 1991, pp. 80–81).

What is then implied is that any homology between social and cultural hierarchies that may have existed in the past – in more 'traditional' forms of society – is now in dissolution. No expectation can be maintained that different patterns of cultural consumption will stand in some systematic relationship to structures of social inequality. The processes that once created and sustained such a relationship – processes of socialisation into distinctive class beliefs, values and practices – have lost their force. In Warde's apt phrase (1997, p. 8), the emphasis shifts dramatically 'from *habitus* to freedom'. Indeed, in more extreme individualisation arguments, such as those advanced by Bauman (1988, 2002), consumption at large becomes celebrated as 'the focus and playground for individual freedom'. And further, in striking contrast to the position taken up by Bourdieu, consumption, in its symbolic aspects especially, is seen not as a field in which social hierarchy is asserted and reproduced but, rather, as one in which a greater proportion of the population than ever before can now engage in 'self-assertion' and without facing 'the danger of imminent and conclusive defeat'. New 'patterns of success' open up for the achievement of symbolic distinction through consumer rivalry and 'taste contests' that can be pursued 'not just in ideologically induced fantasies but in practical life, by the *majority* in capitalist societies' (Bauman, 1988, pp. 58–61).[5]

---

[5] Rather remarkably, in his several references to Bourdieu, Bauman appears not to appreciate how radically their views diverge.

However, while individualisation arguments thus call homology arguments directly into question, their influence on sociologists with research interests in the field of cultural consumption would appear, so far at least, to be rather limited. Two reasons for this can be suggested. First, individualisation arguments are concerned with consumption in general, and although clearly intended to apply to its cultural no less than to its material aspects, the former have not received any special attention. Second, individualisation arguments cannot themselves claim any strong research basis. Their leading proponents are 'social theorists', writing in a largely data-free mode. Thus, while individualisation arguments have been discussed a good deal in both sociological and wider intellectual circles, they could scarcely be regarded as empirically compelling.

From this point of view, then, the second main challenge that has been raised to homology arguments is of a quite contrasting kind. This comes in the form of arguments that are specifically concerned with cultural consumption *and* that are grounded in by now quite extensive social research – that is, what we label as 'omnivore–univore' arguments. As already noted, the work of Wilensky and others in the 1960s revealed that members of higher social strata did not in the main have any aversion to popular culture and were indeed fairly regular consumers of it – together, perhaps, with various kinds of high culture. In the 1990s new research, notably by Richard Peterson and his associates (see esp. Peterson, 1992; Peterson and Simkus, 1992; Peterson and Kern, 1996) led to what were in effect developments of insights that this earlier work provided but that had been largely neglected while homology arguments remained to the fore.

These developments, in the form of omnivore–univore arguments, derive, like individualisation arguments, from the idea that a close mapping of cultural onto social hierarchies no longer exists. But rather than claiming that cultural consumption is now free of *any* systematic relationship with social stratification, proponents of omnivore–univore arguments see a new relationship as having emerged. In present-day societies, they would maintain, members of higher social strata, apart perhaps from a very small minority, do not shun popular or lowbrow culture but, as Wilensky observed, they regularly participate in it; and indeed, if anything, do so yet more actively than members of lower strata. However, a significant difference remains in the consumption of high or more 'distinguished' cultural forms. Such consumption is in fact largely confined to higher social strata – even if being less typical than homology arguments would suggest – while in lower strata consumption tends not to extend beyond more popular forms. In other words, the cultural consumption of individuals in more advantaged social positions differs from that of individuals in less advantaged positions in being both greater *and* wider in its range. It comprises not only more highbrow culture but more middlebrow and lowbrow culture *as well*. The crucial contrast that is created is not then that of 'snob versus slob' but rather that of cultural omnivore versus cultural univore (Peterson, 1992, p. 252).

Since being first advanced, omnivore–univore arguments have in fact aroused wide interest. A good deal of further research, following on from that of Peterson, has been stimulated in a range of modern societies, and with results that have been broadly, if not always entirely, supportive (see e.g. Bryson, 1996, 1997; van Eijck, 2001; López-Sintas and García-Álvarez, 2002, 2004; Coulangeon, 2003; López-Sintas and Katz-Gerro, 2005; van Eijck and Knulst, 2005; Chan and Goldthorpe, 2005, 2007d,e). However, various questions have emerged concerning how exactly omnivore–univore arguments are to be understood and, in particular, concerning the meaning and significance that might best be attached to the idea of cultural omnivorousness and to research findings that document its prevalence among higher social strata.

It has, for example, been observed (see e.g. Sullivan and Katz-Gerro, 2007; Coulangeon and Lemel, 2007) that two different understandings of cultural omnivorousness are possible. It could be taken to refer either to a general cultural 'voraciousness', in the sense of a large appetite for *all* forms of cultural consumption, or, more specifically, to a tendency towards 'taste eclecticism' that finds expression in patterns of cultural consumption that cut across established categories of 'high' and 'low'. In fact, in his early work Peterson himself is quite explicit on this issue: omnivorousness does *not* – or not necessarily – imply a tendency to like everything in a quite undiscriminating way. Rather, what it signifies is simply 'an *openness* to appreciating everything', from which particular tastes and consumption may or may not develop, and is thus primarily to be contrasted with cultural tastes and consumption that are 'based on rigid rules of exclusion' (Peterson and Kern, 1996, p. 904; cf also Peterson, 2005).

Following from this interpretation of omnivorousness, however, it has further been asked whether, insofar as cultural omnivores do display such openness and a consequent disregard for supposed hierarchies of taste, their presence is not largely consistent with individualisation arguments. Omnivore cultural consumption, it has been suggested, may be concerned more with individual self-realisation than with setting down social markers and creating social distinction (see e.g. Wynne and O'Connor, 1998). But it may be noted that Peterson is here again quite unambiguous, at least in the original statement of his position. While omnivorousness should be understood as antithetical to cultural exclusiveness and 'aesthetic distancing', it 'does not imply an indifference to distinctions', and indeed the rise of the cultural omnivore 'may suggest the formulation of new rules governing symbolic boundaries' (Peterson and Kern, 1996, p. 904). In other words, omnivores may be seen as embracing a new aesthetic which, even if more inclusive, democratic and relativist than that which earlier prevailed, can still serve to express cultural *and* social superiority, and especially when set against the far more restricted cultural tastes and consumption of univores (cf. López-Sintas and García-Álvarez, 2002). Furthermore, omnivores may still show discrimination either in the uses that they make of mass or popular culture – for example, through ironic or otherwise condescending uses; or in still rejecting *some* of its particular forms – 'anything but heavy metal' (Bryson, 1996).[6]

Omnivore–univore arguments can then be seen as posing a challenge to homology and to individualisation arguments alike. On the one hand, the idea of a simple matching of social and cultural hierarchies is called into question, as in turn are Bourdieusian claims that cultural taste and consumption closely reflect 'class conditions', via

---

[6] What has, however, to be recognised is that further uncertainty has more recently been created in regard to omnivore–univore arguments as a result of an elaboration suggested by Peterson himself. In recognition of the fact that a very small minority may still be found within higher social strata who do reject popular culture, Peterson (2005) now suggests that this minority should be categorised as 'highbrow univores' in contrast with the more typical 'highbrow omnivores'; and that, correspondingly, 'lowbrow univores' and 'lowbrow omnivores' should also be distinguished. We are ourselves very doubtful about the value of this move. There would seem to be a danger of losing the crucial connotation of omnivorousness as entailing cultural consumption that is relatively wide-ranging in *its extension across*, rather than merely in *its expression within*, generally recognised taste levels.

the mediation of distinctive and exigent forms of *habitus,* and that cultural exclusiveness represents the main form of 'symbolic violence' through which cultural reproduction promotes social reproduction. On the other hand, while over-socialised conceptions of the actor are thus rejected, so too are ideas of cultural consumption as now essentially reflecting no more than the highly personalised choices and self-identity projects that individuals pursue, and in a way that is free of constraints imposed by, and of motivations grounded in, the positions that they hold within structures of social inequality.

It is, then, against the background of the research and theory outlined above that the papers brought together in this volume have been written. A range of questions remain open and are, directly or indirectly, addressed. Have ideas of a homology between social and cultural hierarchies and of cultural exclusiveness serving social reproduction now to be generally abandoned – or may there be some particular societal contexts in which they still apply? Have individualisation arguments been too much neglected, or at least should not more recognition be given to the possibility that in modern societies the relationship between social and cultural stratification has become relatively weak, whatever form it may take? Conversely, even if this relationship, whatever its strength, is now better treated in terms of an omnivore–univore rather than an elite–mass distinction, in which of their possible interpretations do omnivore–univore arguments find most empirical support? And, in any event, may not patterns of cultural consumption and types of consumer be found, at least in particular cultural domains or under particular national conditions, that are not readily characterised in omnivore–univore terms?

We turn next to the approaches and strategies that will be followed in taking up these and related issues, and in regard, first of all, to social stratification.

1.2 The treatment of social stratification: class and status

As we have already remarked, we would see the main weakness of earlier research into the social stratification of cultural consumption as resulting from inadequacies in the way in which stratification has been conceptualised and, in turn, treated in empirical analyses. The source of these inadequacies, we would argue, is a failure to maintain the distinction, classically proposed by Max Weber (1968, vol. 2; pp. 926–939 esp.), between *class* and *status* as two qualitatively different forms of social stratification, the empirical connection between which may vary widely by time and place. In all the papers in the present volume the class/status distinction is explicitly recognised and, as will be seen, plays an important part in the data analyses, and in the interpretations of these analyses, that are presented.

For Weber, and for us, a class structure is one formed by social relations in economic life. Elaborating on Weber, we treat class positions as being ones defined by relations in labour markets and production units and, most immediately, by employment relations. Thus, employers are differentiated from self-employed workers or employees; and salaried employees are in turn differentiated from wage-workers by reference to characteristic features of their employment contracts (cf. Goldthorpe, 2007a, ch. 5). We would not regard classes, understood in this way, as necessarily or even typically forming 'real' sociocultural groupings. In Weber's own words, '"*Klassen*" *sind keine Gemeinschaften*'. Rather, classes are seen as collectivities that exist insofar as 'a number of people have in common a specific causal component of their life-chances' (Weber, 1968, vol. 2, p. 927).[7]

Again following Weber, we would regard a status order as a structure of relations of perceived, and in some degree accepted, social superiority, equality and inferiority among individuals that reflects not their personal qualities but rather the 'social honour' attaching to certain of their positional or perhaps purely ascribed attributes (e.g. 'birth' or ethnicity).[8] The social hierarchy thus created is expressed in

---

[7] It may be noted that our understanding of class is thus clearly different from that of authors, such as Pakulski and Waters (1996) or Kingston (2000) who have claimed 'the death of class', and whose arguments, we believe, also suffer from a failure to distinguish between class and status. In turn, our position differs too from that of Grusky and his associates (see esp. Grusky, 2005; Grusky and Sørensen, 1998; Grusky and Weeden, 2001; Weeden and Grusky, 2005), who, in response to authors such as the above, seek to restore the idea of classes as real sociocultural entities by 'ratcheting down' class analysis to the level of occupations (in this regard, see further Goldthorpe, 2007a, ch. 6). While we ourselves take occupation – along with employment status – as a proxy for class position and again, as will be seen in Chapter 2, as a prime characteristic to which status attaches, we are here concerned, in seeking to make our Weberian approach operational, with quite specific and different aspects of occupations.

[8] Our understanding of status thus differs from that found in some current literature, in particular in more microsociological analysis (e.g. Jasso, 2001),

differential association, and especially in its more intimate forms of what Weber refers to as 'commensality' and 'connubium' – who eats with whom, who sleeps with whom; and further in lifestyles that are seen as appropriate to different status levels. Status affiliations are thus more likely than class affiliations to be 'real' in the sense of ones that are recognised by and meaningful to the social actors involved. None the less, in what Weber refers to as modern 'democratic' societies, status orders may be better thought of as comprising relatively loose networks of social relations, or, in his phrase, 'status circles', rather than sharply demarcated status groups.

The distinction made between class and status is then clear, and, as we will aim to show, it is one that in the analysis of the stratification of cultural consumption takes on a particular relevance and value. First, though, it is of some contextual interest to note how the failure to exploit this distinction in previous work has come about – in fact, in two quite different ways.

On the one hand, and most notably in the American case, this failure reflects a loss of Weberian refinement, already apparent in the 1950s and 1960s, as leading figures in the field of social stratification sought in effect to reinterpret class in terms of status – perhaps on account of anti-Marxist sentiment. Thus, definitions of social classes are offered on such lines as 'strata of society composed of individuals who accept each other as status equals' (Lipset and Bendix, 1959, p. 275) or 'aggregate[s] of persons, within a society, possessing approximately the same status' (Shils, 1975).[9] It is therefore scarcely surprising to find that American authors earlier referred to, such as Gans and Peterson, in advancing homology and omnivore–univore arguments respectively, tend to use the terms 'class' and 'status' as more or less synonymous

where it is in fact on personal qualities and their perceived 'worth' that status chiefly depends. We see value in the distinction suggested long ago by Davis (1949, ch. 4) between status (or 'prestige') and esteem. The former refers to a structure of inequality, while the latter reflects the *conduct* of an individual in a particular position or as the representative of a family, ethnic group etc. In popular English literature in the nineteenth century stock characters were the wicked squire (high on status but low on esteem) with designs on the humble but virtuous serving girl (low on status but high on esteem).

[9] The suggestion of anti-Marxist sentiment would seem to have some warrant here in that both Bendix and Shils were noted Weber scholars and their attempted reduction of class to status – for which they offer no explanation – is otherwise very puzzling.

or to merge them in the idea of 'socioeconomic' status. And while various other stratification 'factors', such as income or education, may then also be taken into consideration, the supposed relationship of these to class and status is left unclear. Thus, either an essentially one-dimensional or, at best, a conceptually quite underdeveloped approach to social stratification is pursued, and one that, we believe, carries serious limitations. While such an approach may readily allow for cultural consumption to be shown to be stratified, in some degree and on some pattern or other, it can provide few insights of relevance to the further task of determining the – possibly quite diverse – social processes or mechanisms through which this stratification is actually generated.

On the other hand, and chiefly in the European case, the distinction between class and status has been elided as a result of efforts not to reduce class to status but rather to reduce status to class – a consequence, in part and at least initially, of the revival of academic Marxism in the 1970s. Status may well be referred to, and in work in the sociology of consumption especially; but status appears then to be treated as little more than an epiphenomenal correlate of class – as, say, in the individualisation arguments of Beck, Giddens or Bauman. Furthermore, with Bourdieu one finds a case made out for treating status in terms of class that is of a quite explicit and elaborated kind.

On Bourdieu's own account, his major work starts out from 'an endeavour to rethink Max Weber's opposition' between class and status (1984, p. xii), and indeed to transcend it. Bourdieu would accept that status is expressed by differential association and above all by style of life. But he then rejects Weber's view of the class positions of individuals or groups as being analytically and empirically separable from their status positions. Rather, status has to be seen as the symbolic aspect of the class structure. And instead of class and status being linked, as Weber puts it, 'in the most varied ways' (1968, p. 932), Bourdieu insists on their necessarily close correspondence – a correspondence which is in fact essential to his homology argument in regard to social and cultural hierarchies. As earlier noted, Bourdieu would see different 'class conditions' as reflected in different forms of *habitus* which in turn create unity within, and differentiation among, lifestyles. And it is then in the cultural field thus constituted that status competition and conflict occur – not as something separate from, and possibly even subversive of, class competition and conflict (cf. Weber, 1968, p. 930) but as their symbolic rather than material expression, and through which cultural reproduction becomes in fact integral to social reproduction. As Weininger (2005, p. 95) has aptly observed, it is when this latter point is understood that 'the full significance of Bourdieu's attempt to yoke together "class" and "status" becomes apparent'.[10]

If, then, in much American work the class/status distinction is lost as a result of what might be seen as conceptual degrading, in the case of Bourdieu, and of others influenced by his work, it is as a result of theoretical *fiat*. But, we would argue, the ultimate outcome is essentially the same, at all events so far as analyses of the social stratification of cultural consumption are concerned. What, for one reason or another, is precluded is any consideration of the idea that class and status, as qualitatively different forms of stratification, may influence cultural consumption in differing degree and in differing ways. Or, in other words, without a clear conceptual distinction between class and status, it is simply impossible to consider hypotheses about their respective effects on cultural consumption.

In our own work, as represented in the papers in this volume, we seek to avoid this limitation. We start out from the Weberian distinction between class and status, and from this we are able to move on directly to an initial theoretical expectation in regard to cultural consumption. That is, the expectation that the stratification of such consumption *will be primarily on the basis of status rather than of class* – and that these two forms of stratification will not, typically, be so closely related to each other as to make it impossible to test whether or not this expectation is borne out.[11] Class position, we would recognise, will tend, through its economic implications, to condition consumption in

[10] The one way in which Bourdieu might be thought to allow for the possibility of some discrepancy between class and status – of the kind to which Weber frequently refers – is where, within what he deems to be the same class, he notes that differences in their command over cultural as compared to economic capital may lead to some 'class fractions' having lifestyles of greater 'distinction' than others. In particular, within the 'dominant class', academics and 'artistic producers' appear to be recognised as in this sense having superior status to industrial and commercial employers, with professionals falling somewhere in-between. However, while, if this interpretation is accepted, it would seem to represent a more substantial concession to Weber's 'opposition' than Bourdieu is ready to acknowledge, it still remains unclear why such differences in status should be seen as only occurring *within* classes – i.e. as relating only to class fractions – rather than, perhaps, cutting across classes.

[11] It is important to note that no claim is here implied that status is *in general* dominant over class in determining the stratification of life-chances or life-choices. Our own position is, rather, that the relative importance of class

general. But since consumption is a major aspect of lifestyle, and in its cultural forms may be thought to take on a particular significance in creating status markers and boundaries, cultural consumption will be more closely associated with status than with class, and in particular insofar as claims to status, as Weber suggests, are often set against the 'pretensions' of mere economic advantage (1968, p. 932). Or, to elaborate somewhat, we would expect that while the social stratification of cultural consumption will to some extent reflect the constraints and opportunities associated with class position, it will be more powerfully shaped by individual motivations *that are grounded in specifically status concerns* – whether these are directed towards status enhancement or exclusion or simply towards confirmation of membership in social networks or circles that are seen as expressing a valued lifestyle.

At the same time, we recognise income and education as other potentially important stratifying forces in regard to cultural consumption that are related to, yet distinct from, class and status. Thus, income may be taken as a good indicator of more immediately available economic resources, and education of cultural resources – although also, perhaps, of individual psychological attributes, such as 'information processing capacity' (cf. Moles, 1971; Berlyne, 1974) that can independently exert an influence on cultural consumption. In our empirical analyses, therefore, separate measures of income and education are in general included, in addition to those of class and status.

By starting from this theoretical position, and by pursuing analyses of the kind that it prompts, our hope then is that we will be able to examine the arguments and still outstanding questions that were reviewed in the previous section in a more illuminating way than hitherto. We now move on to consider a number of more specific methodological issues that arise in our work, under the three headings of data, analysis and comparative strategy.

1.3 Further methodological issues

1.3.1 Data

The arguments that are addressed in this collection are ones that relate to the societal level. They are arguments about the degree, pattern

and status will differ over different areas of social life, and in a theoretically intelligible manner. For empirical evidence supportive of this position, see Chan and Goldthorpe (2007a).

and determinants of the social stratification of cultural consumption in the context of national societies. Consequently, in order to evaluate these arguments empirically, data are needed that likewise relate to this level: i.e. data that are adequate to describing the cultural consumption of individuals representative of national populations, and data that allow these individuals to be located within the different forms of stratification with which we are concerned. Primarily, then, contributors draw on data that are derived from relatively large-scale sample surveys of national populations.[12] However, on account chiefly of the heavy cost of such surveys, in only one of our national cases, that of Netherlands, was it possible for surveys to be designed and carried out by academic sociologists. In all other cases, what is involved is the secondary analysis of survey data collected by governmental or quasi-governmental agencies in connection with their own interests in cultural participation.

With research thus reliant on data not directly tailored to the sociological purposes in hand, problems almost inevitably arise and call for some attention. In the present case, the data on cultural consumption that are most generally available for analysis come from questions put to survey respondents about whether or not, within a given time period, they had engaged in some particular kind of cultural activity: for example, 'Have you in the last twelve months visited an art gallery?', 'Have you in the last twelve months been to the theatre?', 'Have you in the last four weeks listened to classical music, jazz, pop or rock music?', and so on. Such data could be thought to have, and indeed do have, limitations in various ways. However, in some cases at least, these limitations turn out to be less serious for our specific concerns than might at first appear.

To begin with, data resulting from the kinds of question indicated are obviously data that refer to actual cultural consumption rather than to cultural tastes. But, from our point of view, this is scarcely a difficulty at all. The arguments previously reviewed are all ones that, in the end, involve claims about cultural consumption – as a form of social action – rather than about taste per se; and there would, moreover, now appear

---

[12] In fact, most contributors concentrate their attention on prime-age populations, in say, the age-range 20–64, on the grounds that the patterns of cultural consumption of younger – for example, teenage – and older groups are likely to be sufficiently distinctive to warrant separate treatment. The Chilean sample is also limited to the population of urban areas.

to be a growing awareness in the relevant literature of the dangers of seeking to infer consumption simply from verbal expressions of taste.[13] Several of the national surveys on which contributors to this collection draw do in fact include questions on tastes; but data from these questions are used, if at all, only as a supplement to data on consumption.

Further, though, data of the kind that we typically use might be regarded as unduly crude in at least two respects. First, the indications given of the actual extent of cultural consumption could easily be misleading so far as particular individuals are concerned. For example, no distinction may be made between persons who went to, say, an art gallery just once in the last twelve months and those who made many such visits; or again between persons who did not participate in some cultural activity over a given period because of special circumstances, such as, say, illness, and those for whom non-participation would be normal. However, it is important to recognise that individual level 'error' in this form need not prevent the data we have from providing a generally reliable picture of patterns of cultural consumption, and of types of consumer, at the aggregate level of national populations – nor then from creating a basis on which the social stratification of such patterns and types can be reliably investigated.

Second, the data on which we draw tend to be rather crude in a further way that could be of greater concern: that is, in the often rather undifferentiated terms in which cultural genres are specified. For example, we may know that an individual goes to the cinema but not whether he or she favours art films or Hollywood blockbusters; or that an individual listens regularly to pop or rock music or to classical music, but not to which of their many varieties. The amount

[13] Such questionable inference in fact recurs in the work of Bourdieu (1984). Items included in the surveys he undertook refer to cultural tastes to a far greater extent than to what he terms 'cultural practices'; but in his analyses and commentary Bourdieu seems regularly to take the former as indicative of the latter. An illustration of how misleading this may be emerges from a recent paper by Silva (2006) who reports that people expressing a taste for Renaissance art or for Impressionism were far more likely to act on their preferences by visiting art galleries than were those expressing a taste for landscapes, still-lifes or portraits. Of course, for some purposes, a focus on tastes rather than on actual consumption may be appropriate, but the rationale for such a focus should then be spelled out. For further discussion of this issue, see the exchange of views between Peterson (2007) and Wuggenig (2007) and Chan and Goldthorpe (2007b).

of detail that we can bring into our analyses of cultural consumption is therefore restricted. However, while care has always to be exercised in drawing conclusions from such data, the actual limits that are placed on our ability to address the arguments and issues with which we are primarily concerned are less damaging than might be thought. What is typically at stake is whether or not individuals engage in forms of cultural consumption at, in fact, rather broadly defined levels. Do patterns of highbrow, middlebrow and lowbrow cultural consumption map closely onto some structure of social inequality? Or have such patterns dissolved, and likewise their linkages with social stratification? Or is it rather the case that different cultural patterns and structural linkages have now to be recognised? Significant contributions can then be made to answering such questions even if the data available are not adequate to tracing the finer detail of the cultural consumption in which individuals are involved: that is to say, by working in a primarily hypothesis-testing mode (see further Chan and Goldthorpe, 2007b).[14]

Finally, though, we would acknowledge that there is one respect in which survey data from any source are unlikely to be satisfactory: that is, in seeking to determine the various uses that individuals may make of particular forms of cultural consumption or, more generally, the subjective meaning that such consumption carries for them. And, as we have already noted, some insight into these matters could be of importance as, say, in evaluating the omnivore–univore argument. Does listening to pop or rock music have the same significance for omnivores, who also listen to jazz, classical music, opera etc., as it does for univores, for whom pop or rock represent their only forms of musical consumption? In regard to questions of this nature, we can only point to the need for analyses of the kind that we report in this collection to be supplemented by – while creating the framework for – more intensive qualitative studies, and especially, we would suggest, sustained ethnographies.[15]

---

[14] We have elsewhere (Chan and Goldthorpe, 2007d, n. 17 esp.) investigated how far an analysis based on quite highly differentiated categories of popular musical consumption would qualify one based on cruder categories so far as an evaluation of the homology, individualisation and omnivore–univore arguments is concerned. The results are in fact reassuring. And what would merit further attention is the indication that emerges from this exercise that cultural consumption may have a 'fractal' structure: i.e. similar patterns of differentiation may occur at differing levels of detail.

[15] In this respect, we would regard the work of Halle (1993), in the case of the visual arts, as being exemplary; and cf. also Painter (2002).

1.3.2 Analysis

As we have noted, the data on cultural consumption that are drawn on in the contributions to this collection come in most cases from official surveys; and, in these cases, the data have then usually been to some extent analysed by the agencies that initially promoted the research, and the results reported in publications of one kind or another. The question thus arises of how the analyses to be found in the chapters that follow, in being addressed to the particular sociological arguments and issues that we have reviewed, differ from those previously carried out. Differences, and ones of major significance, are indeed to be found in two main respects. And as well as contributors' secondary analyses being in these ways distinguished from the primary analyses that were undertaken, they also, we believe, mark some advance on much earlier academic work in the field.

First of all, and as we have already suggested, it is important, given the nature of our sociological concerns, to move beyond consideration of different kinds of cultural consumption in a more or less piecemeal fashion. We need to explore the extent and nature of the patterning of such consumption and, in turn, to try to identify types of consumer, whether within particular cultural domains or across domains. This would seem an essential preliminary to treating questions of stratification. To this end, therefore, all contributors engage initially in some form of typology construction.

These efforts vary a good deal in their actual form, depending on the structure of the data available and on authors' treatment of their data in previous work. In some cases, patterns of consumption and types of consumer are directly derived from basic data on individual cultural consumption by means of latent class analysis or analogous techniques; in others, typologies of consumers are arrived at more indirectly. However, in all cases the aim is essentially the same: that is, to investigate empirically how far and in what ways it is possible to associate individual respondents to the national sample surveys that are utilised with patterns of cultural consumption of relatively well-defined kinds.

Second, in turning to questions of stratification, it is essential to our sociological purposes to go beyond bivariate analyses, relating one form of cultural consumption to one aspect of stratification, and also beyond other more complex but still primarily exploratory methods – such as multiple correspondence analysis – to multivariate analyses that are undertaken within a regression context.[16] As earlier emphasised, we wish in our work to treat social stratification in a more differentiated fashion than has usually been attempted and, in particular, to maintain the Weberian distinction between class and status. Thus, in investigating the stratification of different types of cultural consumer, taken as the dependent variable in usually multinomial logistic regression models, contributors to this volume apply separate measures of class and status[17] and also of income and education – but with the latter being included in, as it were, their own right rather than as simply elements of some synthetic 'socio-economic status' scale. In this way, then, the aim is to identify the independent, or net, effects of these several explanatory variables and, by estimating probabilities under regression models, to make some assessment of their relative importance.

Furthermore, in following this approach, valuable indications are often gained of the range and nature of the social processes or mechanisms that underlie the statistical dependencies that are demonstrated. Thus, to illustrate, if – as in fact frequently occurs – educational attainment is found to exert an important influence on cultural consumption, *independently* of class and status, this could then be taken to point to some fairly specific linkage between education and such consumption: for example, to a linkage via cultural resources that are not all that closely associated with class or status or via individual differences in 'information processing capacity' of the kind that were earlier referred to.

In regard to this analytical strategy, we may add, the data-sets that are chiefly utilised have major advantages. As well as providing details of respondents' occupation and employment status of the kind needed to implement our measures of class and status (see further Chapter 2) and good information on respondents' personal and/or household incomes and educational qualifications, they also cover a wide range of

---

[16] We do not accept the argument (see e.g. Wuggenig, 2007) that in the evaluation of homology arguments, or at all events of that of Bourdieu, correspondence analysis must be accorded some privileged role while regression methods are inappropriate (see further Chan and Goldthorpe, 2007b).

[17] The one exception is in the case of the Netherlands where, in contrast with the five other national cases covered, the relationship between class and status proved to be so close that measures of both could not be included in the same analysis because of collinearity problems (see further below, p. 181).

their socio-demographic characteristics. In analyses where the prime focus of interest is on the social stratification of cultural consumption, these characteristics – gender, age, marital status, family composition, area of residence etc. – can then be introduced as important control variables.

Moreover, in some, though unfortunately not all, cases, information is available that allows us to establish the social status of respondents' parents or spouses. And, as will be seen, the effect of the status of such 'significant others' on individuals' own patterns of cultural consumption does often prove to be of importance, and even perhaps to outweigh that of their own status (see also Chan and Goldthorpe, 2007c). Thus, the part played in the stratification of cultural consumption by processes of status mobility or exogamy is highlighted, and this is again an area of research in which more intensive, micro-level studies would seem to have a large potential.

1.3.3 *Comparative strategy*

In social stratification research, a tradition has developed of cross-national comparative work in which increasingly high standards have been achieved in the standardisation of key variables and in turn of various analytical procedures (see e.g. Shavit and Blossfeld, 1993; Shavit and Müller, 1998; Arum and Müller, 2004; Breen, 2005; Shavit *et al.*, 2007). We aim to follow in this tradition as far as possible. However, we are not in fact able to do so to the extent that we would ideally wish, chiefly on account of the fact that the social stratification of cultural consumption is still a relatively underdeveloped field of research, at all events in comparison with, say, those of educational inequalities or social mobility.

As already indicated, the stratification variables that are used in the national contributions to this collection are indeed standardised to a large degree, and the same holds true for socio-demographic variables. But in the case of the dependent variable, that is, cultural consumption itself, no such claim can be made. Although the survey questions that are drawn on tend to have a similar form – i.e. to ask about whether or not a particular cultural activity was engaged in over a given time period – the activities to which such questions relate differ quite widely, in both their range and detail, from one national case to another. Thus, whether the concern is with consumption across several cultural domains or only within a single domain, it is not possible to use the same set of survey items from case to case in order to provide the empirical basis for establishing patterns of cultural consumption and types of consumer.[18]

What this means, therefore, is that cross-national comparisons directly at the level of data analysis cannot be provided in any systematic way, and authors of the national chapters do not in fact attempt such comparisons. Rather, a more indirect comparative strategy is pursued on the following lines. Authors of national chapters are left free to exploit the particular data-sets available to them in whatever ways they would believe most effective in addressing the range of arguments concerning the social stratification of cultural consumption that we have earlier reviewed, while all treat stratification in the differentiated way that has been indicated and in which the distinction between class and status is crucial. In other words, cross-national comparability in the papers here brought together is sought through contributors focusing their attention on a shared set of substantive concerns from a shared conceptual position. It will then fall to the editor of the collection to consider in the final chapter how far this strategy has been successful and to assess the results achieved. How far have our theoretical expectations regarding the relative importance of class and status been borne out? In the light of the class–status distinction, do the national chapters point to similar conclusions regarding the validity or otherwise of what we have labelled as the homology, the individualisation and the omnivore–univore arguments? In so far as commonalities are revealed, can their sources be identified? Or, in so far as conclusions appear not to be in accord from one national case to another, can this lack of agreement be traced back beyond merely differences in available data

---

[18] There are questions on cultural consumption in the Eurobarometer survey series that are uniform for all countries or 'candidate countries' of the European Union. But we have deliberately chosen not to use Eurobarometer data for methodological reasons. Chief among these is that the demographic data in the Eurobarometer surveys are relatively thin. Consequently, it would not support the analyses that we wish to carry out. In particular, there is no detailed occupational information which we need in order to implement our social status scale. Also, the education variable in the Eurobarometer surveys is limited to a single measure of when the respondents completed their full-time education. This is a rather crude and unsatisfactory measure, as it elides many important differences in educational qualifications. Finally, and rather obviously, the Eurobarometer surveys do not cover Chile or the US, which are two very interesting and important cases for us indeed.

to real differences in societal contexts, whether of a systematic or a nationally specific kind?

In connection with such issues, one final methodological point has to be made. In the tradition of comparative stratification research to which we have referred, a cross-national perspective has typically gone together with a longitudinal perspective. The question is raised of whether any cross-national differences revealed in the particular aspects of stratification under examination are tending to narrow or to widen over time – or, that is, the question of societal convergence or divergence. Here again we must acknowledge that how far we can follow in this tradition is limited. National surveys that include questions on cultural consumption, of the kind on which contributors to this collection rely, are in most countries still a fairly new development, and in most cases no accumulation of data that would permit repeated cross-sectional analyses over a significant period are available. Thus, studies of the stratification of cultural consumption over time remain rather rare (though see Peterson and Kern, 1996; van Eijck and Knulst, 2005) and we are not ourselves able to take matters forward in this respect – apart from some amount of informed speculation. However, it seems highly probable that in the years ahead the possibilities for the study of change in cultural consumption and in its social stratification, both within and across national societies, will substantially increase, and we would then hope that the present work will at all events be able to serve as a useful baseline.

1.4 The national chapters

The six nations covered in this comparative study can be taken only as an 'accidental sample', and any generalisations made from them must on this account be highly provisional. However, we believe that in various respects the accidents of choice have been happy ones. This we seek to bring out in briefly introducing each national study. In addition to indicating the particular concerns of the authors, we also note features of the case that are likely to be of strategic interest within a comparative perspective.

The first two national studies, those relating to the USA and to France, are alike in that both deal with cultural consumption in one particular domain, that of music. As the authors in both cases stress, music has played a crucial role in debates on the stratification of cultural consumption. For Bourdieu (1984, p. 18), it is in music that one finds the homology between cultural and social hierarchies most clearly expressed – 'nothing more infallibly classifies' than taste in music. However, music also provides the context in which omnivore–univore arguments were first developed (Peterson, 1992; Peterson and Simkus, 1992) and in which they have since been most extensively applied. There is, therefore, some appeal in starting this collection with two studies of musical consumption that are concerned with the evaluation of omnivore–univore and of Bourdieusian homology arguments and that come from the two countries that provide their 'home ground'.

For the USA, Alderson, Heacock and Junisbai take up the question of whether their findings from earlier work (Alderson *et al.*, 2007) on cross-domain cultural consumption – that such consumption is stratified on the basis of status rather than class and on broadly omnivore–univore lines – are replicated when the focus is specifically on music. They discover that while status still emerges as a major stratifying force, together with education and, to a lesser extent, income, the types of musical consumer that emerge from their analyses cannot be adequately captured by a simple omnivore–univore divide. While there is no evidence of a high status and culturally exclusive musical elite, and musical omnivores are clearly in evidence, they would appear to complemented by musical 'paucivores' – individuals with a middling level and range of musical consumption – rather than by univores of any kind. And further, even when data on actual consumption are supplemented by data on tastes, it would seem necessary to recognise a surprisingly large number of individuals, with relatively low status and educational attainment, who are more or less inactive, or at very least unenthusiastic, so far as music is concerned.

In the French case, the data used by Coulangeon and Lemel differ from those available to Alderson *et al.* in that they relate to listening to music only (regardless of whether or not attendance at a live event was involved) but at the same time cover a wider range of genres. However, the findings of the two studies are in many respects similar. In France as in the USA, musical consumption is chiefly stratified by status, rather than by class, and also by education and income, and with higher strata displaying an omnivorous rather than an exclusive style of consumption. But again, too, omnivore–univore as well as homology arguments are called into question. Like Alderson *et al.*, Coulangeon and Lemel discover a substantial group of effective non-listeners, or musical inactives, which, even if not as large as that revealed for the USA, is likewise disproportionately made up of low status, poorly educated and low-income individuals. And although they are able to identify (lowbrow) musical univores, they too find further typological refinement necessary: that is, in separating highbrow from middlebrow omnivores, on lines that seem in fact rather close to those drawn between omnivores and paucivores in the American case. While rejecting the Bourdieusian idea of a close correspondence between social and cultural hierarchies, maintained through the exigencies of *habitus*, Coulangeon and Lemel would still wish to give full recognition to the pursuit of 'distinction' in cultural taste and consumption. In other words, in so far as it is now omnivorousness – or 'taste eclecticism' – that chiefly characterises high status groups, they would ally themselves with those who see this new aesthetic (cf. p. 9 above) as itself serving to symbolise and express social superiority.

The four remaining national chapters differ from those for the USA and France in that they are concerned with cross-domain cultural consumption: all in fact in some way cover music, theatre and the visual arts and in most cases cinema and dance are also included. The first of these studies to be presented is that of Chile. As Torche describes, Chile is characterised by a high degree of economic and social inequality but is at the same time highly homogenous in terms of ethnicity and religion. In being concerned with cultural consumption in a developing society, Torche notes at the outset that levels of such consumption in Chile do not appear to be generally lower than in economically more advanced societies included in the comparative project. However, the results of her analyses of participation in a relatively wide range of public cultural activities are in several respects distinctive. While she finds that a majority of the Chilean population (even in urban areas) has to be regarded as in effect inactive, in most marked contrast to a small minority of omnivores, she also identifies two other types of cultural consumer that do not have obvious counterparts elsewhere: that is, 'movie-lovers' and 'live-performance aficionados'. Further, although the stratification of these types does in general occur on the basis of status, rather than class, and of education and income, with inactives being concentrated in lower strata, the effects of these variables are in some cases quite differentiated. Thus, it is higher status and education that chiefly distinguish omnivores, but higher education and, especially, income that chiefly distinguish movie-lovers. And status does not set apart live-performance aficionados – who could perhaps be regarded as adherents of persisting forms of folk-culture – from other types of consumer. Overall, then, Torche's analysis of the Chilean case brings out the importance of recognising wider variation both in the nature of cultural hierarchies and in their linkages to social stratification than would be apparent if attention were confined to more advanced societies.

The next chapter is of special interest in dealing with a national society, Hungary, that has recently undergone fundamental changes – and ones that have had a major impact on cultural consumption. Bukodi begins by noting that following the regime change from communism, and the withdrawal of previously extensive state subsidies to the arts, an apparently general decline in levels of cultural consumption has occurred. Consistently with this, she finds that around half of her sample of the Hungarian population have to be regarded as culturally inactive, at least in the sense of being non-attenders at cinemas, theatres, classical concerts, pop, rock or jazz events, operas, or museums and galleries. Among those who are culturally active, Bukodi then distinguishes omnivores, univores and, of special interest, cultural 'exclusives' who confine their consumption entirely to highbrow genres. However, while inactives are relatively disadvantaged in terms of status, education and income alike, it is again the case that the stratification of actual consumers is less straightforward. In this regard, it is individuals' education and income rather than status that matter, and it emerges *inter alia* that although exclusives may be a cultural elite, they are not a social elite, tending in fact to have lower education and incomes than omnivores. But further, while individuals' own status is not a significant influence on type of consumer, father's status is: those culturally active have higher parental status than inactives and, further, omnivores have higher parental status than exclusives. Given that omnivores tend also to be younger than exclusives, Bukodi concludes that it is omnivorousness that represents the style of cultural consumption most typical of the more advantaged strata that are now emerging in post-communist Hungarian society.

Turning to the Dutch chapter, Kraaykamp, van Eijck and Ultee point out that although few would consider the Netherlands as a 'class society', participation in 'highbrow' cultural activities, in the form of visiting museums, attending theatres or classical concerts, is in fact just as socially stratified in the Netherlands as elsewhere. At the same time, though, consumption of popular culture, at least insofar as going to pop concerts is concerned, would appear *not* to be stratified by education, income, class or status. In other words, individuals in socially more advantaged positions have no greater aversion to 'lowbrow' culture than individuals in less advantaged positions. This set of results, as Kraaykamp *et al.* point out, is more in line with the omnivore–univore argument than with the homology argument. Two further results of the Dutch chapter are notable. First, class and status in the Netherlands turn out to be very highly correlated. In fact, there would be a multicollinearity problem if both class and status are entered as predictors in a regression model. Thus, Kraaykamp *et al.* have no choice but to model the effects of class and status separately. As it turns out, the effect of class and that of status are broadly comparable in terms of variance explained or substantive magnitude. Second, Kraaykamp *et al.* show that the educational attainment and social status (or class) of a person's partner have independent effects on his or her cultural consumption.

In the last national chapter of this collection, we consider cross-domain cultural participation in England. On account of time and other resource constraints, it is perhaps unsurprising that cross-domain omnivorousness is rather uncommon: only one in ten respondents in our English sample are omnivores in multiple domains. However, we are able to show that social stratification of cross-domain cultural consumption follows largely the same pattern as that of cultural consumption *within* individual domain (cf. Chan and Goldthorpe, 2005, 2007d,e). That is to say, once again it is education, income and social status, but *not* social class, which differentiate levels of cross-domain cultural consumption.

In this chapter, we have set out the theoretical arguments and still outstanding questions that are to be addressed in our research project. And we have explained the analytical framework and comparative strategy that structure our empirical analyses. But before we proceed to review the evidences that are reported in the national chapters, we shall have to take a short detour to report in Chapter 2 the construction of a key explanatory variable of our approach, namely the social status scale, and discuss some of its properties.

2 The social status scale: its construction and properties

TAK WING CHAN

In Chapter 1, John Goldthorpe and I argue that one weakness of previous research into the social stratification of cultural consumption relates to inadequacies in the way in which stratification has been conceptualised and, in turn, treated in empirical analyses. The source of these inadequacies, we further argue, is a failure to maintain the Weberian distinction between *class* and *status* (Weber, 1968, vol. 2; pp. 926–939 esp.). Following Weber, we expect the social stratification of cultural consumption to be based on social status rather than on social class.

The contributors to the present collection all accept this argument. Each national team has constructed a status scale for their country which will be used as a key explanatory variable, along with social class, education and income, in the chapters that follow. Given the pivotal role that is played by social status in our explanatory framework, the aim of this chapter is to describe the status scales in some detail. I begin with a discussion of how the scales are empirically estimated. I then describe some key properties of the status scales, addressing questions such as whether the sub-populations of a society share the same status order, and how social status, in the classical Weberian sense, relates to other stratification variables; principally education, income, 'socioeconomic status' and social class. I will also discuss, albeit in an informal manner, the extent of cross-national commonality and variation in social status. In the concluding section of this chapter, I compare our status scales with other occupational scales that are in use in empirical sociological research.

2.1 Estimating the status order

From the Weberian standpoint, social status, as a hierarchy of social superiority, equality and inferiority, is expressed primarily through patterns of intimate association. Taking this as our starting point, and drawing directly on the work of Laumann (1966, 1973), Goldthorpe and I have already provided some evidence of the persistence of a status order in Britain (Chan and Goldthorpe, 2004). Our approach involves two assumptions. The first is that in modern societies occupation is one of the most salient positional characteristics to which status attaches.[1] We further assume that close friendship implies a relation of basic equality between individuals, one into which status differences are unlikely to intrude.

Specifically, we use data on close friendship from wave 10 (year 2000) of the British Household Panel Survey. To circumvent the problem of data sparsity, we first collapse the 3-digit UK occupational classification into 31 categories.[2] On the basis of this classification, we then construct a contingency table of respondent's occupation by close friend's occupation. Next we generate 'outflow rates' or row percentages of this table, which express the occupational distribution of close friends by occupational groupings of the respondents. We then compute the dissimilarity indices for every pair of outflow distributions and use these as inputs to a multidimensional scaling (MDS) analysis.[3] In effect, the 31 occupational groupings are scaled according to the degree of similarity of their friendship patterns.

The results show that the ordering of the occupational groupings, on the first dimension of our MDS exercise, largely reflects the degree of 'manuality' of the work involved. Thus, non-manual occupations rank above manual occupations, and within the non-manual range, professional occupations rank above managerial occupations. Indeed, managerial occupations in personal service or blue-collar settings are of rather low status given the typical income and educational attainment of their incumbents. For example, Managers and proprietors in services rank 17th out of 31 occupations (hereafter abbreviated as 17/31), and Plant, depot and site managers

[1] That this is indeed the case would appear to be a matter of some consensus among sociologists of otherwise quite differing views (e.g. Blau and Duncan, 1967; Parkin, 1971; Treiman, 1977; Coxon and Jones, 1978; Stewart *et al.*, 1980; Grusky and Sørensen, 1998).

[2] The data sparsity problem arises because our estimation procedure is applied to a square contingency table. Thus, sample size requirement increases quadratically with the number of occupational groupings distinguished.

[3] We have also analysed the respondent by close friend table with Goodman's RC(*M*) models. Generally speaking, very similar results are obtained. Details are available on request.

rank 18/31. These occupations are found at the bottom of the non-manual range, ranking in fact below many secretarial and clerical occupations (Chan and Goldthorpe, 2004, p. 390).

We would argue that this ordering of occupations does indeed express social status rather than homophily alone. This is so firstly because it provides rather clear 'echoes' of the relatively explicit and well-defined status order that prevailed in British society from, say, the later nineteenth through to the mid-twentieth century. Sociologists and historians would appear largely to concur (for useful reviews see Runciman, 1997; McKibbin, 1998) that the non-manual–manual distinction marked a major boundary within this order, and one that was strongly upheld even as the distinction became less consequential in terms of economic conditions; and, further, that professional employment was generally regarded as being socially superior to managerial employment, and especially to managerial employment in industry or 'trade'.

A second argument supporting our interpretation is that the second dimension and, to a more limited degree, the third dimension of our MDS exercise are also interpretable, in terms of occupational sex segregation and occupational situses respectively (see Chan and Goldthorpe, 2004, pp. 387–389). Insofar as these two dimensions capture features of the occupational structure which affect the *opportunities* for friendship formation, the first dimension, being thus 'purged' of these influences, should reflect more directly the dynamics of friendship *choice*. Given these considerations, we believe that the first dimension of our MDS analysis can be most plausibly interpreted as representing social status, in the Weberian sense. Starting from the structuring of a relationship implying social equality, a structure of status *in*equality can be inferred.

Of course, the proof of the pudding is in the eating. In the end, the persuasiveness of our interpretation rests on the strength of the evidence that cultural consumption is indeed stratified on the basis of the estimated status scale. This is one of the main goals which motivates the collective research effort that is reported in this book.

2.1.1 Marriage vs. friendship data

The contributors to this collection have all followed the approach outlined above in order to estimate a status scale for their country.

Table 2.1 *Data used in the estimation of the status scale*

country	data source	data type	N	# occ[a]
Chile	2003 Social Characterisation Survey	Marriage	58,511	28
France	1982–83 Contacts Entre les Personnes Survey	Friendship	1,723	28
Hungary	2001 Census (20% sample)	Marriage	367,300	36
Netherlands	Family Survey of Dutch Population (1992, 1998, 2000, 2003)	Marriage	2,949	26
UK	British Household Panel Survey, 2000	Friendship	9,160	31
US	2000 US Census (5% PUMS)	Marriage	2,297,139	94

Note: [a] number of occupational categories distinguished.

Table 2.1 shows the data sets that they use.[4] In four of the six countries – Chile, Hungary, the Netherlands and the US – the status scale is estimated on the basis of marriage or partnership data, while for France and the UK data on close friendship is used. Does it matter that different kinds of data are used?

To answer this question, I have repeated the analysis for the UK, using marriage/partnership data drawn from the 1991 Sample of Anonymised Records (SARs). The SARs data set ($N = 105,289$) is a one per cent sample of all UK households in the 1991 Census. I extract relevant occupational information of married or cohabiting couples in SARs, and form a contingency table cross-classifying their occupations. By applying MDS analysis to this table, it turns out that the leading dimension that is extracted correlates very highly with the status scale that is based on friendship data, with $r = -0.96$.[5]

[4] Note that, apart from the Dutch case, the data sets used for constructing the status scales are different from those used in the analyses of cultural consumption.

[5] Note that because 'the interpretation ... put upon any MDS solution must be invariant under reflection, translation, and rotation' (Bartholomew *et al.*, 2002,

Similar results are obtained for France. As the 1982–83 *Contacts Entre les Personnes* Survey also contains occupational information of spouses, our colleague Yannick Lemel (2006) is able to compare the two status scales that are constructed on the basis of marriage and friendship data respectively. Again, the correlation is very high, with $r = 0.96$.

These results suggest that status is a pervasive social force which structures both marriage choice and friendship choice. Indeed, Weber speaks of 'commensality' and 'connubium'. Both forms of intimate relationship offer researchers a handle to identify the status order in contemporary societies.

2.1.2 *The status scale in the six countries*

Let us consider the estimated status scales more closely. Table 2.2 lists, for each country separately, the occupational groupings that are distinguished (hereafter as status groups) in descending order of status scores. The dotted lines indicate those status groups which account for (roughly) the top 20% and the bottom 20% of the population in each country. Because of differences in national occupational classification, and also because of various substantive and practical considerations,[6] the status groups that are distinguished in the six countries are not the same. This inevitably hampers formal comparison. But broadly speaking, the general contour of the ordering of the status groups is very similar across countries, and very much in line with the British pattern described above.

For example, professionals are invariably found at the top of the status hierarchies, followed by associate professional occupations and managerial occupations. However, managerial occupations in industry or 'trade' often have rather middling status. For instance, in Chile, Managers in wholesale and retail trade rank 11/28; Middle managers

---

p. 56), the sign of the correlation has no interpretation; it is the absolute magnitude which matters. I have also repeated my MDS analysis of the SARs data with a residual category of 'no occupational information', so as to accommodate the 3.7% of men and 17.9% of women who did not work between 1981 and 1991. Again, the status scale thus derived correlates very highly with that which is based on friendship data, with $r = -0.95$.

[6] For example, the large N of the US sample supports a much more detailed occupational classification.

Table 2.2 *Status groups in descending status score and their relative size in each country*

Chile

Rank and short title	%	score
1 Professionals in science, engineering and health	3.5	1.915
2 Professionals in business, law and others	3.2	1.531
3 Professionals in education	4.7	1.183
4 Associate professionals in business, law and others	5.0	1.078
5 Managers in production, operations and finance	2.3	0.957
6 Associate professionals in others	3.8	0.666
7 Secretaries and numerical clerks	5.1	0.612
8 Other clerical workers	2.5	0.421
9 Cashiers, tellers and receptionists	2.1	0.410
10 Shop sales workers	5.6	0.210
11 Managers in wholesale or retail trade	4.5	0.205
12 Drivers	5.9	0.114
13 Personal service workers	3.1	0.062
14 Welders, blacksmiths, toolmakers and mechanics	4.5	0.000
15 Service workers	3.7	−0.202
16 Plant and machine operatives	2.6	−0.280
17 Construction workers, plumbers and electricians	5.3	−0.328
18 Other skilled manual workers	4.2	−0.472
19 Porters, messengers and doormen	2.5	−0.482
20 Cleaners	2.6	−0.526
21 Stall and market salespersons	1.5	−0.571
22 Street and door-to-door vendors	1.6	−0.636
23 Market corp farmers and forestry workers	2.2	−0.679
24 Labourers in mining, construction and manufacturing	2.0	−0.727
25 Subsistence farmers	1.1	−0.927
26 Domestic servants	8.5	−0.991
27 Field croppers, vegetable growers and gardeners	2.4	−1.125
28 Farm labourers	4.8	−1.418

France

Rank and short title	%	score
1 Liberal professions (self-employed)	1.1	0.36
2 Second- and third-level teachers and scientists	2.8	0.34

(cont.)

Table 2.2 *(cont.)*

France

Rank and short title	%	score
3 Media and entertainment	0.6	0.25
4 Engineers and technical managers	3.0	0.23
5 Sales and administrative managers	4.8	0.22
6 Civil Service officers	1.4	0.20
7 Business owners with 0+ employees	0.4	0.18
8 Elementary school teachers and related	3.6	0.17
9 Social and healthcare workers	3.5	0.12
10 Shopkeepers and related	3.7	0.07
11 Civil service middle managers	1.7	0.04
12 Middle managers in sales and administration	5.0	0.04
13 Technicians	3.4	0.02
14 Office workers	9.0	0.00
15 Farmers	5.1	−0.04
16 Tradesmen	2.7	−0.06
17 Shop assistants	3.8	−0.07
18 Civil Service workers	8.2	−0.08
19 Foremen and labour supervisors	2.7	−0.08
20 Police and military	1.7	−0.10
21 Household helpers	7.6	−0.15
22 Qualified transport, warehousing and maintenance workers	1.5	−0.20
23 Qualified tradesmen	5.3	−0.21
24 Qualified factory workers	6.0	−0.21
25 Drivers	2.1	−0.22
26 Farm workers	1.5	−0.25
27 Unskilled factory workers	6.2	−0.26
28 Unskilled tradesmen	1.6	−0.31

Hungary

Rank and short title	%	score
1 Legal professionals	0.3	1.0383
2 Tertiary-level education teaching professionals	0.2	1.0194
3 Physicians, pharmacists, natural scientists	0.6	0.8992
4 Engineers and computer scientists	1.8	0.8186
5 Cultural professionals, artists, religious professionals	0.7	0.7071

Table 2.2 *(cont.)*

Hungary

Rank and short title		%	score
6	Social science and welfare professionals	0.2	0.6318
7	Business professionals	1.6	0.6248
8	General managers	0.6	0.6232
9	Senior government officials	0.2	0.5068
10	Secondary and primary education teaching professionals	3.9	0.5054
11	High-ranked armed forces officers	0.5	0.4521
12	Department managers	2.8	0.3625
13	General managers of small business undertakings	1.4	0.3385
14	Associate professionals in health	0.3	0.3058
15	Associate professionals in culture, arts and religion	0.4	0.2252
16	Associate professionals in business, law and finance	6.2	0.1202
17	Technicians and related professionals	3.0	0.0179
18	Office clerks	4.9	0.0135
19	Production supervisors, site managers	1.3	−0.0793
20	Associate professionals in health and welfare	3.1	−0.1158
21	Numerical clerks and other clerical workers	1.4	−0.2170
22	Personal service workers	0.8	−0.2307
23	Protective service workers and low-ranked armed forces	2.2	−0.2796
24	Sales workers	6.8	−0.3168
25	Communal and other service workers	0.7	−0.4309
26	Health, welfare, cultural service workers	1.2	−0.4743
27	Hotel and restaurant workers	2.5	−0.4805
28	Skilled handicraft and miscellaneous industrial workers	2.0	−0.5375
29	Transport and postal workers	1.2	−0.5851
30	Skilled metal trade workers	8.3	−0.6258
31	Skilled food and other light industry workers	6.0	−0.7104
32	Skilled construction workers	5.7	−0.7368
33	Machine and plant operatives	12.3	−0.7546
34	Extraction workers	4.4	−0.8519
35	Routine service workers	6.7	−0.8629
36	General labourers	4.0	−0.9206

(cont.)

Table 2.2 *(cont.)*

The Netherlands

Rank and short title		%	score
1	Doctors and other medical professionals	1.5	1.90
2	Business professionals	1.6	1.69
3	Teachers and professionals in education	7.2	1.51
4	Other professionals and executive officers	7.3	0.97
5	Scientists, engineers and technicians	4.0	0.88
6	Nurses and associate professionals in medicine	6.1	0.69
7	Managers and proprietors in sales and services	2.6	0.68
8	Technical professionals	2.8	0.67
9	Senior managers in private or public sector	7.3	0.65
10	Brokers and sales agents	2.1	0.59
11	Transport clerks	6.7	0.30
12	Secretaries and receptionists	3.9	0.22
13	Account clerks	7.0	0.21
14	Mechanics and electricians	3.8	0.06
15	Market traders and travelling salesmen	5.7	−0.29
16	Plumbers and construction workers	3.3	−0.37
17	Personal service workers	3.4	−0.67
18	Farm workers	1.8	−0.72
19	Protective service workers	2.7	−0.74
20	Transport operatives	4.3	−0.84
21	Manual workers in material extraction/processing	2.8	−0.86
22	Machine operatives	2.6	−0.99
23	Care workers	5.6	−1.02
24	Craft workers	0.6	−1.12
25	Manual workers in textiles and clothing	1.6	−1.64
26	Chefs and waiting staff	1.8	−1.75

UK

Rank and short title		%	score
1	Higher professionals	3.3	0.5643
2	Associate professionals in business	2.6	0.5337
3	Specialist managers	2.7	0.5107
4	Teachers and other professionals in education	4.5	0.5017
5	General managers and administrators	2.5	0.4114
6	Associate professionals in industry	3.9	0.3116

Table 2.2 *(cont.)*

UK

Rank and short title		%	score
7	Scientists, engineers and technologists	1.9	0.3115
8	Filing and record clerks	1.9	0.2559
9	Managers and officials, nec	2.0	0.2355
10	Administrative officers and assistants	2.1	0.2274
11	Numerical clerks and cashiers	3.7	0.2238
12	Associate professionals in health and welfare	4.8	0.2228
13	Secretaries and receptionists	3.3	0.1539
14	Other clerical workers	3.5	0.1443
15	Buyers and sales representatives	1.6	0.1193
16	Childcare workers	2.6	0.1097
17	Managers and proprietors in services	4.4	−0.0453
18	Plant, depot and site managers	2.7	−0.0625
19	Sales workers	6.3	−0.1151
20	Health workers	2.6	−0.2121
21	Personal service workers	2.2	−0.2261
22	Protective service personnel	1.9	−0.2288
23	Routine workers in services	6.1	−0.2974
24	Catering workers	2.3	−0.3261
25	Store and dispatch clerks	2.1	−0.3353
26	Skilled and related manual workers nec	3.9	−0.4072
27	Transport operatives	3.3	−0.4114
28	Skilled and related manual workers in construction and maintenance	3.5	−0.5014
29	Skilled and related manual workers in metal trades	3.5	−0.5121
30	Plant and machine operatives	6.2	−0.5589
31	General labourers	2.2	−0.5979

US

Rank and short title		%	score
1	Social scientists and related workers	0.2	0.6264
2	Postsecondary teachers	0.7	0.5580
3	Lawyers, judges and related workers	0.7	0.5557
4	Architects, surveyors, and cartographers	0.2	0.5086
5	Media and communication workers	0.4	0.4846

(cont.)

Table 2.2 *(cont.)*

US		
Rank and short title	%	score
6 Life scientists	0.2	0.4830
7 Physical scientists	0.3	0.4772
8 Mathematical science occupations	0.1	0.4104
9 Entertainers and performers, sports and related workers	0.3	0.4070
10 Librarians, curators and archivists	0.2	0.3980
11 Primary, secondary and special education school teachers	3.7	0.3949
12 Advertising, marketing, promotions, public relations and sales managers	0.9	0.3644
13 Computer specialists	1.9	0.3393
14 Engineers	1.3	0.3148
15 Top executives	1.7	0.3012
16 Other teachers and instructors	0.3	0.2956
17 Health diagnosing and treating practitioners	3.2	0.2944
18 Financial specialists	2.0	0.2912
19 Counsellors, social workers, and other community and social service specialists	0.9	0.2850
20 Other healthcare practitioners and technical occupations	0.0	0.2781
21 Art and design workers	0.6	0.2713
22 Air transportation workers	0.2	0.2590
23 Media and communication equipment workers	0.1	0.2508
24 Sales representatives, services	1.2	0.2500
25 Religious workers	0.4	0.2386
26 Operations specialties managers	2.0	0.2360
27 Business operations specialists	1.9	0.2328
28 Sales representatives, wholesale and manufacturing	1.0	0.2221
29 Other management occupations	5.0	0.2001
30 Other sales and related workers	0.9	0.1872
31 Legal support workers	0.3	0.1747
32 Fire fighting and prevention workers	0.2	0.1613
33 Transportation, tourism, and lodging attendants	0.1	0.1594
34 First-line supervisors/managers, protective service workers	0.3	0.1395
35 Law enforcement workers	0.9	0.1055

Table 2.2 *(cont.)*

US		
Rank and short title	%	score
36 Supervisors, office and administrative support workers	1.3	0.0844
37 Life, physical and social science technicians	0.2	0.0486
38 Drafters, engineering and mapping technicians	0.5	0.0332
39 Supervisors, sales workers	2.7	0.0327
40 Occupational and physical therapist assistants and aides	0.0	0.0327
41 Supervisors, personal care and service workers	0.1	0.0144
42 Electrical and electronic equipment mechanics, installers and repairers	0.5	0.0013
43 Funeral service workers	0.0	0.0006
44 Secretaries and administrative assistants	2.8	−0.0060
45 Supervisors of installation, maintenance and repair workers	0.4	−0.0267
46 Other education, training and library occupations	0.8	−0.0505
47 Health technologists and technicians	1.3	−0.0511
48 Rail transportation workers	0.1	−0.0522
49 Supervisors, construction and extraction workers	0.8	−0.0540
50 Information and record clerks	2.7	−0.0578
51 Other office and administrative support workers	2.1	−0.0612
52 Supervisors, transportation and material moving workers	0.2	−0.0633
53 Animal care and service workers	0.1	−0.0657
54 Financial clerks	2.2	−0.0767
55 Plant and system operators	0.2	−0.0795
56 Water transportation workers	0.1	−0.0797
57 Other healthcare support occupations	0.6	−0.1191
58 Other protective service workers	0.5	−0.1276
59 Supervisors, building and grounds cleaning and maintenance workers	0.2	−0.1434
60 Other construction and related workers	0.2	−0.1497
61 Retail sales workers	3.3	−0.1585
62 Fishing and hunting workers	0.0	−0.1704
63 Supervisors, farming, fishing and forestry workers	0.1	−0.1734
64 Other personal care and service workers	1.2	−0.1783
65 Supervisors, production workers	1.1	−0.1783

(cont.)

Table 2.2 *(cont.)*

US		
Rank and short title	%	score
66 Other installation, maintenance and repair occupations	1.7	−0.1791
67 Personal appearance workers	0.6	−0.1839
68 Entertainment attendants and related workers	0.1	−0.1844
69 Not in labour force	10.0	−0.1890
70 Material recording, scheduling, dispatching and distributing workers	2.1	−0.2001
71 Printing workers	0.3	−0.2008
72 Vehicle and mobile equipment mechanics, installers and repairers	1.5	−0.2124
73 Construction trades workers	4.1	−0.2137
74 Communications equipment operators	0.1	−0.2242
75 Supervisors, food preparation and serving workers	0.4	−0.2262
76 Extraction workers	0.1	−0.2348
77 Other transportation workers	0.1	−0.2656
78 Motor vehicle operators	3.0	−0.2924
79 Woodworkers	0.2	−0.2977
80 Grounds maintenance workers	0.5	−0.3048
81 Forest, conservation and logging workers	0.1	−0.3366
82 Metal workers and plastic workers	1.9	−0.3486
83 Other production occupations	2.5	−0.3588
84 Food and beverage serving workers	1.0	−0.3880
85 Helpers, construction trades	0.0	−0.3926
86 Agricultural workers	0.6	−0.3947
87 Assemblers and fabricators	1.1	−0.3974
88 Material moving workers	2.0	−0.4050
89 Food processing workers	0.4	−0.4092
90 Building, cleaning and pest control workers	2.0	−0.4470
91 Nursing, psychiatric and home health aides	1.0	−0.4515
92 Other food preparation and serving related workers	0.2	−0.4780
93 Cooks and food preparation workers	1.1	−0.5263
94 Textile, apparel and furnishings workers	0.9	−0.5342

in sales and administration in France rank 12/28; and Production supervisors and site managers in Hungary rank 19/36.

Status groups found at the other end of the hierarchies are typically manual labourers or machine operatives. Examples include Unskilled factory workers and Unskilled tradesmen in France (rank 27/28 and 28/28 respectively), General labourers in Hungary (36/36), and Manual workers in textiles and clothing in the Netherlands (25/26). Routine personal service workers also have rather low status. For example, Domestic servants in Chile rank 26/28; Chefs and waiting staff in the Netherlands rank 26/26; and Nursing, psychiatric, and home health aides in the US rank 91/94.

There are exceptions to the general pattern outlined above, but most of these are quite readily understandable. For example, due to the relatively large agricultural sector in Chile, Florencia Torche quite sensibly distinguishes four categories of farmers and farm labourers for Chile, which are all found at the bottom of the Chilean status hierarchy. Correspondingly, some manual occupations in Chile are of relatively high status ranking (e.g. Welders, blacksmiths, toolmakers and mechanics rank 14/26 and Plant and machine operatives rank 16/26).

However, some cross-national differences are harder to interpret. For example, Transport operatives, Drivers, or other similarly named status groups tend to have very low status in most countries: 25/28 in France, 20/26 in the Netherlands, 27/31 in the UK, and 78/94 in the US. But they have relatively high ranking in Chile at 12/28. Such discrepancies might reflect national idiosyncrasies to some extent. But it is likely that in some cases they are artefacts due to the banding of quite disparate occupations into a nominal status group, which, in turn, is an unfortunate though unavoidable consequence of the sample size constraint (see note 2 above).

2.2 Further properties of the status scales

2.2.1 Is the status order common to all sub-populations?

In a previous paper, Goldthorpe and I have shown that the status order in the UK is gender-neutral (Chan and Goldthorpe, 2004), in the sense that the status scale that is derived from the friendship choice of our male respondents correlates quite highly with that which is

Table 2.3 *Correlation of status scales estimated for different sub-populations in the UK and the US*

country	sub-groups under comparison	r
UK	white couples and ethnic minority couples	0.917
US	black couples and all couples	0.914
	married couples and cohabiting couples	0.945
	gay couples and heterosexual couples	0.884

based on the friendship choice of our female respondents ($r = 0.75$). Moreover, where discrepancies between these two scales are found (and there are only two outliers), they can reasonably be regarded as artefacts that are due to the relatively small sample size of that study ($N = 9,160$, see Chan and Goldthorpe, 2004, pp. 388–389). But is it generally the case that the status order is shared by *all* sub-populations within a society? This question is interesting in its own right. But it carries further significance because, in addition to occupation, social status is likely to have other social bases. Ethnicity, for example, often has important status-conferring effects. Thus, in societies where ethnic divisions are salient, are there ethnically specific status orders?

Table 2.3 provides some relevant evidence. For the UK, I turn again to the SARs data set. Because of its relatively large N, I am able to carry out separate analyses for white couples and for ethnic minority couples.[7] It turns out that these two status scales are very highly correlated, with $r = 0.92$. Similar results are obtained for the US. Alderson *et al.* (2005) have estimated a separate status scale for black couples using the 2000 US Census data, which correlates very highly with that based on the whole US sample ($r = 0.91$).

Indeed, we see high correlations when other comparisons are made, as between married and cohabiting couples ($r = 0.95$) or between gay and heterosexual couples in the US ($r = 0.88$). These results corroborate earlier findings of Laumann (1973), who shows that while ethnoreligious affiliations are of key importance to social status in

---

[7] Ten ethnic groups are distinguished in SARs. But despite its relatively large N, the sample size of SARs still would not support separate analyses for *individual* ethnic groups.

Table 2.4 *Bivariate correlation between status and education and between status and income, and standardised regression coefficients when status scores are regressed on education and income*

| | individual level | | aggregate level | | | | |
| | correlation | | correlation | | multiple regression | | |
	edu[a]	inc[b]	edu[c]	inc[d]	edu	inc	R^2
Chile	0.634	0.317	0.911	0.872	0.650	0.294*	0.85
France	0.651	0.441	0.895	0.895	0.468	0.461	0.83
Hungary	0.726	0.352	0.931	0.845	0.754	0.211*	0.88
Netherlands	0.528	0.137	0.877	0.687	0.784	0.130*	0.78
UK	0.440	0.248	0.784	0.554	1.000	−0.264*	0.64
US	0.531	0.317	0.956	0.708	0.848	0.171	0.93

Note: [a] measured as year of schooling, [b] measured as labour market income, [c] measured as proportion with post-secondary education, [d] measured as proportion found in top income quintile as defined by the whole sample.* *not* significant at 5% level.

contemporary American society, occupation-based status ranking is largely replicated *within* each ethnoreligious group.

2.2.2 Status, education, income and SEI

How is social status related to other arguably more 'basic' factors such as education or income? A certain level of income is necessary in order to sustain the lifestyle characteristic of a certain level in the status hierarchy, and the preferences that shape the form and content of lifestyles are likely to be influenced by education. Thus, we would expect status to be correlated, to some degree, with both education and income. But if these correlations prove to be *very* high, the question would arise of whether status is anything more than a mere epiphenomenon of differences in income and education.

In the first column of Table 2.4, I report the correlation, measured at the individual level, between social status and education (operationalised as years of schooling). The magnitude of this correlation is quite variable across countries, ranging from $r = 0.44$ for the UK to $r = 0.73$ for Hungary. The correlations between income and status, measured again at the individual level, are weaker, but again variable, ranging from $r = 0.14$ for the Netherlands to $r = 0.44$ for France.[8] Overall, these correlations are strongest for Hungary and France, weakest for the Netherlands and the UK.

The status–education and status–income correlations can also be calculated at the aggregate level. I measure education as the proportion within each status group with post-secondary qualifications, and income as the proportion found in the top income quintile (as defined for the whole sample). The results are reported in columns 3 and 4 of Table 2.4. Three points are notable. First, the aggregate level correlations are, as would be expected, much stronger than those calculated at the individual level. Second, the aggregate correlations are less variable across countries.[9] However, thirdly, at the aggregate level the UK again stands out as having the weakest status–education and status–income correlations. Goldthorpe and I have previously observed that in the UK 'the connection between education and status, like that between income and status, would not appear to be especially strong' (Chan and Goldthorpe, 2004, p. 391). From a cross-national comparative viewpoint, it is now clear that this is not true for other countries and that the UK is an outlier in this regard.

To help visualise the aggregate level correlations reported in Table 2.4, Figures 2.1 and 2.2 show respectively the distribution of education and income *within* status groups for the six countries. In these two figures, status groups are ranked in descending order from left to right on the axis which runs from north-west to south-east, while levels of education (or income in the case of Figure 2.2) go from the lowest level to the highest level on the axis which runs from south-west to north-east. Each 'slice' of Figure 2.1 (Figure 2.2) is then a histogram of the distribution of education (income) for a status group. The unevenness of the surfaces in these two figures would then indicate

[8] The very low status–income correlation for the Netherlands is probably due to the fact that more than 80% of Dutch women, even those employed in high status occupations, work part time. If income is measured at the household rather than the individual level, then the status–income correlation for the Netherlands would be higher at $r = 0.34$. I thank Gerbert Kraaykamp for this piece of information.

[9] This is probably because the aggregate measures average out some measurement errors that are found at the individual level. For example, because educational systems vary between countries, our individual level measure of education as years of schooling is not strictly appropriate in all cases.

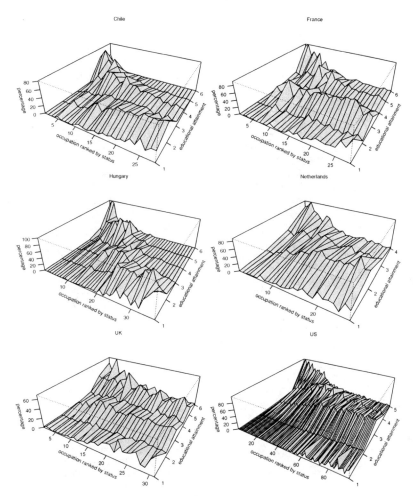

Chile   France
Hungary   Netherlands
UK   US

Fig. 2.1 Distribution of educational attainment within status group

the extent of discrepancy between social status on the one hand, and education or income on the other.

Finally, in the last three columns of Table 2.4 I report the standardised regression coefficients and R^2 when social status scores are regressed on aggregated measures of education and income as defined above. It can be seen that the income coefficient is *not* statistically significant for four countries, namely Chile, Hungary, the Netherlands

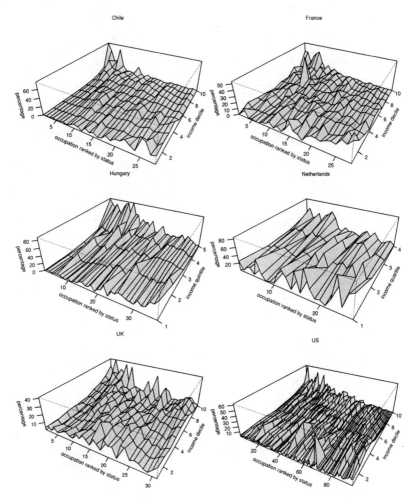

Fig. 2.2 Distribution of income within status group

and the UK. Recall that for measures such as Duncan's SEI or Ganze-boom and Treiman's occupational status scale, the income and educa-tion coefficients would both be statistically significant in a comparable regression, and that the coefficient for income would be of similar mag-nitude to that for education (Duncan, 1961; Blau and Duncan, 1967, p. 125) or only slightly less (Ganzeboom and Treiman, 2003, p. 161). Our results would suggest that social status, in the classical Weberian sense, is empirically as well as conceptually different from synthetic

Table 2.5 *Seven-fold version of the CASMIN class schema*

I	Higher level salariat
II	Lower level salariat
III	Routine non-manual employees
IV	Petty bourgeoisie
V	Technicians and supervisors of manual workers
VI	Skilled manual workers
VII	Nonskilled manual workers

'socioeconomic status' scales, in at least four of the six countries considered here.

In terms of R^2, it can be seen that once again UK stands out as having the weakest relationship between social status on the one hand, and education and income on the other. At the other end of this comparison is the US, where education and income together explain 93% of the variance in social status.

2.2.3 Status and class

In this section, I turn to the key question of how class and status map onto each other. By social class, I refer to the EGP or CASMIN class schema (Erikson *et al.*, 1979; Erikson and Goldthorpe, 1992; Breen, 2005), which has in recent years become the 'industry standard' in comparative sociological research (see e.g. Shavit and Müller, 1998; Breen, 2004; Blossfeld *et al.*, 2006; Shavit *et al.*, 2007). It is also the basis of the official British National Statistics Socio-Economic Classification (NS–SEC) (Rose *et al.*, 2005).

Table 2.5 shows a seven-fold version of the CASMIN class schema. According to Erikson and Goldthorpe (1992, pp. 35–47), a key dimension underlying their class schema is employment status, i.e. the distinction between employers, self-employed workers and employees. But among employees, which typically account for 85–90% of the economically active population, a further distinction between 'labour contract' and 'service contract' is important. Labour contracts refer to 'relatively short-term and specific exchange of money for effort'. Individuals employed on labour contracts typically work under quite direct and close supervision, and often they are compensated according

Table 2.6 *Variance of social status between classes and within class for the seven countries*

	between	within	ρ	# classes
Chile	2567706	1223502	0.677	7
France	3791.3	1049.0	0.783	5
Hungary	2601.58	546.54	0.826	7
Netherlands	2786.43	1301.36	0.682	6
UK	847	317	0.728	7
US	224047	100527	0.690	7

Note: ρ is the proportion of total variance in status that is explained by social class.

to a piece rate or a time (hour, day or week) rate. In contrast, service contracts 'involve a longer-term and generally more diffuse exchange'. Employees render service to the employer and are rewarded not just with an annual salary but also a long-term career (see Erikson and Goldthorpe, 1992, p. 41). The distinction between labour contract and service contract can, in turn, be understood in terms of concepts in personnel economics, specifically 'human assets specificity' and 'difficulty in monitoring effort' (Goldthorpe, 2007a, pp. 108–119). For our present purpose, suffice it to note that higher and lower level salariat (classes I and II of Table 2.5) are composed of individuals employed on the basis of service contracts as well as employers of medium and large establishments, while individuals in classes III, V to VII are workers employed on the basis of labour contracts.

As a rough indicator of the closeness of the class–status link in the six countries, Table 2.6 reports the proportion of the total variance in social status that is *between* social classes, ρ.[10] It can be seen that the class–status link seems broadly comparable in four of our six countries: Chile, the Netherlands, the UK and the US, with ρ ranging from 0.68 (Chile) to 0.73 (UK). But the value of ρ is somewhat higher for Hungary (0.83) and for France (0.78).[11] For Weber, class and status can be

---

[10] Note that because of practical constraints, our colleagues in Chile, France and the Netherlands have to use variants of the seven-fold class scheme. Thus, the ρ values reported in Table 2.6 are not strictly comparable, and should be taken as rough indicators only.

[11] Note that because only five social classes are distinguished in France, its ρ value is likely to be an underestimate.

'linked in the most varied ways'. From Table 2.6, and also from the status–education and status–income correlations reported in Table 2.4, it would seem that the class–status link or, more generally speaking, the link between the economic and the social–cultural hierachies, is closer in France and Hungary than in the other four countries.

While ρ is a useful one-number summary, it might also mask local variation in the class–status link. Thus, in Figure 2.3, we show boxplots of status by class for the six countries. Three points are notable. First, it is clear that in all cases there is a status gradient across class. In terms of the median or the interquartile range, the salariat (classes I and II) have higher status than the intermediate classes (III, IV and V), which in turn tend to have higher status than the working classes (VI and VII). Second, the dispersion of status *within* class can be quite large, especially for the petty bourgeoisie (class IV) and lower level salariat (class II).[12] Consequently, and this is the third point, there are considerable overlap in status *between* certain classes. This means that although class and status are, as would be expected, correlated with each other, they are, generally speaking, *not* measuring the same thing. There are many instances where the status of individuals is not congruent with their class position. Indeed, as the following chapters will show, apart from the Netherlands, it is possible to include status as well as class, along with education and income, in regression analyses of cultural consumption, without introducing significant multicollinearity problems.

Further inspection of Figure 2.3 confirms our observation, based on Table 2.6, that class and status are more tightly linked in France and Hungary. But it would seem that the same would also be true for Chile, if not for its relatively large urban petty bourgeoisie (IVab). For the other three countries, the Netherlands, the UK and the US, there is considerable overlap in status between manual classes (V, VI and VII) and between higher and lower level salariat (I and II).

2.3 Social status and other occupational scales

Let us now consider how our status scale relates to other occupational scales that are commonly used in sociological research, namely

---

[12] The Netherlands is an outlier here in that its class II has an unusually narrow status range.

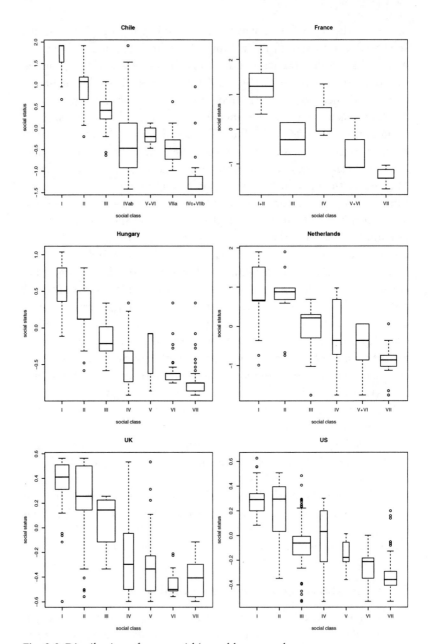

Fig. 2.3 Distribution of status within and between classes
Note: The boxes are drawn such that their widths are proportional to the
square-root of *N* of the classes.

Treiman's Standard International Occupational Prestige Scale (SIOPS), the Hope–Goldthorpe scale (H–G scale), the International Socio-Economic Index (ISEI) and the Cambridge (now called CAMSIS) scale. Although these scales are all very highly correlated with each other, they are conceptualised and operationalised in quite different ways.

2.3.1 SIOPS and Hope–Goldthorpe scale

To begin with, occupational prestige scales are based on ratings of 'social standing' of occupations by respondents of sample surveys (see e.g. Reiss, 1961; Nakao and Treas, 1994). It turns out that it does not matter very much the way respondents are asked to rate occupations: different research protocols yield very similar results. Also, it does not matter very much who is asked to rate the occupations, with different sub-populations as defined by gender, race or social positions generally giving similar ratings (Hauser and Warren, 1997, pp. 188–190). Treiman (1977) reviews 85 occupational prestige studies from 60 countries, and reports a high degree of cross-national commonality and over-time constancy in prestige scores. Indeed, Hout and DiPrete (2006, pp. 2–3) refer to this finding as the 'Treiman's constant'. Subsequently, Ganzeboom *et al.* (1992) develop a Standard International Occupational Prestige Scale (SIOPS) to facilitate cross-national comparison.

While the empirical results of occupational prestiage studies are clear, the meaning of what they measure is contested (see e.g. Sørensen, 2001, p. 289). Goldthorpe and Hope (1972, 1974) argue that prestige ratings are 'better interpreted as representing popular evaluations of the general "goodness" (in the broad sense of "desirability") of occupations'. As it does not involve notions of social superiority, equality and inferiority, SIOPS and its many variants, including Hope and Goldthorpe's own H–G scale, should be distinguished from the status order in the classical Weberian sense. The bottom row of Table 2.7 shows that, for the UK, the status order correlates with SIOPS and the H–G scale at a comparatively modest level, with $r = 0.77$ and $r = 0.76$ respectively.

It is instructive to consider where the discrepancies between these scales arise. On the lefthand panel of Figure 2.4, the SIOPS scores of the 31 status groups that are distinguished in the UK are plotted

Table 2.7 *Correlation between various occupational status scales for the UK*

	ISEI	SIOPS	H–G	CAMSIS
SIOPS	0.948			
H–G scale	0.893	0.933		
CAMSIS	0.903	0.902	0.887	
social status	0.806	0.774	0.758	0.895

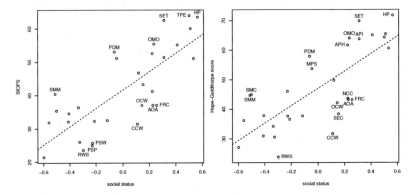

Fig. 2.4 SIOPS and H–G scale plotted against social status scale

against their social status scores. It can be seen that SMM (Skilled and related manual workers in metal trade), PDM (Plant, depot and site managers) and SET (Scientists, engineers and technologists) have high SIOPS scores relative to their status scores, while the opposite is true for many routine non-manual occupations or personal service occupations, such as FRC (Filing and record clerks), AOA (Administrative officers and assistants), CCW (Childcare workers), PSW (Personal service workers), PSP (Protective service workers) and RWS (Routine workers in services). A similar pattern can be found when the H–G scale is plotted against social status (see the righthand panel of Figure 2.4).

This pattern suggests that the non-manual–manual distinction is indeed maintained rather more sharply in the social status scale than in either SIOPS or the H–G scale. Managerial occupations in industrial settings (e.g. PDM) and certain skilled manual occupations (e.g. SMM) are rather well-paid occupations, and they are quite desirable in that sense. But they also have relatively low rankings on the status order because of their 'manual' nature or milieu. The opposite applies to many clerical occupations. For similar results based on data taken from the 1972 Oxford Social Mobility Survey, see Goldthorpe (1981, p. 10).

2.3.2 International Socio-Economic Index

As to the International Socio-Economic Index or ISEI, it should first be noted SEI was originally developed as a way to 'fill in' scores for occupations that are not rated in occupational prestige surveys (Duncan, 1961).[13] Furthermore, it is well known that apart from a few occupations, notably farmers who tend to have relatively low income and education as compared to the prestige rating that they receive, SEI scores and occupational prestige scores are generally very similar (Featherman and Hauser, 1976). In developing ISEI, Ganzeboom *et al.* (1992, p. 8) note that they 'have discarded the interpretation of SEI as an indirect and therefore imperfect measure of prestige'. Instead, they suggest that ISEI captures those attributes of occupations which convert the main resource held by individuals (i.e. education) to their main reward (i.e. income). Nonetheless, it can be seen in Table 2.7 that ISEI correlates quite highly with both SIOPS and H–G scales, at $r = 0.95$ and $r = 0.89$ respectively. With our social status scales, however, the correlation is substantially lower at $r = 0.81$. Furthermore, the outliers in Figure 2.5 are largely the same as those found in Figure 2.4. This underlines the point made in Section 2.2.2 above that our status scale is empirically as well as conceptually different from 'socioeconomic status'.

2.3.3 Cambridge Social Interaction and Stratification scale

Finally, Table 2.7 shows that social status correlates more highly with the CAMSIS scale ($r = 0.90$) than with ISEI, SIOPS or the H–G scale.

---

[13] Specifically, for those occupations where prestige ratings do exist, their prestige scores are regressed on some aggregate measures of the income and education characteristics of their incumbents. The regression coefficients thus obtained are then used to generate scores for those occupations that are not included in occupational prestige surveys.

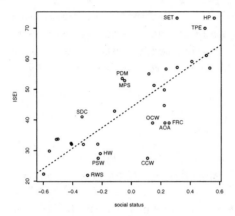

Fig. 2.5 ISEI plotted against social status scale

This is to be expected because our status scale and CAMSIS are constructed in very similar ways (see e.g. Stewart *et al.*, 1973; Prandy and Lambert, 2003). What sets us apart, though, is a rather fundamental conceptual difference. For Prandy and his colleagues, 'the Weberian distinction of classes... from status groups... is neither useful nor necessary' (Stewart *et al.*, 1980, p. 28). More recently, Bottero and Prandy (2003, p. 180) maintain that 'research has tended to eliminate the distinction between class and status, or the economic and the cultural, which was once seen as central analytically to conventional stratification theory'.[14] The implication then is that the CAMSIS scale is 'a hierarchical structure of generalized advantage/disadvantage related to the differential distribution of resources of different kinds' (Prandy, 2002, pp. 594–595).

One problem of Prandy's position is that it is unclear quite what the generalised hierarchy of 'stratification arrangements' is. But, more importantly, the Weberian class–status distinction is a conceptually cogent one, and is of potential empirical importance. Thus, instead of rejecting it by *fiat*, the questions of whether a status order is still

---

[14] However, Prandy and Lambert (2003, p. 401) take up a weaker position: 'Of course, hardly anyone, from Weber onwards, has ignored the close links between the material, or economic, and the cultural, or social – between, conventionally, class and status... Even accepting the argument that this is an important *analytical* distinction that should be maintained, in practice it is a difficult one to make'.

identifiable in contemporary societies and whether class and status have differing explanatory power in different areas of social life are matters for empirical investigation. The six national chapters that follow provide some evidence in this regard.[15]

2.4 Summary

In this chapter, I have described how the status order, in the classical Weberian sense, can be estimated empirically with survey or census data. I have then explored the properties of the status scales, and reported the following results. First, marriage choice as well as friendship choice are structured by social status. This speaks to the pervasive nature of status as a social force. It also implies that both types of data offer us a handle to identify the status order in contemporary societies.

Second, the status order of a society seems to be shared by all subpopulations within it. Apart from occupation, there are indeed other bases for social status, most notably ethnicity. But the occupation-based status ranking that we develop is largely replicated *within* each ethnic group.

Third, the general contour of the status order is very similar across countries. In all six countries that are included in this collection, occupations are ordered according to the degree of 'manuality' of the work involved. This means that non-manual occupations rank above manual occupations, and within the non-manual range, professional occupations generally rank above managerial occupations, especially those in industry or 'trade'.

However, and this is the fourth point, there is considerable cross-national variation in the strength of the correlations between social status on the one hand, and education or income on the other. These correlations are strongest for France and Hungary, and weakest for the UK. When status is regressed on both income and education, it turns out that the coefficient for income is *not* statistically significant at the conventional 5% level for four of the six countries: Chile, Hungary, the Netherlands and the UK. This underlines the empirical as well as conceptual difference between social status, in the classical Weberian sense, and 'synthetic' scales of socioeconomic status.

---

[15] See also Chan and Goldthorpe (2007a) for further evidence for the UK.

Fifth, social status is associated with social class in sensible ways. But the mapping of social status onto class is rarely so high as would preclude the inclusion of both class and status as predictors in regression analyses of cultural consumption. (The only exception here is the Netherlands.) Having introduced the key explanatory variable of our research project in this chapter, we can now proceed to the national chapters.

3 | Social stratification and musical consumption: highbrow–middlebrow in the United States

ARTHUR S. ALDERSON, ISAAC HEACOCK
AND AZAMAT JUNISBAI

3.1 Introduction

In earlier research (Alderson *et al.*, 2007), we used the *General Social Survey* (Davis *et al.*, 2003) to identify and analyse styles of cultural consumption that emerge *across* domains of cultural activity in a nationally representative sample of US residents. Motivated theoretically by three broad views of the relationship between stratification and cultural consumption – the homology, individualisation and omnivore–univore arguments (see Chapter 1) – we examined responses to a set of survey items regarding respondent participation in activities as diverse as reading, attending the theatre, visiting an art museum and attending a rock, country, or rap performance. We found that contemporary cultural consumers cluster into a small number of recognisable patterns, patterns that are more consistent with the omnivore–univore thesis than they are with the alternatives. When we modelled these styles of consumption, we found that an explicit measure of social status emerged as the central 'stratification-related' variable defining such styles, and that the role of social status was large relative to other socio-demographic and compositional factors. For instance, individuals at the highest social status were 8.3 times more likely to be 'omnivores' across these domains than they were to be members of a comparatively inactive group of cultural consumers. By comparison, individuals with the highest educational credentials were 5.4 times more likely and individuals at the highest income were 3.7 more likely.

In this chapter, we move from the analysis of cross-domain styles of cultural consumption to examine consumption within a single domain – that of music. Our choice here is purposive. The question of music is particularly sociologically interesting and theoretically charged. As DeNora (2003, p. 2; see also DeNora, 2000) has stressed, there is a long line of inquiry in social theory, stretching back at least to Plato's *Republic*, that is concerned with the social functions of music and, indeed, with its *effects* on social organisation. While, today, perhaps more visible outside of the academy in moral panics surrounding the alleged malign influence of various developments in popular music such as 'rap' and 'heavy metal' (e.g. Binder, 1993) or grist for the self-improvement industry mill (e.g. the 'Mozart effect'), such concerns were central to much social thinking on culture throughout the last century, culminating in the agenda-setting musicological work of Adorno (1976, 2002). Music also figured prominently in the turn away from 'grand theory' in the sociology of culture that began in the 1970s, exemplified in work such as Peterson's (1976) *Production of Culture* and Becker's (1982) *Art Worlds* (e.g. Peterson and Berger, 1975; Peterson, 1990, 1997). This turn, which, as Peterson and Anand (1994, pp. 311–312) relate, had coalesced by the early 1980s into a self-conscious alternative to 'the then-dominant ideal that culture and social structure mirror each other', used the tools of organisational, occupational, and network analysis to reveal how culture was 'not so much societywide and virtually unchanging as it is situational and capable of rapid change'. Finally, music has emerged as a prime 'proving ground' for a contemporary sociology of culture that, among other findings, has largely overturned an older view of high-status Americans as exclusive 'snobs' who reject middlebrow and lowbrow cultural practices and products (e.g. Lynes, 1954; Sontag, 1966; Bourdieu, 1984; Murphy, 1988). In place of high–low, elite–mass divisions, this work on music indicates that contemporary high-status Americans tend toward 'omnivorousness', not only exhibiting more of a taste for 'high' culture than others, but also for 'middle' and 'low' culture (e.g. Peterson, 1992; Peterson and Simkus, 1992; Peterson and Kern, 1996; Bryson, 1996).

Our focus on music is also motivated by the place it is accorded in Bourdieu's (1984, p. xii) 'endeavor to rethink Max Weber's opposition between class and *Stand*' in *Distinction*. As detailed in Chapter 1, one of the goals of the larger project to which this paper contributes is precisely to reassert the classic Weberian (1968) distinction between class and status that Bourdieu, among others, elides (see also Chan and Goldthorpe, 2007a). If there is any domain of cultural activity in which Bourdieu's rethinking of Weber and the model of the relationship between stratification and lifestyle he derives from this holds, it should be that of music. Interrogating aesthetic criteria of 'disinterestedness', 'purity' and 'difficulty', Bourdieu argues that the Kantian aesthetic (1986) should be viewed as the polar opposite of aesthetic conceptions that prevail among middle- and lower-class groups. The distancing from 'vulgarity' or 'natural enjoyment' that this 'bourgeois ethos' demands is thus far from innocent – it 'classifies' and legitimates social differences. If the bourgeois ethos is one that requires from all forms of art 'the negation of the world, and especially the social world', then music is the 'purest' or most 'spiritual' art, as, he claims, 'it says nothing and has *nothing to say*' (1984, p. 19, emphasis in original). As the pure art *par excellence*, then, 'nothing more clearly affirms one's "class", nothing more infallibly classifies than tastes in music' (1984, p. 18).

This chapter thus makes three main contributions. First, moving beyond the study of musical taste to that of musical consumption, we look within a single domain of cultural activity, exploring whether the styles of consumption that we earlier observed *across* domains – and the conclusions we drew regarding the centrality of social status to the definition of such styles – can be found *within*. Second, while the contemporary, music-centred sociology of culture touched on above regularly identifies 'status' as a key factor distinguishing styles of cultural consumption, research in this area has in fact never employed an overt measure of status. Rather, proxies such as education, income, occupation or SES are assumed sufficient to capture status effects. In this chapter, we employ an explicit measure of social status (see Chapter 2). This allows us to determine how social status – as distinct from social class, education, or income – is associated with styles of musical consumption in the US and to assess the magnitude of its association relative to other factors. Finally, in meeting one influential alternative to a classical Weberian conceptualisation of the stratification system (i.e. Bourdieu, 1984) on its 'home field', our results should be seen as those of a conservative test of the utility of distinguishing analytically between social status and social class in the contemporary US. If nothing more infallibly classifies than music, then any finding of independent, substantively significant status effects on styles of musical consumption would be especially compelling evidence in favour of one of the broader goals of this project.

Our analysis proceeds in two parts. First, we analyse the patterns of response to a range of items regarding musical consumption fielded in the August 2002 *Public Participation in the Arts* supplement to the US *Current Population Survey* (US Department of Commerce, Bureau of the Census, 2004). Using latent class cluster analysis (hereafter LCA), we identify and characterise contemporary styles of musical consumption. We also offer some validation of our characterisation of the LCA results, using information on musical taste and a range of distinct (non-musical) activities that is also available in the *Survey of Public Participation in the Arts* (hereafter SPPA). Second, we model these styles of musical consumption with our status scale and a range of variables relating to social stratification in concert with a set of socio-demographic controls. In examining the multinomial logistic regression results, we also give particular attention to the relative magnitude of the observed associations between variables of interest and styles of musical consumption.

3.2 Styles of highbrow–middlebrow musical consumption

As noted above, our data on musical consumption come from the SPPA. In August 2002, face-to-face interviews were conducted with a total of 17,135 non-institutionalised individuals, 18 years of age or older, identified via a probability sample of US households. The response rate was 70%. We restrict our analysis to the 12,280 persons aged 24–64.[1] Owing to missing data on a number of variables – especially occupation and the presence of children in the household – the regression results presented below are based on the analysis of 9,914 cases.

The SPPA queries respondents on their participation in a range of artistic events and activities. It also surveys respondents about participation in a variety of leisure activities and about taste for various musical and artistic events. As regards musical consumption, respondents were queried on their activities in relation to four genres: opera, classical, jazz and musicals. We thus focus on the consumption of two generally recognised 'highbrow' genres – opera and classical – and two 'middlebrow' genres – jazz and musicals. Of the four, our characterisation of jazz as 'middlebrow' – while strictly irrelevant for the analysis – is

---

[1] Unfortunately, age is categorical in the SPPA and we are forced to depart here from the convention in the larger comparative project of restricting the analysis to persons aged 20–65.

clearly the most troublesome. Very simply, 'jazz' is a peculiar genre. While today taught at conservatories of music, for instance, as 'high art', it is organically 'lowbrow' and much of the research on jazz, as Peterson and Kern (1996, p. 901) relate, suggests that it is presently 'middlebrow', owing in some part to the fact that popular definitions of jazz vary dramatically from person to person.[2]

One very nice feature of the SPPA for our purposes is the level of detail that the survey provides on participation in artistic activities. As regards music, one could analyse: (1) attendance at musical performances (e.g. 'Did you go to a live classical music performance, such as symphony, chamber, or choral music in the last 12 months?'), (2) listening to music (e.g. 'During the last 12 months did you listen to classical music on records, tapes, or compact disks?' *and* 'During the last 12 months did you listen to classical music on the radio?'), or (3) viewing musical performances (e.g. 'During the last 12 months did you watch a classical music performance on television, a video (VHS) tape, or a video (DVD) disk?'). In this paper, we fully exploit the data at hand and analyse all three; that is, we analyse attendance, listening and watching across opera, classical, jazz and musicals.

Table 3.1 lists the percentage of SPPA respondents who report that they have engaged in the twelve activities listed in the past year. We rank the items in terms of their popularity, from least to most popular. Note that there is a distinct gradient, with the percentage of respondents reporting listening to classical music in the last year being an order of magnitude larger than those reporting attending opera. By activity, opera is least popular in terms of *attending* (3.2%), while musicals are most popular (19.4%); musicals are least popular in terms of *listening* (5.8%), classical is most popular (31.4); and opera is least popular in terms of *watching* (4.9%), classical most popular (17.5%).[3]

To identify styles of musical consumption among the SPPA respondents, we subject their response patterns on the twelve items above to latent class cluster analysis (e.g. Magidson and Vermunt, 2001).

---

[2] In short, 'jazz', to some, is Ornette Coleman, while, to others, it is Kenny G. See DiMaggio and Ostrower (1990) and Peterson and Simkus (1992), cited in Peterson and Kern (1996, p. 901), for evidence for the 'unusually diffuse evaluation of what is called "jazz" by different people'.

[3] As for the place of jazz as a genre, one can note that it is no more popular across attending, listening and watching than classical music.

Table 3.1 *Percentage of respondents who have attended live music events, listened to music (recording/radio), or watched a musical performance (television/vcr/dvd) in the last twelve months*

Activity	%
Opera attended	3.2
Opera seen	4.9
Musical listened	5.8
Opera listened	8.3
Musical seen	12.0
Jazz attended	12.7
Classical attended	12.8
Jazz seen	17.5
Classical seen	17.5
Musical attended	19.4
Jazz listened	30.7
Classical listened	31.4

In broad outlines, the idea behind LCA is elegant in its simplicity. Starting from the observation that the binary responses to the twelve manifest variables in Table 3.1 will exhibit some degree of association (e.g. among those SPPA respondents who report that they attended an opera performance in the past year, 62% also report attending a classical music performance, while, among those reporting that they did not attend an opera performance, just 11% report attending a classical performance), the goal of LCA is to determine the number of latent classes T – in our case, styles of musical consumption – that are necessary to account for the association that exists among the manifest variables. Assuming that an independence model – one that places all observations in the same latent class (i.e. $T = 1$) – does not fit the data, the analyst would proceed to fit $T = 2, \ldots, n$ models until such association is accounted for by the model. Once a solution is found, one typically then assigns respondents to the latent class for which they have the highest posterior membership probability (e.g. if $T = 2$ and the membership probabilities are, given the respondent's response pattern, 0.8 and 0.2, one would assign the respondent to the first class). Our latent class analysis was performed using the program *LatentGOLD 3.0* (Statistical Innovations Inc, 2003).

Table 3.2 *Latent class models fitted to SPPA musical consumption items*

Models	BIC_{LL}	L^2	df	p	% reduction in L^2
1 class	92727.499	21234.795	4083	0.000	0.0
2 class	77893.188	6280.770	4070	0.000	70.4
3 class	76221.306	4489.173	4057	0.000	78.9
4 class	75464.868	3613.019	4044	0.999	83.0
3 class[a]	75655.412	3914.070	4056	0.940	81.6

Note: [a] A residual direct effect between jazz listened and jazz seen is added.

The LCA results are presented in Table 3.2. As one can note, by a standard approach to LCA, neither a two- nor three-class solution adequately fits the data; that is, we must specify four latent classes to account for the association that exists among the manifest variables. In fitting these models, we paid close attention to the residual associations among items after fitting the $T = 1$ through $T = 4$ models. In examining the three-class solution, we find that there is a very large and distinct residual correlation between those who report *jazz listening* and *jazz watching*. When we re-estimate the three-class model, specifying a direct effect between the two items, the three-class model, as one can note in Table 3.2, fits the data well.

How do the final two models differ? The four-class model differs mainly in identifying a group of 'jazz aficionados', respondents who are most distinctive for doing a good bit of jazz listening and watching, and, secondarily, attending. In the three-class solution that allows a direct effect between jazz listening and watching, this group is largely folded into a group of middling consumers that we will describe below. Given that the fit of both models is quite acceptable, and not clearly distinguishable, in the interests of parsimony, we analyse the three-class model with direct effects.[4]

[4] Two points concerning this strategy are important to note. First, jazz aficionados aside, we otherwise identify the same classes in the four-class solution that we do in the three-class solution. Second, except as noted below, none of the conclusions that we draw from the regression analysis below are different when we model the four-class solution.

Table 3.3 *Relative size of latent classes and conditional probabilities of consuming each item in last twelve months*

	Omnivore	Paucivore	Inactive
Class size	0.110	0.325	0.564
opera attended	0.184	0.031	0.003
opera seen	0.324	0.035	0.003
musical listened	0.376	0.051	0.001
opera listened	0.548	0.069	0.000
musical seen	0.752	0.168	0.014
jazz attended	0.396	0.228	0.017
classical attended	0.561	0.187	0.010
jazz seen	0.541	0.301	0.032
classical seen	0.752	0.266	0.011
musical attended	0.552	0.304	0.061
jazz listened	0.776	0.568	0.065
classical listened	0.963	0.577	0.036

Table 3.3 presents the profiles of these classes and the labels that we employ to characterise them. The three-class solution divides the SPPA respondents into three groups constituting 11%, 33%, and 56% of the sample. Again, as in Table 3.1, items are presented in increasing order of overall popularity. The first class, the smallest, consists of people who have comparatively high probabilities of having done all across attending, listening and watching. We label them 'Omnivores'. The third class – the largest – consists, in contrast, of people who have comparatively low probabilities of having done any of the activities considered. We label them 'Inactive'. In between – literally and figuratively – is the second class, with middling probabilities of attending, listening and watching. We label them 'Paucivores'. So, for instance, the probability of a Paucivore watching opera in the last year is an order of magnitude greater than that of an Inactive, while, in turn, the probability of an Omnivore watching opera is an order of magnitude greater than that of a Paucivore. Our labelling is motivated by these relative probabilities. The Omnivores are 'omnivorous' in the precise sense that they are considerably more active than others across all items, ranging from the popular, such as classical listening, to the unpopular, such as attending the opera. Similarly, the Paucivores are

Table 3.4 *Estimated overall probability and conditional (row) probabilities of consuming each item*

	Omnivore	Paucivore	Inactive	Total
Overall probability	0.110	0.325	0.564	1.000
Opera attended	0.629	0.316	0.055	1.000
Opera seen	0.731	0.235	0.034	1.000
Musical listened	0.710	0.286	0.004	1.000
Opera listened	0.728	0.272	0.000	1.000
Musical seen	0.482	0.455	0.064	1.000
Jazz attended	0.343	0.583	0.073	1.000
Classical attended	0.482	0.475	0.043	1.000
Jazz seen	0.340	0.558	0.101	1.000
Classical seen	0.473	0.493	0.034	1.000
Musical attended	0.314	0.509	0.177	1.000
Jazz listened	0.279	0.602	0.119	1.000
Classical listened	0.339	0.598	0.064	1.000

'paucivorous' in the sense that they are 'in-between' across all items, with considerably higher odds of being active across attending, listening and watching than the Inactives, but with considerably lower odds relative to the Omnivores. Finally, the Inactives, who, it bears emphasising again, constitute roughly 56% of the SPPA sample, are distinct for their relative inactivity across all items.

We take two steps to interrogate our interpretation and labelling of the latent classes. First, in Table 3.4, we examine the partial conditional probabilities formed from the row percentages, which tells us from which class consumers of each item are drawn. So, for instance, while Omnivores make up just 11% of the sample, we find that they make up 63% of the audience for live opera and, in contrast, while Inactives make up 56% of the sample, they make up just 6% of the same audience. Examining the row probabilities, it is clear, first, that the Inactives are appropriately named. This group is distinctive, in essence, for being the modal class for those who *have not* engaged in any of the activities under consideration. The Omnivores, in contrast, are distinctive for being the modal class for those consuming opera – in all its forms – and listening to musicals: 73% of those who have seen opera, 73% who have listened to opera, 71% who have listened

Table 3.5 *Characteristics of latent classes*

	Omnivore	Paucivore	Inactive
Peterson's omnivorous taste (max = 8)	4.135	3.329	1.958
lowbrow genres liked (max = 5)	2.566	2.262	1.547
middlebrow genres liked (max = 3)	1.568	1.067	0.411
proportion using Internet for music	0.387	0.284	0.141
proportion taking part in sports	0.466	0.457	0.275
proportion taking part in outdoor activity	0.591	0.507	0.316
proportion jog, walk, exercise	0.858	0.780	0.480
proportion taking part in volunteer activity	0.614	0.466	0.218
proportion gardening	0.757	0.656	0.437
proportion weave/needlework/sew	0.324	0.220	0.116
proportion making home improvement	0.701	0.637	0.451
hours worked last week	39.363	40.022	40.492
proportion top quartile hrs wrk last week	0.414	0.366	0.324
hours of television per day	2.030	2.230	2.609
proportion top quartile TV hrs per day	0.108	0.161	0.244

Note: except as indicated by italics, all (row) comparisons significant at $p < 0.01$.

to a musical and 63% who have attended an opera in the last year fall into the Omnivore class. This class is, thus, most distinctive for its participation in activities that are least popular: While the Omnivores are more likely to consume all items than others (i.e. Table 3.3), what especially sets them apart is their participation in opera and in listening to musicals. The Paucivores are most distinctive for being the modal class for the consumption of jazz, classical listening and musical attendance, overall, the most popular activities: 60% of those listening to jazz, 60% of classical listeners, 58% of those attending live jazz, 56% of those watching jazz and 51% of those attending musicals last year fall into this class.

Second, in Table 3.5, we examine how far our relative, minimalist characterisation and labelling might extend into other domains, including that of musical taste. We see two main issues here. First, is the labelling of the first class as 'Omnivores' defensible? While this group exhibits a relatively broad and intense style of consumption within these four genres of music, these are, after all, highbrow and middlebrow genres. Might we, perhaps, be mistaking a cultural elite for omnivores? Second, are the Inactives inactive in any more general sense, outside of the domain of highbrow and middlebrow musical consumption? Populism runs deep in US culture, and 'art music' is surely thought more than a little precious by many Americans. Very simply, then, while our Inactives may not go to the opera, are they not likely to be active in other domains? And might this not give us some additional insight into this style of musical consumption?

As noted earlier, the SPPA is a comparatively rich source and we can begin to address these questions. Stepping outside of our 'revealed preferences' framework, we can, for instance, investigate the musical tastes of each class, determining whether our Omnivore and Paucivore musical consumers are likewise omnivorous or paucivorous in their musical tastes. Peterson and Kern (1996, p. 901) operationalise omnivorousness as the number of middlebrow and lowbrow musical genres that respondents report liking. Peterson's lowbrow genres are country, bluegrass, gospel, rock and blues, and the middlebrow genres are easy listening, musicals and big band. As one can note from Table 3.5, Omnivore musical consumers are indeed significantly more omnivorous in their tastes by this metric than Paucivores who, in turn, are more omnivorous than Inactives. Omnivores, on average, report liking 4.1 middlebrow and lowbrow genres, while Inactives report liking 2.0. This is very similar to the difference in omnivorousness that Peterson and Kern (1996) report between a segment they identify as 'highbrows' (i.e. those who report liking classical and opera) and 'others' (i.e. those who do not) in the 1992 SPPA. Disaggregating Peterson's omnivorous taste, it is also worth noting that Omnivores are significantly more likely to report liking middlebrow and lowbrow genres than Paucivores and Inactives. This suggests that Omnivores in the domain of highbrow and middlebrow musical consumption are not a cultural 'elite' or 'nobility' who reject lowbrow and middlebrow musical genres, but rather exhibit omnivorous taste.

Regarding the Inactives, we consider a number of possibilities. Might the Inactives be musically active in new media that are not well-captured by the items we examine?[5] Table 3.5 suggests not; rather,

---

[5] Perhaps they do not attend live performances or listen to compact discs, but rather spend their evening swapping pirated mp3 files on the Internet?

Omnivores are significantly more likely to report using the Internet for music than Paucivores or Inactives. Interestingly, the same general conclusion can be drawn regarding any number of non-musical activities as well: Omnivores are not only more likely to consume opera, classical, jazz and musicals, they are also more likely to take part in sports, in outdoor activities, to exercise, to take part in volunteer activities, to garden, to sew or to busy themselves with home improvement. Paucivore musical consumers fall squarely 'in-between' in terms of these activities as well.[6]

Musical consumption and participation in the other activities listed in Table 3.5 of course require time. Perhaps Inactives face distinctive time-constraints? Might they simply work more than others? As one can note, on average, they do work more, about an hour more than Omnivores and a half-hour more than Paucivores in the week preceding the interview. However, we also note that the standard deviation of hours worked is considerably larger for Omnivores than it is for Inactives and, moreover, that a larger proportion of Omnivores appear in the top quartile of hours worked than Inactives (i.e. 0.41 vs. 0.32

[6] Sullivan and Katz-Gerro (2007, p. 125) revisit the omnivore concept (e.g. Peterson, 1992; Peterson and Kern, 1996) and contrast *voraciousness*, understood as involving the 'frequency of participation in specific cultural activities', with *omnivorousness*, understood as involving 'a broad range of cultural tastes'. Based on their analysis of time use data for the UK, they find that the correlates of the former are very similar to those observed in studies of the latter. They conclude that a design combining time-use data with information on cultural tastes would be required to rigorously establish the conceptual distinction between these 'separate but related dimensions of cultural consumption' (2007, p. 133). While we agree with Sullivan and Katz-Gerro (2007) that it is important to distinguish analytically between *what* people consume and the way in which they consume it, the SPPA unfortunately affords us no opportunity to draw such a distinction in any detail. Clearly, the Omnivore musical consumers we identify are more 'voracious' than other types of consumers. As we have found, they are more likely to attend opera, jazz, classical and musical performances outside of the home than others *and* more likely to engage in any number of other activities. Beyond this, however, we can only recapitulate: The segment we label as 'Omnivores' not only exhibit a relatively broad style of highbrow and middlebrow musical consumption, but they are also more likely to exhibit *omnivorous musical tastes*. Based on these results, we conclude that this class of musical consumers is appropriately labelled and speculate that omnivorousness and voraciousness may be less orthogonal to one another in the US than Sullivan and Katz-Gerro suggest they are in the UK.

respectively).[7] Again, the Paucivores are 'in between'. Inactives, then, are not only inactive in highbrow and middlebrow musical consumption and less omnivorous in their musical tastes than others, they are relatively inactive across a variety of other activities and this would not appear to be a straightforward result of the demands of work. In the end, we were able to find just one activity in the SPPA in which Inactive musical consumers were significantly more active than Omnivores or Paucivores: television viewing. As one can note in Table 3.5, Inactives report watching just over a half-hour more television a day than the Omnivores, and nearly a quarter appear in the top quartile of hours of television viewing.[8]

In sum, our latent class cluster analysis identifies three classes of musical consumers: a class of Omnivores who are notable for their relatively high probabilities – across attending, listening and watching – of consuming opera, classical, jazz and musicals, a Paucivore class of middling consumers and a class of Inactives who exhibit remarkably low probabilities of participating in any of the twelve forms of musical consumption we examine. Omnivores are most distinctive for their consumption of opera (in all forms examined) and listening to musicals, the least popular activities overall. Paucivores, in contrast, are the modal class for jazz (again, in all forms), classical listening and musical attendance, the most popular activities. Inactives are most distinctive for being the modal class for those who have not engaged in any of the twelve forms of musical consumption we examine. Omnivore musical consumers also exhibit omnivorous musical tastes and are more active than other classes across a range of activities from

---

[7] It is worth noting that the *Current Population Survey* 'hours worked' item we use here is arguably the highest quality available in the US on individual working time.

[8] While the information presented in Table 3.5 is certainly suggestive of the idea that Inactives in the domain of highbrow and middlebrow musical consumption partake of a broader 'low-activity' style of cultural consumption – an intriguing possibility that is deserving of further research – it should not be taken to imply that Inactives do not attend, listen, or watch music of *any* type or, indeed, that they do not have rich musical lives outside of the domains under consideration in this paper. Our aim here, it bears repeating, is simply to explore the extent to which Inactives in this domain might be 'inactive' in a more general sense, beyond highbrow and middlebrow musical consumption. As the results indicate, our identification of a class of Inactives is not simply an artefact of our focus on the specific musical genres under consideration.

gardening to sport. Inactive musical consumers are least omnivorous in their musical tastes and are comparatively inactive in other domains, while, again, Paucivore musical consumers are 'in between' in these senses as well.

3.3 Social stratification and musical consumption

What factors distinguish these styles of musical consumption? To answer this question, we treat the latent classes just discussed as the dependent variable in a multinomial logistic regression analysis. Rather than model the responses to the twelve manifest variables, then, we model the types of consumers that are identified by LCA. We do so with a number of covariates relating to social stratification in concert with a set of socio-demographic controls. Prime among the former is the measure of social status that we detail below. Our argument is that social status can be distinguished analytically from social class and that status, as distinct from class, is the stratificatory linchpin of contemporary US lifestyles and patterns of cultural consumption. To estimate the associations of social status with such patterns, we also include measures of educational qualifications, social class, family income, gender and race. We also control for marital status, in the expectation that the married will be less likely to be active musical consumers than the unmarried; the presence of children in the household, by the same rationale as that for marital status; region of the country, based on the expectation that opportunities for consumption may vary by region; the size of the locale in which the respondent resides, based on the same rationale as that for region; nativity, with no strong prediction; and age, in the expectation that age will be positively related to active musical consumption.

We measure respondent's educational level as *BA Degree* and *Graduate Degree* (with Less Than BA Degree as the reference category).[9] We form a seven-class version of the Goldthorpe class scheme (*IIIab – Routine Non-Manual, IVab – Petty Bourgeoisie, IVc – Farmer, V+VI – Skilled Workers and Foremen, VIIa – Non-Skilled Workers, VIIb – Farm Labourers*, with *I+II – Higher and Lower Salariat* as the reference category). *Family Income Per Capita (log 10)* is created

---

[9] Details regarding variable construction are available from the authors upon request.

from a categorical income variable.[10] *Female* is an indicator variable coded 1 for female, 0 otherwise. *Married* is coded 1 for currently married, 0 otherwise. *Child (0–5)*, *Child (6–13)*, and *Child (14–17)* code for the presence of dependent children in the household. *Midwest*, *West* and *South* (with *Northeast* as the omitted category) code for region. *Mid-Size City* and *Big City* code for MSAs or CMSAs with populations, respectively, between 250,000–999,000 and greater than 1,000,000 (with MSA/CMSAs with less than 250,000 as the omitted category). *Foreign Born* codes for whether the respondent was born outside of the US. *Age 35–44*, *Age 45–54* and *Age 55–64*, with *Age 24–34* as the reference, code for respondent age. Finally, *Black*, *Hispanic* and *Other Race* (with *White* as the reference category) code for race.

The variable of central interest is our measure of *Social Status*. As detailed elsewhere (Alderson *et al.*, 2005), our approach is to allow a status order to emerge from patterns of differential association in tables of occupations in which rows and columns are partners to married or cohabiting couples. Inspired by Chan and Goldthorpe (2004), our approach builds on that of Laumann (e.g. Laumann and Guttman, 1966) and, earlier still, Warner's 'associational approach' to the US stratification system (e.g. Warner *et al.*, 1949). It is motivated by the fundamental insight that intimate association is an indicator of social equality and, thus, that status differences can be read off patterns of *differential association*. Our results indicate that one can readily identify a status order in the contemporary United States, one that is reasonably distinct from the social class system. We also find that this status order is remarkably similar across sub-populations (e.g. the status order that emerges from the analysis of gay cohabiters is very similar to that which emerges from the analysis of married couples, see Table 2.3 in Chapter 2).

Social Status is derived from the multidimensional scaling of the row-dissimilarities of a symmetrised 94 × 94 table of 'minor occupation groups' defined by the 2000 US Standard Occupational

---

[10] For the thirteen bounded categories in the SPPA income variable, before standardising by the number of persons in the respondent's household, we pursue a fairly standard practice with such categorical income items and set the respondent's income to the middle of the defined range (e.g. a respondent in category '$5,000–$7,499' is recoded as $6260) and set the open-ended top category to 150% of the lower bound.

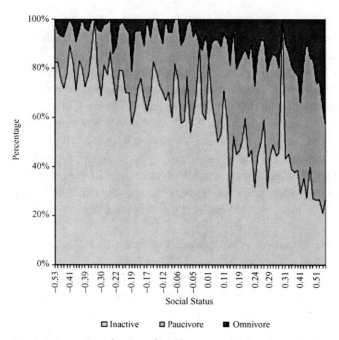

Fig. 3.1 Area plot of styles of highbrow–middlebrow musical consumption by social status

Classification in which the rows (men) and columns (women) are partners to 2,297,139 marriages. (A supplementary analysis that employs 'gender-specific' status scales was derived, via the same procedure, from asymmetric tables of the marital choices of the same men and women.) The 5% Public Use Microdata Sample of the 2000 US Census was used to create the scale. We restrict our analysis to persons aged 20–64, exclude those employed in military occupations (less than 0.1% of the PUMS sample aged 20–64), and introduce a category for those who were not in the labour force at the time of the Census. Status scores for occupations defined in the 2000 Standard Occupational Classification were assigned to SPPA respondents using the 1980 Census Occupational Classification of the respondent's 'primary job' and a cross-walk developed by the Census Bureau (Scopp, 2003).

Figure 3.1 reveals how the SPPA respondents are distributed across latent classes by social status. At the minimum status, 83% are Inactive and about 1% are Omnivores. At the maximum, in contrast, 27%

are Inactive and 43% are Omnivores. While the proportion of Inactive declines fairly linearly, the proportion Omnivore remains fairly constant across the first forty percent or so of the range of status and rises thereafter. Unconditionally, then, there is a clear relationship between social status and styles of highbrow and middlebrow musical consumption.[11]

In Table 3.6, we present the regression results. As one can note, most of the variables have statistically significant effects on at least one of the comparisons. Before discussing these, we can begin by noting the null findings. The most important in this regard is that we find no significant class effects in these data.[12] In terms of the descriptives, there is also no strict class gradient to styles of musical consumption, wherein, relative to the salariat (i.e. classes I+II), the odds of Omnivore vs. Inactive (hereafter O|I), Paucivore vs. Inactive (P|I) and Omnivore vs. Paucivore (O|P) would decline monotonically as one moves toward the unskilled (i.e. VIIa – Non-Skilled Workers and VIIb – Farm Labourers). Rather, for instance, the petty bourgeois exhibit higher odds of O|I, P|I and O|P than the salariat. While the absence of significant class effects may be surprising to some readers, it is consistent with what we have observed in earlier work on cultural consumption in the United States (Alderson *et al.*, 2007). In addition to social class, we also have null findings regarding the presence of children in the household and the Midwest vs. Northeast regional comparison.

Among the significant parameters, the findings for our status scale are of central interest. As one can note, social status is found to play a significant role in distinguishing styles of musical consumption: higher status individuals are more likely to be Paucivores than Inactives, and are especially more likely to be Omnivores than Inactives. Interestingly, at conventional levels, social status does not distinguish between Omnivores and Paucivores. Social status thus appears most important for the distinction between those who do *something* in the way of

---

[11] The large 'spike' at social status 0.3012 results from the classification of the two chief executives in the sample as 'Inactive'. No other occupational category has a smaller number of respondents.

[12] In the case of the 'jazz aficionados' identified in the four-class LCA solution (see Table 3.2), there is one qualification to this conclusion: Relative to *I+II – Higher and Lower Salariat*, we find that *VIIa – Non-Skilled Workers* are significantly less likely to be jazz aficionados than Inactive.

Table 3.6 *Multinomial logistic regression predicting latent class membership*

	O vs. I		P vs. I		O vs. P	
	$\hat{\beta}$	s.e.	$\hat{\beta}$	s.e.	$\hat{\beta}$	s.e.
Social Status	1.270***	0.245	0.839***	0.163	0.432	0.249
BA Degree	1.233***	0.098	0.707***	0.066	0.526***	0.100
Graduate Degree	1.847***	0.123	1.078***	0.093	0.769***	0.119
IIIa+b	−0.011	0.121	−0.033	0.079	0.022	0.123
IVa+b	0.249	0.173	0.126	0.119	0.123	0.175
IVc	−0.345	0.415	−0.396	0.254	0.050	0.446
V+VI	−0.204	0.205	−0.151	0.115	−0.054	0.213
VIIa	−0.285	0.220	−0.223	0.124	−0.062	0.229
VIIb	0.242	0.523	−0.624	0.428	0.867	0.607
Family Income	0.604***	0.135	0.546***	0.085	0.058	0.140
Female	0.592***	0.080	0.266***	0.054	0.325***	0.081
Married	−0.421***	0.083	−0.154**	0.057	−0.267**	0.084
Child (0–5)	−0.098	0.153	0.101	0.092	−0.199	0.155
Child (6–13)	0.032	0.149	−0.032	0.090	0.065	0.152
Child (14–17)	−0.109	0.132	0.018	0.085	−0.127	0.135
Midwest	−0.095	0.113	−0.013	0.075	−0.082	0.115
West	0.395***	0.109	0.344***	0.076	0.051	0.109
South	−0.316**	0.113	−0.213**	0.076	−0.103	0.115
Mid-Size City	0.385**	0.111	0.251**	0.072	0.134	0.114
Big City	0.430***	0.093	0.376***	0.060	0.054	0.095
Foreign Born	0.239	0.148	−0.087	0.106	0.326*	0.151
Age 35–44	0.282*	0.114	0.067	0.069	0.215	0.116
Age 45–54	0.770***	0.116	0.195**	0.074	0.575***	0.117
Age 55–64	0.929***	0.132	0.239**	0.089	0.691***	0.133
Black	−0.506**	0.184	0.360***	0.092	−0.865***	0.184
Hispanic	−0.365	0.186	−0.288*	0.115	−0.077	0.194
Other Race	−0.507**	0.194	−0.549***	0.141	0.042	0.202

Note: $^{*}p < 0.05$, $^{**}p < 0.01$, $^{***}p < 0.001$ (two-tailed tests).

highbrow and middlebrow musical consumption (i.e. are Omnivores or Paucivores), and those who do not (i.e. are Inactives).[13]

---

[13] Supplementary analyses reveal that it is the control for social class that drives our results for social status in the O|P contrast. In a model in which social class

As regards the other significant parameters, we find that, relative to those with less than a BA degree, those holding a BA degree are more likely to be Omnivores or Paucivores than Inactives and, in terms of the O|P contrast, are more likely to be Omnivores. The same conclusions hold for those holding a graduate degree, and the effects on each contrast are notably larger. We interpret these results in light of the 'information processing hypothesis' (e.g. Ganzeboom, 1982; Chan and Goldthorpe, 2007c) discussed elsewhere in this volume.[14] Family income per capita affects styles of musical consumption in a fashion that is consistent with a straightforward resource-based explanation: We find that those with more income are more likely to adopt *some* participatory style, but income does not distinguish between such styles; that is, income has positive effects on the O|I and P|I contrasts, but does not distinguish between Omnivores and Paucivores. Gender has effects that are consistent with earlier research which suggests that women are more likely to be active cultural consumers than men (e.g. Bihagen and Katz-Gerro, 2000). Women are found to be more likely to be Omnivores or Paucivores than Inactives, and more likely than men to be Omnivores than Paucivores as well.

Marital status has negative effects on all three contrasts, a result we interpret as reflecting, *ceteris paribus*, the greater constraints on cultural activity faced by the married relative to the unmarried. Region does not distinguish between Omnivores and Paucivores, but it does have effects on the O|I and P|I contrasts, with the West more likely, and South less likely, to be active musical consumers relative to residents of the Northeast. Relative to individuals residing in small towns or rural areas, those in larger cities have more opportunity to pursue an active style of musical consumption, and 'Mid-Size City' and 'Big City' have appropriately ordered effects on the O|I and P|I contrasts.

---

is not included, status has a significant effect in the expected direction on the Omnivore–Paucivore contrast.

[14] Very simply, with the effects of social stratification – social status, social class, income, race, gender – netted out, the effects of educational qualifications can be interpreted in terms of the varying levels of information content desired by individuals in their cultural activities. Relative to those less educated, more highly educated individuals are expected to display an affinity for styles of musical consumption that make greater demands in terms of information content (e.g. comparatively broad and intense consumption that includes complex musical forms).

City size, however, does not distinguish between Omnivores and Paucivores, suggesting that the effects of population are largely those of
a constraint on access. While we had no strong directional hypothesis, we thought it nonetheless important to control for nativity given
current levels of immigration to the United States. Foreign born has a
significant positive effect on the P|O contrast, but does not significantly
affect the O|I or P|I contrasts. The results for Age 35–44, Age 45–54,
and Age 55–64 indicate that, relative to respondents under thirty-five
years of age, older individuals are more likely to be Omnivores or
Paucivores than Inactives, and more likely to be Omnivores than Paucivores. Finally, as regards the effects of race and ethnicity, Black has
a significant negative effect on the O|I contrast, a positive effect on
the P|I contrast, and a negative effect on the O|P contrast. Relative to
non-Hispanic whites, Hispanics are found significantly less likely to be
Paucivores than Inactives. Other Race has significant negative effects
on the O|I and P|I contrast. In short, while Hispanics and members of
other non-Hispanic white groups are more likely to be Inactive than
they are Omnivores or Paucivores – that is, disconnected from highbrow and middlebrow musical consumption – blacks are more likely
to be Paucivores than they are Inactives or Omnivores.[15]

How large are these effects, in and of themselves and relative to one
another? Given the large number of coefficients and contrasts to attend
to, we think it most efficient to graphically summarise the information
in Table 3.6 in the fashion suggested by Long and Freese (2006). We
do this in Figure 3.2. In this figure, the Omnivore class is indicated with
an 'O', Paucivore with a 'P' and Inactive with an 'I'. In interpreting this
figure, there are just three things to note: First, the factor change for
each outcome relative to the Inactive category is scaled across the top
of the figure. The distance of O and P from I is thus the change, on the
upper scale, in the odds ratio associated with a min-max change in the

---

[15] This is a notable contrast with the findings of our earlier, cross-domain
examination of cultural consumption which indicate, *ceteris paribus*, that
African Americans are disconnected from the dominant culture in the United
States (Alderson *et al.*, 2007). In supplementary analyses, we determined that
this finding is driven by the folding of the jazz aficionados into the Paucivore
class that, as detailed above, is the practical result of specifying a direct effect
between *jazz listening* and *jazz watching*. In other words, when we model the
four-class solution, we find that Black has a significant positive effect on the
Jazz Aficionado vs. Inactive contrast, and a significant negative effect on the
O|I and P|I contrasts.

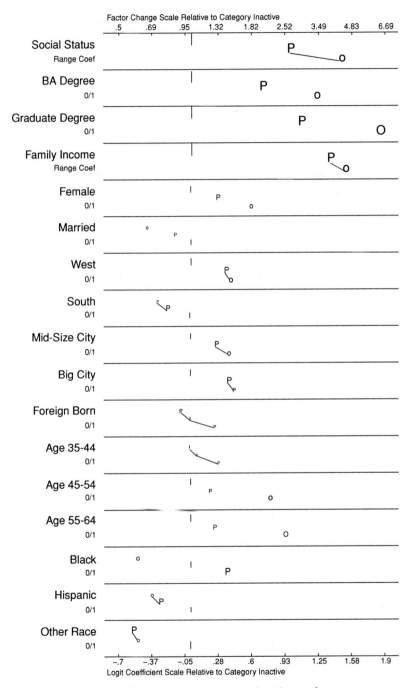

Fig. 3.2 Factor change/discrete change associated with significant parameters

explanatory variables. Second, when lines connect points, this indicates that the variable in question does *not* have a significant effect on the contrast. So, for instance, social status does not distinguish between Paucivores and Omnivores at the 5% level, so they are connected. Finally, the elements themselves are sized to indicate the magnitude of the discrete change (or change in predicted probability) in each outcome associated with a min-max change in the variable of interest, holding all other variables at their means and modes.[16]

Taking each outcome in turn, we can begin with the Inactive style. As indicated by the size of the Is, social status, educational qualifications and family income are clearly associated with the largest discrete change in the Inactive outcome of any of the significant variables. Behind the graphics, we find that graduate degree reduces the probability of I by 28% for an individual at the means and modes. Family income has the second largest effect, reducing the probability of I by 23% across its range, followed by social status (−0.20), and BA degree (−0.18).

Turning to the Omnivore style, it is clear from Figure 3.2 that the same factors again have the largest effects. Those who hold a graduate degree are approximately 6.3 times more likely to be Omnivores than Inactives, while, across their range, family income and social status raise the odds of O|I by factors of 4.5 and 4.4, respectively. In terms of discrete change in the Omnivore outcome − and, again, behind the sizing of the elements in Figure 3.2 − graduate degree raises the probability of O by 9%, BA degree by about 5% and social status by 4%.

These same variables likewise heavily shape the Paucivore outcome. Those at the maximum income are 3.9 times more likely than those at the minimum to be Paucivores than Inactives. Those with a graduate degree are 2.9 times more likely than those without a tertiary degree to be Paucivores, and, across its range, social status raises the odds of P|I by a factor of 2.7. Income is also associated with the largest discrete change in the Paucivore outcome, raising the probability of P by 19% with a min-max change, followed in magnitude by the effects of graduate degree (0.18) and social status (0.16).

---

[16] The modal respondent is a white, 35–44 year old, married man, with no children in the household, salariat class, with less than a BA degree, who resides in a big city in the South.

In sum, the regression results indicate that social status, along with educational qualifications and income, is central to the definition of the styles of highbrow and middlebrow musical consumption that we identify with latent class analysis. As noted above, the status scale that appears in Table 3.6 and Figure 3.2 is based on the scaling of a symmetrised table in which the rows and columns are partners to marriages; that is, we apply the status scores derived from married couples to, for instance, cohabiters and elide the small differences that emerge when we scale the dissimilarities of cohabiters or of men and women separately. In our work on the US status scale (Alderson *et al.*, 2005), we have also produced distinct scales for married men and women, for cohabiting couples, and for black Americans (among other sub-samples). The fairly large sample that the SPPA provides affords us the opportunity to apply these more specific scales to the relevant sub-samples. How robust are the results to such a move? Interestingly – and reassuringly – when we assign the unmarried the scores derived for cohabiters or assign black Americans scores derived for blacks, the results are substantively identical, up to and including the rank-order of the factor changes and discrete changes associated with social status and other main factors. We do, however, find some notable differences when we assign gender-specific status scores to men and women (i.e. scales derived from separate analyses of the dissimilarities of men and women).[17]

In Figure 3.3, we graph these results along with those of other important variables. Note first that, by the gender-specific scale, social status now has a significant effect on the O|P contrast, in addition to the O|I and P|I contrasts; that is, status now significantly distinguishes between Omnivores and Paucivores. Second, it is noteworthy that inclusion of the gender-specific status has no real effect on the relationship of *gender* with styles of musical consumption: Gender again has significant effects on all contrasts and the effects are of approximately the same magnitude. In terms of discrete change, we find that social status has the second largest effect on the Omnivore outcome (after graduate degree), the second largest effect on the Paucivore outcome (after income), and the second largest effect on the Inactive outcome

---

[17] This is especially interesting given the high correlations among the scales. The measure of social status that we use above is correlated at 0.94 with that for men and 0.96 with that for women.

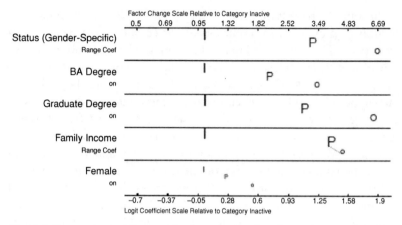

Fig. 3.3 Factor change/discrete change associated with gender-specific status measure and other key parameters

(after graduate degree). Finally, as one can note from Figure 3.3, the status scale is now associated with the largest change in the odds of O|I and the second largest change in the odds of P|I.

3.4 Discussion and conclusions

In earlier research (Alderson *et al.*, 2007), we looked *across* domains of cultural consumption in the US and found that contemporary cultural consumers cluster in patterns that are more consistent with the omnivore–univore thesis than they are with the alternatives. Modelling these styles of cross-domain consumption, we found that social status is central to the definition of these styles and that the effects of status are large relative to other factors. In this paper, we look within a single domain – that of music – asking whether the styles of consumption we observed in earlier work, and the conclusions that we drew regarding the central role of status, might be likewise found within a single domain. Our choice of music is purposive, motivated by the place that music has been accorded in cultural sociology, especially its status as a 'proving ground' in much recent work in the sociology of culture. Our focus on music is also motivated by its place in Bourdieu's (1984) effort to 'rethink' Weber's (1968) distinction between status and class. As the 'purest' or 'most spiritual' art, there is, for Bourdieu, no more unambiguously 'classificatory' realm of cultural activity. Consequently, if a

Weberian conceptualisation of the stratification system merits rethinking, this should be nowhere more obvious than in the domain of music. We thus think the study of musical consumption presents us with an especially conservative test of the utility of reasserting the analytical distinction between status and class.

Latent class cluster analysis of highbrow and middlebrow music attendance, listening and watching identifies three distinct groups of musical consumers: a group of Omnivores notable for the relative intensity and breadth of their musical consumption, a group of Inactives notable for their low level of activity across all items, and a group of middling consumers – Paucivores – who exhibit moderate levels of consumption. Using information on musical tastes and a variety of distinct (non-musical) activities, we find that highbrow and middlebrow musical Omnivores likewise exhibit omnivorous musical *taste* and are more active than others across a range of distinct activities. Paucivore musical consumers fall 'in-between' in these senses as well. They are more omnivorous in their musical tastes than the Inactive, but less omnivorous than the Omnivores. They are more active across activities ranging from exercise to sewing than the Inactive, but less active than the Omnivores. Examination of the LCA results reveals that, while Omnivores are more likely to consume all items considered than others, they are most defined by their consumption of the least popular items (e.g. opera attendance). Paucivores, in contrast, are most defined by their consumption of the most popular items (e.g. classical listening), while the Inactive class is defined by its status as the modal class for those who have not engaged in highbrow and middlebrow consumption of any sort.

Of the three views of the relationship between stratification and cultural consumption briefly touched on above, these findings are most consistent with the omnivore–univore thesis (e.g. Peterson, 1992; Peterson and Simkus, 1992; Peterson and Kern, 1996). As regards the individualisation argument (e.g. Featherstone, 1991; Lash, 1988; Bauman, 1988), the fact that LCA identifies a small number of clusters of cultural consumers – rather than the multitude of disjoint segments that would reflect the release of styles of consumption from moorings to the stratification system and to other social institutions – would seem to argue strongly against it. The findings present multiple challenges to the homology argument (e.g. Gans, 1999; Bourdieu, 1984). First, we find no evidence for a 'cultural elite' or 'cultural nobility', a group that would consume 'high' culture and reject popular or mass culture as crude or disreputable. Their closest analogue in our data, as the regression results reveal, are the Omnivores, defined by their high status, income and educational attainment. However, rather than rejecting middlebrow and lowbrow musical genres, this group is significantly *more likely* than others to report 'liking' them. Just as we find no cultural elite in these data, we find no clear evidence for the 'mass' posited by the homology argument. Again, as the regression results reveal, their closest analogue are the Inactives, defined by their low status, income and educational attainment. Their remarkably low level of highbrow and middlebrow musical consumption could conceivably be taken as evidence of their rejection of high culture in favour of popular forms. In a supplementary analysis, we estimated each latent class's odds of reporting liking any number of Peterson and Kern's (1996) five lowbrow genres. We found that Inactive musical consumers do not exhibit significantly greater odds of liking any discrete number of such genres, including reporting liking just one (i.e. they are no more likely than others to display a univorous taste for a single lowbrow genre). Rather than a mass segment defined by a commitment to popular forms and a rejection of others, this group, while literally 'mass' in size at 56% of the SPPA sample, is most distinctive for its inactivity across all genres, highbrow, middlebrow and lowbrow alike. As for the omnivore–univore thesis, we do indeed find a class of Omnivores, a group defined by a relatively broad and intense style of musical consumption. However, aside from the jazz aficionados identified in the four-class solution, we do not find much evidence for the existence of a set of clusters defined by particularistic musical consumption patterns (i.e. univores). Rather, in the Inactives (and the Paucivores), we find group(s) not clearly anticipated in Peterson's (1992) omnivore–univore distinction.

The multinomial logistic regression results reveal that these styles of cultural consumption have strong roots in the stratification system, but in social status rather than social class. We find that, while social class is not significantly associated with any of the contrasts, social status is central to the distinction between those who are active highbrow and middlebrow musical consumers – Omnivores or Paucivores – and those who are Inactive. Educational qualifications also have substantively large effects on all of the contrasts, distinguishing Omnivore and Paucivore from Inactive, and from each other.

Income has effects that are consistent with a straightforward resource-based explanation: those with income are more likely to engage in musical consumption but, beyond enabling an Omnivorous or Paucivorous style, it does not distinguish between such styles of participation. Gender is positively associated with all contrasts: women are more active musical consumers than men. Hispanics and members of other (non-black) racial minorities are found to be more likely to be Inactive than they are to adopt any active style. African Americans, in contrast, are more likely to be Paucivores than Inactives, and more likely to be Inactives than Omnivores. The effects of gender and race (among other variables) are relatively small compared to those of social status, educational qualifications and income. We also find that a gender-specific status scale better fits the data than a scale that averages the differences between men and women in partner choice and that, in that context, the role of status in defining styles of musical consumption is even more pronounced. In sum, the regression results establish (1) the utility of an explicit measure of status that allows one to move beyond commonly employed proxies that themselves, through other mechanisms, may have independent effects on cultural consumption (e.g. education or income), (2) the necessity of distinguishing analytically between social status and social class when attempting to understand or explain cultural consumption in the contemporary United States, and, most generally, (3) the deep roots of current styles of cultural consumption in features of the US stratification system.

4 | Bourdieu's legacy and the class–status debate on cultural consumption: musical consumption in contemporary France

PHILIPPE COULANGEON AND YANNICK LEMEL

Music has long been a research focus in the sociology of taste and cultural practice (Schuessler, 1948, 1981; Bourdieu, 1984; Peterson, 1992; Peterson and Kern, 1996; Bryson, 1996, 1997; Relish, 1997; van Eijck, 2001; Coulangeon, 2005). In fact, the idea that musical consumption is influenced by social factors could even be regarded as a truism. Why then have sociologists paid so much attention to music? One probable reason is that music is not part of the culture that is taught and learned in school, at least not in the same way as litera- ture is. Instead, music is a cultural domain in which the influence of primary groups, e.g. family, peer group, ethnic community, remains strong. This is probably the reason why Bourdieu (1984) considered musical taste as particularly revealing about social class. Furthermore, the development of digital technology has gone hand in hand with the diversification of the use of music, e.g. from solitary listening and attending concerts to actively playing, to decorative functions (back- ground or mood music in public places – transports, restaurants, etc.), the influence of music in everyday life is very pervasive. At any rate, the stratification of musical tastes has long interested sociologists (Gans, 1974, 1985; Levine, 1988).

4.1 Perspectives on the social stratification of cultural and music listening habits

Much of current research in the sociology of cultural taste and practice are empirical or theoretical appraisals of Bourdieu (1984). The most productive critique, originally formulated in relation to music, is the omnivore–univore thesis (Peterson and Simkus, 1992; Peterson and Kern, 1996). However, the extent to which Peterson's views really challenge Bourdieu's theoretical construct is still contested and the meaning of omnivorousness remains controversial.

4.1.1 Homology *and* habitus

Bourdieu's view of cultural consumption and lifestyles is structured by two concepts: *structural homology* and *habitus*. The former refers to an isomorphic relationship between social class on the one hand and aesthetic preferences on the other. According to this view, people's tastes and aesthetic judgment are determined by their position within the class structure, which in turn is characterised by the composition and volume of capital that is found in different classes. This gives rise to a double process. Individuals not only share the tastes and judgment of members of their own class, they also share their distastes, and this reciprocity plays a crucial role in the structural dimension of Bourdieu's concept of homology (Bourdieu, 1984). The dialectic of tastes and distastes constitutes the symbolic dimension of 'class struggle', and tastes are organised hierarchically as a 'highbrow/lowbrow' opposition (Gans, 1974, 1985; Levine, 1988). In the area of music, the contrast is between the preference of the upper classes for elite music – i.e. classical music, opera and, to some extent, jazz – against the preference of the working classes for popular genres, such as pop music, rock, rap and dance.

Habitus is the second and complementary concept in Bourdieu's sociology of taste and cultural practice. Introduced by Marcel Mauss (1934) as *techniques du corps*, it can be understood as those aspects of culture that are incorporated in the body and everyday practices of individuals, groups, societies and nations. It is the totality of learned habits, *techniques du corps* and other non-discursive knowledge that could be said to 'go without saying' for a specific group (Héran, 1987). And, in contrast to class consciousness as understood by Marxists, it operates mainly at a subconscious level. Bourdieu's claim was that the concept of *habitus* introduces a sense of agency to structuralist anthropology. However, since this concept was originally defined as a set of dispositions that durably generate practices and perceptions (Bourdieu, 1990), it does imply a deterministic view of dispositions. Moreover, as the effect of *habitus* is largely due to informal socialisation, it does not involve a genuine learning process. This characteristic appears especially salient in the particularly ineffable sphere of music where the production and transmission of dispositions involve largely implicit processes (Bourdieu, 1984).

Structural homology and *habitus* are both integral parts of the cultural legitimacy theory in *Distinction*. This theory proposes that in all cultural or artistic domains, the dominant tastes and practices are always those of the dominant classes. Furthermore, the symbolic power attached to dominant culture contributes to the process of reproduction of the class structure. Because our data allow us to address the notion of *habitus* in an indirect manner only, in this paper we deal with the structural component of Bourdieu's analyses, i.e. his theory of *structural homology*.

Bourdieu's theory has generated considerable criticism. There are some radically individualistic arguments which deny the social dimension of taste and lifestyles (Featherstone, 1987; Bauman, 1988; Giddens, 1991; Beck, 1992). But these have generally failed to demonstrate their veracity empirically. Then there is the 'omnivore–univore' hypothesis, which was originally proposed by DiMaggio (1987) and then systematised in a seminal article by Richard Peterson and Peter Simkus on the musical tastes in contemporary America (Peterson and Simkus, 1992). This posits that the main social distinction today is a matter of cultural diversity rather than one of highbrow versus lowbrow culture.

4.1.2 The meaning of the omnivore–univore thesis

Since Peterson and Simkus's work, much evidence has been gathered in the field of music in both North America and Europe (Peterson and Kern, 1996; Bryson, 1996, 1997; Relish, 1997; van Eijck, 2001; Coulangeon, 2005; Chan and Goldthorpe, 2007d). They show that cultural elites tend to have eclectic tastes, while the working class tend to be rather more univorous in their cultural consumption. Furthermore, similar results have been reported in other fields, such as reading (van Rees *et al.*, 1999) and the performing arts (López-Sintas and García-Álvarez, 2002; Chan and Goldthorpe, 2005).

Although the omnivore–univore thesis appears to be empirically well founded, the interpretation of this theoretical construct remains quite controversial. It is possible to identify two slightly different meanings here. The first highlights the cumulative property of cultural consumption and is expected to depend mainly on wealth and time availability, whereas the second emphasises taste eclecticism. In this second sense, omnivorousness is more concerned with the variety of tastes than with the quantity of cultural goods consumed. As stated by Peterson, omnivorousness is the shift 'from intellectual snobbism . . . based on the glorification of arts and the contempt of popular entertainments, . . . to a cultural capital that appears increasingly as a disposition to appreciate the aesthetic of a wide variety of cultural forms, not only including arts, but also a large range of folk and popular expressions' (Peterson, 2004). A specific ability is required to overcome the cultural and aesthetic boundaries between genres and repertoires, and this ability is expected to depend on education or social status. Empirical analyses of taste eclecticism are often restricted to a specific domain within which tastes can be measured across at least a list of genres, as in the case of music. Given the relative heterogeneity of such lists, it could be argued that a list of artists or even of specific works of arts, literature or musical pieces would allow a better appraisal of taste eclecticism. However, it is rarely possible to collect such data. As previously mentioned, music is an area for which large data sets on taste are currently being collected in surveys on cultural practices.

4.1.3 The class–status debate

We now turn to examine the extent to which Weber's well-known distinction between class and status is relevant to the sociology of cultural consumption. While Bourdieu tends to merge the two concepts of class and status group (Bourdieu, 1984; Lemel, 2004), some recent work gives credence to the idea that cultural consumption is much more a matter of status than of class (Chan and Goldthorpe, 2005).

From the Weberian standpoint, while class situation is defined by positions in the organisation of production, property and markets, status relates to social esteem or honour that is based on lifestyle, education, heredity or occupation. In other words, one of the main differences between class and status is that the former is production-based while the latter is consumption-based. Indeed, according to the theory of conspicuous consumption (Veblen, 1994), social status is derived, in part, from the kind of goods people consume, the leisure activities they pursue, the clothes they wear, the food they eat, etc. Moreover, the impact of status on cultural consumption operates through the tendency of people of equal status to interact with each other (status

homophily or status homogamy). This generates relatively homogeneous status groups in terms of lifestyles, cultural consumption and
so on. A class-based theory of cultural consumption, on the other
hand, assumes either a strong class consciousness or a very efficient
socialisation process. The argument of class–culture homology implies
that individuals' cultural practices reinforce their class commitment.
Finally, it is important to stress that there is no a priori reason for
prioritising class or status in research into the social determinants of
musical consumption.

Previous research on musical taste also showed that the omnivore–
univore contrast was correlated not only with class, social status and
occupation, but also with age and cohort. While older members of
the upper classes tend to be more exclusively highbrow in their tastes,
younger generations appear to be more omnivorous (Peterson and
Kern, 1996; van Eijck, 2001; Coulangeon, 2005). Therefore, when
exploring the class–status debate, we need to control for the influence
of other socio-demographic characteristics, such as age, generation,
gender or ethnicity. In other words, multivariate analysis is required.

4.1.4 *The French context*

When analysing musical consumption in France, it is worth keep-
ing in mind some features of contemporary French cultural policies.
The traditional emphasis on the highbrow–lowbrow divide echoes the
orientation of André Malraux, the distinguished French writer and
intellectual who became the first Minister of Culture of the Fifth
Republic from 1958 to 1969. In Malraux's views, the task of cultural policy was mainly to democratise the masterpieces in classical
and contemporary arts. This political agenda, in which there was no
place for popular arts and mass culture, was dominated by a strict
definition of the 'legitimate' culture field (Looseley, 1997). A series
of surveys on cultural participation since 1973 has shown the limits of this policy.[1] In the late 1990s, the audience of concert halls,
museums, operas, theatres and so on remained as socially stratified as
they were in the early 1970s, despite the amount of public subsidies
that had been given to the arts and cultural sector, often perceived
as the quintessence of the so-called French 'cultural exception'. This

---

[1] The French Ministry of Culture has made four national surveys on cultural
participation in 1973, 1981, 1988 and 1997.

persistent inequality has long been interpreted as a failure of Malraux's doctrine. The growing awareness of the limits of the democratisation policy gave way, since the mid 1980s, to an alternative strategy that has been personified by Jack Lang, socialist Minister of Culture of François Mitterrand, from 1981 to 1986, and from 1988 to 1993. Since then, cultural policy in France has become more open to an increasingly diverse conception of the arts, especially in the domain of music, with growing support given to some 'illegitimate' genres, jazz in particular. This alternative strategy highlights the cultural bridging from mass and popular culture to elite culture, the cultural mediation between the arts and its audience, and artistic and cultural education. This contrasts with earlier cultural policy, that seemed more concerned with giving financial support to the artists.

4.2 Data and methodology

The data set under consideration stems from the 'Permanent Survey on Life Conditions' (*Enquête permanente sur les conditions de vie* – EPCV) carried out by INSEE (the French National Institute for Statistics and Economic Studies). This biannual survey has a core section that contains standard questions on income, family, health, work, consumption and housing, and a variable section with a thematic focus. The May 2003 edition of the survey includes a thematic module on sport and cultural practices. This module, inspired by previous surveys on cultural practices of the French Ministry of Culture in 1973, 1981, 1988 and 1997, covers a wide variety of activities, such as reading, music listening, cultural outings (theatre, concert, etc.), television viewing, artistic hobbies (drawing, painting, playing music, etc.) and sports activities.

4.2.1 The population under consideration

The EPCV sample is representative of the French population aged 15 or above ($N = 5,626$). But since we are interested in the social stratification of music listening, we restrict our analyses to people who are, or have been, economically active, i.e. people with valid occupational information. In other words, people who have never worked, mainly students and some housewives, are excluded from the analyses. These restrictions obviously limit the analyses; particularly the omission of teenagers who constitute a market of primary importance for the music industry. Furthermore, their omission might lead to a serious bias in the statistical analysis if the minority of young people aged 15 to 25 who have already entered the labour market are retained in the sample. This is because in France today the majority of people in this age group are still attending school or university. Also, treating the occupation of people who are currently working as equivalent to the last occupation of people who have retired for, say, ten years or more might be problematic. For these reasons, we restrict our analyses to people aged 25 to 64, and who are, or have been, economically active ($N = 3,744$).

The stratification variables that we consider are social class (specifically, the EGP class schema), social status (see Chapter 2), personal income[2] and education (considered as a three level ordinal variable: elementary general or vocational education, intermediate general or vocational education, and tertiary general or vocational education). Apart from these stratification variables, we also include the following variables as controls: age, gender, area of residence and working time.

4.2.2 Musical consumption or musical taste

The EPCV module on sports and cultural practices includes a question on the musical genres that the respondents listen to most frequently.[3] Respondents are invited to name up to a maximum of three genres from the following list:[4] (1) pop, (2) international pop, (3) techno, (4) world music, (5) rap, (6) rock, (7) jazz, (8) classical music and opera.[5]

---

[2] The EPCV data set includes information on household income. The personal income variable included in the following analysis is estimated by the ratio of household income to household size.

[3] Survey data on music listening usually lacks precision, as they generally document the broad musical genres that people listen to, but not the finer segmentation within each genre. This may yield a misleading view of the social stratification of musical preferences by underestimating the diversity of people's tastes. The survey on the social background of musical tastes carried out by Karl F. Schuessler in the late 1940s using an audio-test device, in which people's tastes were approached through the rating of eight musical pieces on a like/dislike scale, constitutes one notable exception (Schuessler, 1948).

[4] Note that this restriction underestimates the degree of omnivorousness (e.g. those who listen to everything). However, previous surveys on French cultural practices, in which the relevant question did not contain such a restriction, show that fewer than 10% of the respondents reported more than three genres. Thus, this restriction is not too unrealistic (Coulangeon, 2005).

[5] There is also a residual category of 'other genres' and respondents can report listening to no particular genres. In the subsequent analyses, we will focus on the eight named genres, because the residual category of 'other genres' does not allow any analysis of its content.

Since the label of musical genres is not socially and culturally neutral, one can argue that direct questions on the genres that people listen to are better measures of their true preference than more abstract questions about their taste. This will be the case if people are more likely to adjust their response according to what they perceive to be the culturally legitimate answer when asked in an abstract manner about musical taste. On the other hand, inferring taste on the basis of practice is also subject to criticism (Hugues and Peterson, 1983; Peterson, 1992). Moreover, measures of taste might make more sense when actual consumption is subjected to exogenous constraints, such as geographic accessibility. These constraints are very important for, say, museum visits or concert and theatre attendance. But they might be less important in the case of listening to recorded music.

4.3 Results

There are two dimensions to musical consumption: the specific genres that people listen to, and the range and diversity of their choice. Together these two dimensions lead to a richer typology of musical consumption than by considering the *number* of genres consumed alone. Obviously, a person who listens to jazz and classical music is not the same as a fan of rock and rap; and a fan of world, techno and jazz is not the same as a fan of rock, pop and international pop.

4.3.1 Basic features of the distribution of musical taste

The first and most obvious question to address is which musical genres people listen to. The left-hand panel of Figure 4.1 shows that over half of the respondents (54%) named 'pop music' as one of the genres they most often listen to. A slightly lower proportion (45%) named 'international pop'. These two genres are rather broad categories. 'Pop' includes music ranging from *chanson à texte* in French (literary songs by Brassens, Ferré, Brel, etc.) to 'disco'. The same holds true for 'international pop'. The only difference between these two genres is a linguistic rather than a strictly musical one (i.e. French vs. other languages, mainly English). Apart from these two categories, only four genres attain a score of at least 10%: world music, classical

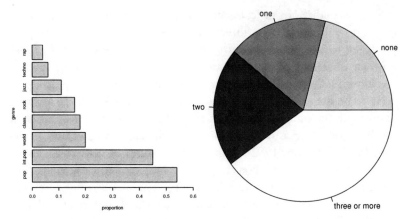

Fig. 4.1 Musical genres most often listened to (left panel) and the distribution of respondents by number of genres listened to

music and opera, rock and jazz. In sum, music listening tends to be concentrated on the two genres of pop music, and, on average, the audiences for the other genres appear to be quite small.

As regards diversity, the right-hand panel of Figure 4.1 shows that 22% of the respondents do not listen to any kind of music, 17% mentioned one genre, 21% two and 41% three genres (i.e. the maximum possible, see above).

In order to synthesise these basic descriptive statistics, we carry out a multiple correspondence analysis (MCA). MCA is a descriptive technique for analysing contingency tables. It is rather similar to standard factor analysis but deals with nominal variables rather than continuous variables. MCA decomposes the overall chi-square statistic (or inertia) of a contingency table into successive 'dimensions'. It is therefore possible to select a lower-dimensional representation of the association between the variables. The distances between the row (column) categories in the associated two-dimensional display are such that two points that are close to each other are similar in their relative frequencies across the columns (rows).[6]

We consider nine variables in our MCA: the eight musical genres, which are entered as dummy variables, plus the number of genres

---

[6] These methods were originally developed by Jean-Paul Benzécri in France in the early 1960s. They have gained ground since. See, for example, Greenacre and Blasius (1994); Clausen (1998).

that are mentioned by the respondent, which ranges from 0 to 3. Thus, the analysis takes into account both the overall 'omnivorousness score' of the respondents and their specific tastes. According to the eigenvalue matrix (see Table 4.1), which indicates the proportion of inertia accounted for by each factor, we could limit our analyses to the first three factors. Together, these three factors capture about 45% of the inertia observed in the data.[7] Three main points emerge from the MCA results.[8]

First, factor 1 appears to be structured primarily by the number of musical genres specified, contrasting the more eclectic respondents (those who specified three genres) against those who did not specify any genre (from left to right in Figure 4.2). Factor 2 probably contrasts those who only listen to the most popular genres ('pop' and 'international pop') against those who listen to less popular ones ('classical music' and, even more so, 'jazz', 'world', 'techno' and 'rap').

As opposed to the first two factors, which seem to be consistent with the omnivore–univore thesis, factor 3 (not shown here) clearly contrasts 'classical music and opera', and 'jazz' on the one hand, with 'rap' and 'techno' on the other. The other genres, i.e. 'pop', 'international pop' and, to a lesser extent, 'rock', assume intermediate positions on this third axis.

4.3.2 Types of musical listeners

Based on individual coordinates on the first three MCA factors, we then carry out a cluster analysis in order to identify types of music listeners.[9] The four-cluster solution, which maximises the inter-cluster inertia and minimises the intra-cluster inertia, is the optimal solution for this sample.

The four types of music listener that we distinguish are of comparable size. Table 4.2 gives more detail about their characteristics, and shows, for each cluster, the proportion of respondents who

---

[7] While the elbow criteria should lead us to consider the first factor only, which explains over 20% of the variance, we continued until the second elbow, which separates the third factor from the subsequent ones.

[8] Further details of the MCA can be found in Coulangeon and Lemel (2007).

[9] The cluster analysis is based on Ward's method, which calculates the total sum of squared deviations from the mean of a cluster. The criterion for fusion is that it should produce the smallest possible increase in the error sum of squares.

Table 4.1 *Correlation of factors to initial variables and MCA eigenvalues*

	factor					
	1	2	3	4	5	6
pop	0.674	0.461	0.086	−0.017	0.094	−0.049
international pop	0.681	0.283	−0.217	0.122	−0.117	−0.005
techno	0.201	−0.175	−0.445	−0.451	−0.069	0.371
world music	0.387	−0.385	−0.116	−0.085	0.072	−0.760
rap	0.108	−0.198	−0.435	−0.481	−0.009	0.160
rock	0.332	−0.268	−0.207	0.673	0.136	0.378
jazz	0.220	−0.475	0.540	−0.009	−0.072	0.143
classical music, opera	0.214	−0.103	0.714	−0.307	−0.082	0.196
# genres mentioned	0.973	−0.136	0.060	−0.044	−0.009	0.039
eigenvalue	0.254	0.152	0.147	0.116	0.112	0.106
% variance explained	0.208	0.125	0.120	0.095	0.092	0.087
cumulative percentage	0.208	0.333	0.453	0.548	0.640	0.727

	factor				
	7	8	9	10	11
pop	0.037	−0.007	0.054	0.555	−0.044
international pop	0.092	−0.032	0.434	−0.424	−0.044
techno	0.545	0.178	−0.237	−0.001	−0.020
world music	0.008	0.021	−0.297	−0.084	−0.035
rap	−0.694	−0.095	0.093	0.048	−0.018
rock	−0.173	−0.093	−0.347	−0.017	−0.033
jazz	−0.128	0.604	0.164	0.011	−0.028
classical music, opera	0.032	−0.497	−0.164	−0.139	−0.035
# genres mentioned	−0.028	−0.026	−0.035	−0.008	0.105
eigenvalue	0.101	0.086	0.080	0.065	0.002
% variance explained	0.083	0.070	0.066	0.053	0.002
cumulative percentage	0.809	0.879	0.945	0.998	1.000

Source: EPCV, INSEE, 2003.

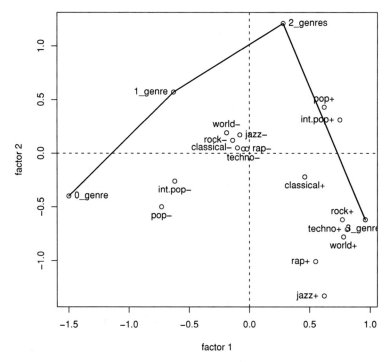

Fig. 4.2 MCA results

mention listening to the eight genres and also the number of genres they listen to.

The first cluster represents approximately 25% of the sample. Its members are rather eclectic listeners, 95% of whom mention three genres. A large majority of the respondents in this cluster listen to pop (79%) and international pop (81%). The proportion of rock, techno, world or rap music fans is also much higher in this cluster than in the other three clusters. However, very few members of this cluster listen to 'highbrow' music (jazz, classical music and opera). As a result, this cluster can be labelled as 'middlebrow omnivores' (MO).

Members of the second cluster, which represents around 18% of the sample, are also rather eclectic in their listening habit: 90% report listening to at least three genres of music. Furthermore, this is the only cluster where a majority of its members listen to jazz and classical music. At the same time, over 50% of its members are fans of pop and international pop. Thus, it makes sense to label this cluster

Table 4.2 *Percentage of respondents within each cluster listening to various genres of music and reporting different number of genres*

	cluster			
	1 MO	2 HO	3 U	4 NL
relative size	0.25	0.18	0.28	0.28
pop	78.64	64.32	79.29	0.00
international pop	80.67	51.34	54.53	0.00
techno	21.16	0.00	1.13	0.54
world music	47.30	27.20	7.16	3.25
rap	13.59	0.00	0.00	1.07
rock	40.27	17.34	5.99	2.74
jazz	1.66	56.61	0.00	1.49
classical music and opera	1.74	66.50	11.92	6.06
mention 3 genres	95.39	89.55	0.00	0.00
mention 2 genres	4.61	10.45	63.24	0.34
mention 1 genre	0.00	0.00	36.76	17.55
mention none	0.00	0.00	0.00	82.12

Note: MO: middlebrow omnivores, HO: highbrow omnivores, U: univores, NL: non-listeners.

as 'highbrow omnivores' (HO). The fact that two distinct groups of omnivores can be identified is consistent with previous findings in this field (Peterson, 2005).

The third cluster, which includes 28% of the respondents, relates to people who generally specify no more than two genres, which are mainly pop and international pop. Members of this cluster have a very low probability of listening to all other genres. Given the way it contrasts with the first two clusters, we refer to this cluster as musical 'univores' (U). The last cluster covers 28% of respondents, 82% of whom reported not listening to any kind of music. Thus, we refer to them as 'non-listeners' (NL).

4.3.3 Characteristics of the four types of listener

Table 4.3 shows the distribution of the four types of listener within social groups as defined by various demographic and stratification

Table 4.3 *Distribution of types of listener by age, gender, area of residence, hours worked per week, class, status, income and education*

		MO	HO	U	NL
overall		0.25	0.18	0.28	0.28
age	25–29	0.50	0.09	0.25	0.17
	30–39	0.35	0.17	0.30	0.18
	40–49	0.19	0.22	0.30	0.28
	50+	0.08	0.22	0.28	0.43
gender	male	0.25	0.17	0.26	0.32
	female	0.24	0.20	0.31	0.24
area of residence	rural	0.22	0.14	0.31	0.34
	< 20, 000[a]	0.24	0.15	0.32	0.29
	20,000–100,000	0.25	0.18	0.27	0.31
	>100,000	0.28	0.21	0.27	0.23
	Paris area	0.24	0.21	0.28	0.28
	Inner Paris	0.30	0.37	0.16	0.18
hours worked per week	not working	0.18	0.18	0.28	0.35
	< 20	0.21	0.28	0.30	0.21
	20–35	0.27	0.21	0.30	0.22
	35–40	0.29	0.16	0.31	0.25
	40–55	0.29	0.20	0.25	0.25
	>55	0.21	0.20	0.27	0.32
class	I+II	0.24	0.32	0.24	0.21
	III	0.27	0.14	0.33	0.25
	IVab	0.18	0.18	0.22	0.42
	IVc	0.08	0.04	0.28	0.60
	V+VI	0.27	0.13	0.30	0.30
	VIIa	0.25	0.09	0.31	0.36
	VIIb	0.29	0.04	0.23	0.44
status quartile	Q4 (highest)	0.23	0.33	0.23	0.22
	Q3	0.26	0.18	0.27	0.30
	Q2	0.26	0.14	0.34	0.27
	Q1 (lowest)	0.25	0.09	0.31	0.36
income quartile	Q4 (highest)	0.23	0.29	0.25	0.23
	Q3	0.27	0.20	0.27	0.26
	Q2	0.26	0.15	0.30	0.30
	Q1 (lowest)	0.23	0.11	0.31	0.35

(*cont.*)

Table 4.3 *(cont.)*

		MO	HO	U	NL
education	tertiary	0.29	0.30	0.22	0.18
	intermediate	0.29	0.17	0.28	0.26
	elementary	0.16	0.10	0.34	0.40

Note: [a] number of inhabitants.

variables. It can be seen that over 40% of those aged 50 or over are non-listeners, whereas half of those aged 25–29 are middlebrow omnivores. Thus, cluster membership is clearly associated with age. It is also associated with area of residence. Generally speaking, the larger the city, the greater the proportion of omnivores. This is also true, to a lesser degree, for middlebrow omnivores. Conversely, the proportion of univores and non-listeners is higher in smaller cities and rural areas. In contrast, cluster membership does not vary much by gender. The distribution of the four types of listener is very similar for men and for women, except that there seems to be more non-listeners among men. Also, cluster membership seems unrelated to hours worked.

Table 4.3 also shows that cluster membership is highly socially stratified. For example, 30% of respondents with tertiary education are highbrow omnivores, as compared to 10% of those with elementary education. Similar gradients are also observed for class, social status and income: 32% of the salariat (class I+II) are highbrow omnivores, as compared to 9% of unskilled manual workers (class VIIa); one third of those found in the top status quartile, as compared to 9% of those in the bottom status quartile; and 29% of those in the top income quartile as compared to 11% of those in the bottom income quartile. An opposite gradient by education, income, status and class can be observed for the share of non-listeners.

The EPCV survey also contains information of other types of cultural consumption. Table 4.4 shows the rate of participation in these other activities for respondents in each cluster. Overall, the classification which we derive from music listening appears quite consistent with the general pattern of cultural participation. The comparison between the two types of omnivores is particularly enlightening and confirms the different orientations of these two groups. Generally, highbrow

Table 4.4 *Cultural consumption characteristics of the four clusters of music listeners*

	MO	HO	U	NL
go to opera	0.03	0.16	0.04	0.06
go to concert	0.66	0.93	0.33	0.33
go to theatre	0.30	0.68	0.21	0.21
go to ballet	0.21	0.38	0.16	0.16
go to circus	0.15	0.18	0.12	0.09
visit museum	0.57	1.10	0.45	0.45
visit historical monument	0.88	1.44	0.81	0.67
visit music hall	0.26	0.35	0.16	0.15
go to cinema	1.08	1.10	0.68	0.50
go to sport events	0.42	0.31	0.31	0.26
read sport magazines	0.62	0.39	0.40	0.32
read national daily newspaper	0.59	1.08	0.39	0.41
read regional daily newspaper	1.51	1.57	1.62	1.45

Note: These cultural consumption indicators come from a set of questions on the frequency of the corresponding practices during the year preceding the survey. These questions included four possible answers (never, rarely, sometimes, frequently), converted to a 4-point scale, from 0 to 3.

omnivores are more active than middlebrow omnivores. 'Sports activities', in which MOs are clearly the most active group, is the only exception. The gap is particularly marked in favour of the highbrow omnivores in activities with a clear 'highbrow' connotation, e.g. going to the opera, theatre, ballet or reading a national newspaper. But even for more 'popular' activities such as visiting a music hall or going to the circus, the participation rate of our highbrow omnivores is still higher than that of middlebrow omnivores, univores or non-listeners. This confirms the HO label that we give to this cluster: not only do they listen to popular as well as highbrow music, they are generally more active across a whole range of activities.

To conclude this section, we would stress that, even if taste eclecticism is a core characteristic of the cultural profile of the highest status group, the well educated or the most advantaged classes (i.e. the salariat), it is very far from being the dominant cultural type in any of them. Indeed, although the share of highbrow omnivores is higher

Table 4.5 *Multinomial logistic regression on cluster membership*

	MO vs. U		HO vs. U		NL vs. U		MO vs. HO		NL vs. HO		NL vs. MO	
	$\hat{\beta}$	s.e.	$\hat{\beta}$	s.e.	$\hat{\beta}$	s.e.	$\hat{\beta}$	s.e.	$\hat{\beta}$	s.e.	$\hat{\beta}$	s.e.
Intercept	-2.421*	0.992	-4.250**	1.069	1.830	1.130	6.285**	1.077	2.035*	0.909	4.455**	1.020
20 to 29[a]	0.451**	0.131	-0.614**	0.192	1.065**	0.180	0.785**	0.208	0.171	0.163	-0.280	0.152
40 to 49	-0.578**	0.127	0.333*	0.141	-0.911**	0.144	0.104	0.152	0.437**	0.132	1.015**	0.138
50 & over	-1.427**	0.161	0.224	0.153	-1.651**	0.176	0.738**	0.159	0.962**	0.137	2.390**	0.167
Female	-0.236*	0.114	0.004	0.121	-0.239	0.127	-0.425**	0.123	-0.422**	0.108	-0.186	0.119
I+II[b]	-0.059	0.195	0.196	0.206	-0.255	0.216	0.034	0.215	0.231	0.195	0.290	0.209
IVab	0.254	0.271	0.490	0.275	-0.237	0.294	0.193	0.259	0.684**	0.230	0.430	0.260
IVc	-0.946*	0.446	-0.823	0.540	-0.123	0.632	1.604**	0.525	0.781**	0.269	1.727**	0.433
V+VI	-0.104	0.160	0.194	0.186	-0.297	0.194	-0.234	0.191	-0.040	0.156	0.064	0.170
VIIa	-0.183	0.210	0.174	0.259	-0.358	0.272	-0.127	0.262	0.048	0.197	0.231	0.219
VIIb	0.451	0.438	0.032	0.752	0.420	0.753	0.485	0.731	0.516	0.398	0.065	0.412
Status	-0.833	0.672	1.720**	0.690	-2.553**	0.725	-2.377**	0.715	-0.658	0.663	0.175	0.714
Elementary[c]	-0.465**	0.123	-0.673**	0.142	0.208	0.155	0.640**	0.143	-0.033	0.111	0.432**	0.127
Tertiary	0.144	0.144	0.240	0.153	-0.097	0.157	-0.203	0.157	0.037	0.150	-0.107	0.154
log-income	0.266**	0.089	0.330**	0.096	-0.064	0.101	-0.575**	0.097	-0.244**	0.082	-0.511**	0.092
0 hour[d]	0.072	0.134	0.341**	0.145	-0.269	0.156	-0.151	0.147	0.190	0.122	0.118	0.139
<20 hr/wk	-0.075	0.296	0.625*	0.284	-0.699*	0.315	-0.755*	0.310	-0.130	0.287	-0.056	0.329
20-35 hr/wk	0.140	0.179	0.292	0.196	0.166	0.218	0.117	0.212	-0.018	0.184	-0.158	0.199
40-55 hr/wk	0.162	0.135	0.011	0.154	-0.152	0.205	-0.310	0.211	0.073	0.137	-0.090	0.143
>55 hr/wk	0.008	0.192	-0.158	0.206	0.151	0.156	0.062	0.159	-0.041	0.182	-0.049	0.202
rural area[e]	-0.331*	0.131	-0.416**	0.146	0.084	0.155	0.492**	0.150	0.077	0.126	0.408**	0.140
< 20000 inhab	-0.305*	0.148	-0.415*	0.168	-0.450	0.244	-0.651*	0.273	0.045	0.143	0.351*	0.159
20000-100000	-0.126	0.165	0.006	0.179	-0.132	0.187	0.288	0.179	0.294	0.157	0.420*	0.169
Paris suburb	-0.210	0.155	-0.144	0.162	0.109	0.179	0.460**	0.173	0.257	0.151	0.467**	0.164
Inner Paris	0.471	0.281	0.920**	0.275	-0.066	0.171	0.401*	0.167	0.269	0.304	-0.202	0.285

Note: [a] aged 30–40 is ref.cat.; [b] class III is ref.cat.; [c] intermediate education is ref.cat.; [d] 35–40 hours/week is ref.cat.; [e] >100000 inhabitants (except Paris) is ref.cat.

in the salariat than in other classes, only a minority of the salariat are highbrow omnivores (32%). The same holds true for the highest status group (33%) and the best educated category (30%).

4.4 Multivariate analysis

In this section, we turn to multivariate analysis. The four-cluster partition of the sample is the dependent variable in a multinomial logistic regression (see Table 4.5). The main independent variables of interest are class, status, education and income. We also include age, gender, area of residence and hours worked per week as control variables. We shall first summarise the effects of the control variables before discussing the main stratification variables.

4.4.1 Age, gender and area of residence

Whilst it is not easy to summarise the pattern of association between age and cultural consumption, of most interest to us is the contrast between the two types of omnivores: among the omnivores, older individuals are more likely to be highbrow rather than middlebrow omnivores. This might be interpreted as either a generation effect or an ageing effect (see below). It is also notable that individuals in the 50–65 age group are more likely to be non-listeners rather than univores, highbrow omnivores or middlebrow omnivores.

As shown in Table 4.5, gender affects listening habits. Women are less likely to be non-listeners rather than univores or highbrow omnivores, and they are more likely to be univores rather than middlebrow omnivores.

Finally, area of residence also has a significant net effect on music listening. The probability of being either a non-listener or a univore rather than a highbrow omnivore or a middlebrow omnivore is higher in small cities and rural areas. Conversely, urban environment favours the probability of being a highbrow omnivore. One interesting point concerns the difference between inner Paris and its suburbs. While inner Parisians and inhabitants of other cities of more than 100,000 inhabitants do not seem to differ from each other in their probability of being middlebrow omnivores rather than non-listeners, suburban Parisians are less likely to be middlebrow omnivores. Moreover, inner

Parisians distinguish themselves from others by a higher probability of being highbrow omnivores.[10]

4.4.2 *Class, social status, education and income*

In comparison with age and gender effects, the net effect of class is quite limited. The only clear and consistent class effect that we see is that farmers (class IVc) are more likely to be non-listeners rather than any of the other three types. Since we have controlled for area of residence in the model, this result cannot be interpreted as arising from the distance between rural communities and locations where cultural products are sold. Rather, we suspect that farmers do have a specific lifestyle, at least insofar as music listening is concerned.

By comparison, there are statistically significant effects for social status, education and income. Regarding education, it can be seen that compared with those with secondary education, respondents with elementary education are *less* likely to be highbrow or middle-brow omnivores rather than univores or non-listeners. Those with tertiary education are more likely to be highbrow omnivores rather than univores. But education does not differentiate between high-brow omnivores and middlebrow omnivores, or between univores and non-listeners.

As for status, it can be seen that higher social status is associated with higher probabilities of being a highbrow omnivore rather than a member of any of the other three types of listeners. This result, taken together with the relatively patchy class effect discussed above, supports the claim of Chan and Goldthorpe (2005) that cultural consumption is stratified more by status than by class. It is also worth stressing again that the two kinds of omnivores are differentiated by status and not by education.

Perhaps the most unexpected result is the net effect of income. Higher income is associated with higher probabilities of being a highbrow omnivore or a middlebrow omnivore rather than a non-listener or a univore. Univores also seem to have higher income than

---

[10] Consistent with what we have seen in bivariate analyses, in a multivariate framework, hours worked per week is generally not associated with music listening.

non-listeners, but there is no statistically significant difference in income between highbrow omnivores and middlebrow omnivores. Another way to summarise the income effects is that lower income increases the probability of being a non-listener as opposed to all other kinds of listeners. We elaborate this point later.

Finally, it should be noted that the effects of income and education on the probability of being a highbrow omnivore or a middlebrow omnivore rather than a univore or a non-listener are in the same direction. This is inconsistent with one of the main arguments advanced by Bourdieu, namely that social space is partitioned by both the amount and the nature of the capital that people hold. Specifically, the contrasts between economic capital and cultural capital and that between economic elites and cultural elites are crucial for Bourdieu. This is not borne out by empirical data on musical taste in France.

4.5 Possible mechanisms

With respect to the class–status debate, our statistical analyses clearly show that omnivorousness in musical taste is a matter of social status rather than class. We deal with possible interpretations of this 'status effect' later. First, we examine the effects of age, education and income in turn.

4.5.1 The impact of age on musical tastes

First, omnivorousness appears to be negatively correlated with age: older respondents are less omnivorous in their music listening habits. Second, non-listening is also correlated with age: older respondents are more likely to be non-listeners. These two results could be interpreted in terms of either ageing or cohort effects.

One possible consequence of ageing is a tendency to concentrate one's interest on a limited number of genres that one has known and experienced in the past. This contrasts with youngsters who may be more keen to experiment with a variety of genres. Nonetheless, the opposite effect might also apply. As people get older, they accumulate new cultural experiences that are partly added to previous ones. Some but not all of these earlier experiences would disappear in the course of this process.

Nevertheless, because of the globalisation of the record industry, a generation or cohort interpretation is also plausible. The youngest cohorts are exposed to and could try out an incomparably wider range of musical genres than their elders. Together with the growing international circulation of music, the economic characteristics of the contemporary music industry promote the eclecticism of the younger generations.

4.5.2 Why education fosters omnivorousness

The second point that emerges from the analysis concerns the impact of education on musical taste. Education fosters eclecticism but this result does not lend itself to a straightforward interpretation. There are at least three possible mechanisms.

First, students might acquire certain culturally relevant skills and habits at school. This interpretation can be expressed in terms of Gary Becker's idea of consumption capital (Stigler and Becker, 1977). As the frequency and intensity of exposure to music increases, the ability to appreciate music also increases. However, what makes this interpretation problematic is that music constitutes only a very small part of the curriculum in French schools. Furthermore, it is not clear how the narrow range of musical education in school could explain the omnivorous taste of the better educated.

Nonetheless, school influence on cultural habits is not only a matter of skill transmission but also one of socialisation. Students learn not only from the formal instructions given by their teachers, but also informally from their interaction with each other, particularly in the cultural domain. With regard to music, school is clearly one of the main sites where teenage crazes flourish. Thus, the longer individuals stay in education, the greater the opportunity for them to experience a variety of cultural repertoires and musical genres, which then account for the positive effect of education on eclecticism.

The third interpretation of the education effect concerns the general competence learned at school. Indeed, what school instills in students is not only a set of specific skills, but also some general information-processing ability (Ganzeboom, 1982). In that sense, we could explain why the proclivity towards non-academic *avant-garde* or even mass cultural products is correlated with school attainment. This explanation is all the more convincing since it applies not only to the musical field. As we have seen, highbrow omnivores are eclectic in other cultural fields.

4.5.3 How to explain that income matters

Higher income raises the probability of being an omnivore rather than a univore, and reduces the probability of being a non-listener as opposed to all other kinds of listeners. This impact of income suggests that omnivorousness is structured not only by social and cultural resources, but also by economic constraints. Although free music is available, listening to a wide variety of musical genres usually implies consuming a lot of musical goods (CDs, concerts tickets, etc.) and thus requires considerable sums of money. Moreover, omnivorousness in musical consumption could also be interpreted as a kind of conspicuous consumption: displaying one's social rank by consuming a large amount and a diverse range of musical products (Veblen, 1994). More generally, in a context of commodification of culture, cultural attitudes are often mediated by the consumption of commercial goods.[11]

4.5.4 Status effects

Overall, our statistical analyses confirm the importance of the status effect, and that there is no net class effect once status, education, income and other demographic variables are controlled for. Social status particularly affects the probability of being a highbrow omnivore.

It must be underlined that a technical artefact might partly explain this result. In our analysis, education is measured as a categorical variable with only three levels. Obviously, the diversity of the social and cultural contexts that characterise different kinds of school or tracks within the three education levels are not captured. This diversity could have been picked up as status effect. Having said that, it seems reasonable to argue that omnivorousness has become a signal of high social status.

---

[11] Of course, the reference to the commodification process does not necessarily imply a critical approach, as stated by the philosophers of the Frankfurt school (Horkheimer and Adorno, 1972). It may also simply be understood as an extension of the access to music listening by people who could not access before the advent of mass-culture industry.

An alternative interpretation of the status effect could be sought in the dynamic of interpersonal relationships. Both theoretical and empirical research suggests that the range and diversity of a person's social networks tends to increase with social status (Marsden, 1987; Lin and Dumin, 1986). The more contacts an individual has, and the more diverse those contacts are, the greater the range of that individual's cultural repertoire (DiMaggio, 1987; Erickson, 1996; Relish, 1997; Warde and Tampubolon, 2002). As people of high social status tend to have more and more diverse social ties, they would also tend to be culturally more eclectic. Furthermore, higher status is generally found to be correlated with the number of 'weak ties' (Granovetter, 1973; Degenne *et al.*, 2003). Whereas strong ties tend to encourage cultural uniformity, weak ties foster cultural diversity.

4.6 Conclusion

Clearly, individualisation arguments which deny any social structuring of cultural behaviour are not supported by our results. Musical consumption in contemporary France remains socially stratified, which contributes to the definition of the social identities of both individuals and social groups.

Our results show that the organisation of musical tastes is along the omnivore–univore line rather than that of highbrow–lowbrow. This is reflected in the evolution of French cultural policies (see Section 4.1.4 above). Jack Lang's policy of including all musical styles in the '*Fête de la Musique*' (Music Festival) of the 1980s contrasts strongly with the almost exclusive support given to 'great' music by his predecessors during the 1960s and 1970s. Indeed, for many commentators, the policy shift from Malraux to Lang is one from a 'cultural democratisation' that is highly compatible with the highbrow–lowbrow hierarchy to one which is more compatible with the growing omnivorousness of cultural consumption (Santerre, 2000).

The omnivore–univore thesis has often been interpreted as an refutation of Bourdieu's theory of 'cultural legitimacy'. The idea is that changes in the behaviour and attitude of the elites in the cultural domain must be considered as a weakening of the symbolic boundaries between social groups, which in turn would contradict the idea of cultural domination. This interpretation is nonetheless not straight-forward.

First, omnivorousness could be a way to assert symbolic domina-tion. For high-status groups, borrowing cultural habits and tastes from lower-status groups might be a way to express their social superior-ity. Although this is difficult to verify through data analysis, it could be argued that, consistent with Bourdieu, social distinctions not only concern the kind of things people consume but also the way they con-sume them (Bourdieu, 1984). In that sense, there are many examples in the history of music where the same musical work or genre are appraised in different ways. The history of how jazz has been received, for example, illustrates this process. Having originated from the dance and entertainment tradition of the African-American working classes, jazz has been progressively reappraised since the 1920s, first by the radio and the record industry and later in intellectual circles (Leonard, 1962), following the pop/folk/fine arts process suggested by Peterson (1972).

A second argument stems from our data analysis. Social status not only differentiates omnivores from other listeners, it also differentiates highbrow omnivores from middlebrow omnivores. Being an omni-vore seldom means listening to all kinds of music (Bryson, 1996). According to the French data under consideration, both highbrow and middlebrow omnivore can be considered as particular modes of refinement. Nonetheless, highbrow omnivores, who have higher social status, could be considered as the contemporary incarnation of cultural distinction.

Finally, at least in the French case, the cultural legitimacy the-ory needs to be amended in three ways. First, Bourdieu's homology thesis, interpreted strictly as implying a one-to-one correspondence between class position and lifestyle, is not supported. For example, highbrow omnivores constitute only one third of upper-class respon-dents, and nearly 25% of them are univores and more than 20% are non-listeners.

Second, the supposed division of the social space in terms of cultural versus economic capital, which is of great importance in Bourdieu's theory, is not supported by our analysis. Most of the time, economic and cultural factors (i.e. income and education) have congruent effects on the structure of musical consumption.

Another controversial issue concerns the very manner with which class is conceived in Bourdieu's works. Weberian and Marxist approaches are more or less conflated and status groups and classes are not clearly distinguished by Bourdieu. What Bourdieu interprets as class effects could also be expressed in terms of social status. Consistent with Chan and Goldthorpe (2005), some primacy of status appears in our data on musical taste.

5 | Social status and public cultural consumption: Chile in comparative perspective

FLORENCIA TORCHE

5.1 Introduction

This chapter studies the stratification of cultural consumption in Chile, that which takes place in public space rather than at home. In particular, it explores whether individual status position affects cultural consumption patterns, net of other measures of socioeconomic advantage such as education, income or class. Status is understood in the Weberian sense as an intersubjective evaluation of social superiority, equality and inferiority (Weber, 1946, pp. 186–88; Chan and Goldthorpe, 2004), which expresses itself doubly in patterns of intimate association such as marriage and friendship, and in shared lifestyles (Weber, 1968, p. 306). These two dimensions of status distinctions provide an internal sense of social solidarity (horizontal integration) and a way to express difference from others (vertical differentiation) (DiMaggio, 1994).

Status distinctions are constructed in explicit opposition to pure market relations. Even though similar economic positions can lead to the formation of status groups, status membership rejects 'the pretensions of sheer property' (Weber, 1968, p. 932; Scott, 1996, pp. 32–33). If a status order exists, it should have a substantial effect on cultural consumption, as the latter usually expresses lifestyle distinctions. In order to test this hypothesis I empirically construct a status order based on the marriage patterns of occupational incumbents in Chile and test if status expresses itself in cultural consumption patterns.

Much research on the social basis of cultural consumption, with its focus on the three hypotheses of homology, omnivore–univore and individualisation, has been confined to a few industrialised nations. But there could be significant international variation in the stratification of cultural consumption by, for example, levels of economic development, extent of inequality, levels of government subsidies, cultural traditions, or the presence/absence and size of a cosmopolitan elite (Peterson, 2005). Specifically, Chile departs from the industrialised countries in ways that provide unique opportunities to test the validity of these hypotheses and to explore the sources and contours of the stratification of cultural consumption.

Firstly, Chile is highly stratified. With an income gini coefficient of 0.571, Chile is the 11th most unequal country in the world (United Nations, 2005). To the extent that access to cultural consumption is determined by economic resources, it should be much more segmented in Chile than in the industrialised world. Furthermore, wide economic disparities have a clear symbolic correlate in patterns of interaction (Barros and Vergara, 1978; Tironi, 1999). While in the industrialised world visible expression of superiority and inferiority through, for instance, deference and curtseying have virtually disappeared (Chan and Goldthorpe, 2004), they are still prevalent in Chile.

This does not necessarily mean, however, that status is a key determinant of cultural consumption in Chile. As I explain below, given the high level of cultural homogeneity in the country, status might be a mere symbolic correlate of socioeconomic differences in educational attainment and income, and may therefore lack an autonomous effect on cultural consumption. The Chilean case therefore provides a strong test of the autonomous influence of status vis-à-vis the economic dimension of stratification.

Secondly, the very organisation of the cultural consumption field, and in particular, the boundaries between 'high' and 'popular' culture may be different in less industrialised countries. The Chilean case highlights important instances of variation. For example, I show that going to the movies – a clear example of popular culture in the industrialised world (Alderson *et al.*, 2007; Chan and Goldthorpe, 2005; Lizardo, 2006) – is highly stratified in Chile, whereas attending plays and concerts appear not to be restricted to the elite. These differences provide a window to explore economic, institutional and cultural sources of variation in the stratification of cultural consumption. In order to analyse the Chilean case in a comparative perspective, this chapter proceeds as follows: Section 5.2 describes the Chilean society; Section 5.3 introduces the data, methods and hypotheses; Section 5.4 presents the analysis, and Section 5.5 concludes.

5.2 The Chilean context

Chile has undergone dramatic change in the last three decades, trans-
forming from a closed economy with heavy state intervention into one
of the most open and market-based economies of the world (Ffrench-
Davis, 1999). Historically one of the poorest countries in Latin America, Chile has experienced remarkable economic growth in the last two
decades. Per capita Gross National Income reaches US$5,870 in 2005,
which is far below the average of US$36,715 of the rich OECD coun-
tries, but the highest in Latin America (World Bank, 2006). Recent
economic growth has led to a significant reduction in poverty rate
from 38.6% in 1990 to 13.7% in 2006, and to an unprecedented
improvement of living standards.

In some respects Chilean society is very similar to industrialised
countries. It has a high urbanisation rate of 84%, and its occupational
structure is largely service-based, with 63% of the workforce engaged
in services, 23.4% in manufacturing and 13.6% in agriculture (World
Bank, 2006). Significant variation exists, however, in other respects.
Educational attainment is growing swiftly but it is still comparatively
low. The mean years of education is 11.6 for those aged 25–29, but
only 9.8 for 45–49-year-olds, and 6.0 for 70–74-year-olds. Another
point of departure from the industrialised world is the very high level
of economic inequality. Inequality is characterised by the concentration
of income at the top of the income distribution associated with high
returns to post-secondary education, with a small professional elite
receiving a substantial portion of the national income (Portes and
Hoffman, 2003; Torche, 2005b).

The wide economic differences in Chilean society have a clear symbolic counterpart in the prevalence of relations of deference and expressions of derogation and superiority between social strata (Barros and
Vergara, 1978; Tironi, 1999; Stabili, 2003). In addition, while in other
countries there are diverse sources of differentiation that compete with
economic advantage as the basis for group distinction – for instance, in
the US, Spain or India, race, language, religion or region are important
markers of identity – Chile is highly homogeneous in these respects.
Spanish is universally spoken, the proportion of indigenous population
reaches only 4.6%, the share of those with African and Asian descent
is less than 0.01%, and the proportion of the population that is foreign

born is only 0.75% (INE, several years). Regional cleavages are absent, and 85% of the population identify themselves as Christian – 82% of them as Catholics. In contrast to the elite fragmentation that has historically characterised other Latin American countries, Chile has a homogeneous social elite (Stabili, 2003). In sum, sources of cultural diversity that are significant in other national contexts are less relevant in Chile, and socioeconomic position stands alone as the main source of social differentiation. The combination of vast inequality with cultural homogeneity of Chilean society suggests that the status order derived from patterns of intimate association might be isomorphic with socioeconomic differences in education, income or class. In other words, the economic and cultural dimensions of stratification might be indistinguishable in Chile.

The recent improvement in living standards has expanded access to cultural consumption that was historically reserved to a small elite (Brunner, 2005). The decline in economic constraints is evident in household budget trends. While in 1987 Chilean households spent only 2.6% of their budget on leisure, in 1997 this had risen to 5.5% (National Institute for Statistics, 1989, 1999). Although many Chileans may still be unable to access cultural goods (Murray and Ureta, 2005), this is much less the case than two decades ago. Expansion in access is acknowledged by the population, with 63.2% indicating that access to cultural activities is easier than five years ago, and only 18.2% indicating that it is more difficult (National Council for Culture and the Arts and National Institute for Statistics, 2005).

However, participation appears to be highly domain-dependent. While engagement with reading material such as books, magazines and newspapers is quite low compared with industrialised nations (Murray and Ureta, 2005; Torche, 2007), the gap is narrower in public expressions such as theatre, concerts, movies and art exhibitions, the focus of this analysis. Figure 5.1 presents the proportion of the urban adult population in Chile, Britain, the Netherlands and France that has gone to different events in the last 12 months.

Interestingly, attendance at the theatre, dance performances, or concerts is not significantly lower in Chile than in the three European countries, in spite of difference in national incomes. Only for movie attendance are participation rates much lower in Chile. While between one-half and two-thirds of the citizens of European nations have gone to the movies in the last 12 months, only one-third of Chileans have

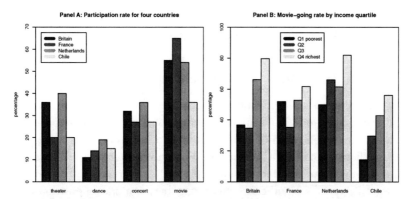

Fig. 5.1 Cultural participation rate in four countries: overall rates (left-hand panel) and movie-going rate by income quartile (right-hand panel)
Source: Eurobarometer 56.0 (2001) and Chilean Survey of Cultural Consumption and Time Use (2004–05)

done so. Furthermore, the right-hand panel of Figure 5.1 presents movie-going rates by income quartile and shows that this practice is much more stratified in Chile. The ratio between the wealthiest and poorest quartile reaches 3.9 in Chile, substantially higher than the 2.2, 1.6 and 1.2 ratios in Britain, France and the Netherlands, respectively.

A paradigmatic form of 'popular culture' in the industrialised world, going to the movies appears to be a mark of economic advantage in Chilean society. Two recent trends may contribute to the distinct status of cinema in comparison to live performances in Chile. First, since the 1990s, in a context of democratisation after an authoritarian regime, the Chilean government has provided support and subsidies to the production and consumption of culture (Weinstein, 2005), particularly to theatre and other stage performances (Piña, 2006, p. 196). In 2004, for instance, only 2.2% of movie tickets used in the country were free, while as many as 48.3% of live performance tickets were at no cost, most of them funded by government subsidies (National Institute for Statistics, 2004). Secondly, live performances are more likely to include popular and traditional productions which fit local tastes and which can be staged in local venues without substantial economic expenditures. In sum, this preliminary comparative analysis suggests that attendance at live performances is not restricted to a small elite, and that movie attendance is sharply stratified in Chile. In what follows I explore the multidimensional nature of the stratification of cultural consumption in the domain of movies and performances and exhibition in the public domain, with a focus on the role of status.

5.3 Hypotheses, data, variables and methods

In addition to adjudicating between the 'homology', 'omnivore–univore', and 'individualisation' arguments, three specific hypotheses about the stratification of cultural consumption emerge from the previous discussion of the Chilean case. First, given that status differences are more salient and pervasively expressed in everyday interaction in Chile, I expect a significant association between status position and cultural consumption to emerge. Second, if, however, the status order is merely an epiphenomenon of educational or economic inequality, we may find a substantial bivariate correlation between status and cultural consumption, but this association should disappear when education, income and social class are controlled for in a multivariate framework. Third, the standing of different cultural consumption practices may depart from the industrialised world. In particular, access to live performances such as theatre or dance appears not to be restricted to the elite, whereas movie attendance appears to be much more stratified than in the industrialised world.

My data comes from the 2004–2005 Survey of Cultural Consumption and Time Use (SCCTU), conducted by the Chilean National Council of Culture and the Arts and the National Institute for Statistics. This probabilistic, stratified and multistage sample is representative of urban areas in Chile ($N = 4,603$), and has a response rate of 86.2%. After selecting individuals 18 years old or older and currently employed, to whom an occupational status score can be attached, the analytical sample size is 2,073. In order to retain observations with missing data without introducing bias a multiple imputation procedure was used (Allison, 2002). Five complete data sets were created using the imputation software Amelia (Honaker *et al.*, 2003). The analysis was replicated with each data set; the parameter estimates and standard errors were then combined.[1]

The SCCTU asks respondents about a diverse set of cultural consumption and leisure activities, ranging from whether they have read

---

[1] This approach provides unbiased estimates, assuming that the data are missing at random (MAR).

newspapers and played instruments to how often they have attended craft fairs and watched TV. This analysis focuses on the domain of live performances and movie attendance, captured by questions of whether the respondent has attended the following six activities in the last 12 months: art exhibitions, dance performances, theatre, concert, other live performance (pantomime, poetry, comedy) and cinema.

Given that the focus of this chapter is to explore the role of status and other features of the stratification system on cultural consumption, the key independent variables are socioeconomic. The status order was empirically obtained from the patterns of marriage/cohabitation of incumbents of 28 detailed occupational groups, using a multidimensional scaling technique (typical occupations within each the occupational group are reported in Table 5.8, see also Chapter 2 and Torche, 2005a). The status hierarchy is strongly correlated with measures of socioeconomic advantage such as social class, income and particularly education (Torche, 2005a), which supports the hypothesis that status differences in Chile may be indistinguishable from socioeconomic inequality.

In addition to status, I include respondent's educational attainment, income, and social class, and father's educational attainment. Educational attainment is an ordinal variable with the following categories: 0–3, 4–8, 9–12, 13–17 and 18 or more years of schooling. Given that respondent's income is not available in the SCCTU, an index of household assets was used as a proxy. This index is based on 18 dichotomous indicators on the possession of: colour TV, car, phone, cell phone, radio, microwave, CD player, VCR, DVD, computer, internet, cable, home video, heating system, dishwasher, and building materials used for the roof, floor and walls. It was constructed using the first component in a principal component analysis, i.e. the linear combination that captures the largest amount of variation common to all indicators, and it has a mean of 0 and a standard deviation of 1 by construction.[2] Social class is measured by a modified 5-class version of the Goldthorpe

---

[2] The asset index has been shown to be a robust proxy for permanent income (Filmer and Pritchett, 1999, 2001). It has important measurement advantages: it is likely to be much less affected by recall bias or mis-measurement than income, it does not suffer from the notorious difficulties associated with measuring income for the self-employed and agricultural workers due to seasonality and accounting issues, and it is much less affected by suspicion or refusal by the respondent (McKenzie, 2004, 234–235). The constructed index has a close-to-normal distribution (skewness = 0.23, kurtosis = 2.42).

schema (Erikson and Goldthorpe, 1992, pp. 35–44), distinguishing: professional and managers (I+II), clerical workers (III), self-employed (IVab), skilled manual workers (V+IV) and unskilled manual workers and farmers (VIIa, VIIb+IVc).[3]

The analysis also includes the following demographic controls: age, gender, marital status (distinguishing single from married/ cohabitating, and widowed/divorced/separated respondents), whether the respondent has children younger than 18 years old, and region. This last variable identifies 13 geographical units that exhaustively divide Chile. Since these regions are characterised by different levels of cultural supply and economic development, this variable taps access to cultural consumption (see Table 5.1 for variable descriptions).

5.4 Analysis

5.4.1 *Latent class analysis of cultural consumption patterns*

Table 5.2 reports the proportion of the population who have taken part in each of the six activities in the past 12 months. Although this set includes activities typically regarded as 'high culture' (dance performances, theatre and art exhibitions), and others widely seen as popular (movies), it is remarkable that there is not a wide variation in their popularity. Attendance varies only from 15% for dance performances to 36% for movies. No sharp dichotomy between universal and restricted activities emerges, at least in the domain examined and given the level of data aggregation.

To analyse whether there are distinct patterns of cultural consumption and therefore types of cultural consumers in Chilean society, I use latent class analysis (LCA). LCA is a multivariate technique that extracts latent constructs from a set of categorical indicators. The technique assumes a model in which the indicators are uncorrelated with each other given the scores on the latent variable (conditional independence). Once latent classes are controlled for, only random association between the variables remains (McCutcheon, 1987; McCutcheon and

---

[3] The class of farmers (IVc+VIIb) was collapsed with the class of unskilled manual workers (VIIa) given the small number of respondents engaged in agriculture in this urban sample.

Table 5.1 *Descriptive statistics*

Variable	Mean	s.d.	Min.	Max.
Male	0.56	0.50	0	1
Age	41	13.87	18	89
Single (Ref. category)	0.30	0.46	0	1
Married/cohabiting	0.55	0.50	0	1
Widowed/separated	0.15	0.36	0	1
Children < 18	0.66	0.47	0	1
Education	3.11	0.88	1	5
0–3 years	0.04			
4–8 years	0.18			
9–12 years	0.46			
13–17 years	0.29			
18+ years	0.03			
Income (asset index)	0	1	−2.02	3.19
Status	0.15	0.77	−1.43	1.92
Father's education	2.45	1.03	1	5
0–3 years	0.20			
4–8 years	0.32			
9–12 years	0.34			
13–17 years	0.11			
18+ years	0.03			
Class I+II (Ref. category)	0.17	0.38	0	1
Class III	0.21	0.40	0	1
Class IVab	0.30	0.46	0	1
Class V–VI	0.10	0.30	0	1
Class VIIab–IVc	0.22	0.42	0	1

Mills, 1998). Based on the theoretical approaches to cultural consumption in contemporary societies, one of three outcomes is expected. The homology approach suggests the emergence of a clear distinction between 'elite' and 'popular' activities. The univore–omnivore hypothesis, in contrast, indicates that a group of respondents will consume all activities whereas another cluster will concentrate in the most popular one. Finally, the individualisation argument would suggest that LCA would produce no clear clusters of activities, signalling the diversification of individual consumption styles.

Table 5.2 *Percentage of respondents who have taken
part in various cultural activities in the last 12 months*

Cultural events or practice	%
attended a dance performance	15.0
attended other live performance (pantomime, poetry, comedy, etc.)	15.4
visited a theatre	20.0
visited an art exhibition	24.2
attended a concert	27.4
been to the movies	35.7

Table 5.3 *Latent class analysis of six indicators of cultural
consumption*

# class	χ^2	G^2	df	p^a	$ABIC^b$
1	7608.1	1425.0	57	0.000	14050.3
2	150.5	136.3	50	0.000	12793.1
3	76.9	75.3	43	0.002	12763.8
4	47.7	48.2	36	0.084	12768.3

Note: [a] p-value associated with the G^2 statistic; [b] -2 log-likelihood $+$ $df \times \ln(n^*)$ where $n^* = (n + 2)/24$.

Results of LCA for 1 to 4 latent classes are reported in Table 5.3. Solutions identifying 1 and 2 classes have a very poor fit. The 3-class model does not fit the data under standard statistical criterion ($p > 0.05$) but it is preferred by ABIC, which rewards parsimony.[4] A 4-class solution fits the data well at the cost of parsimony. To decide between the 3-class and 4-class solutions, a Wald test for the combination of the outcome categories in the 4-class solution was performed in the multinomial regression context. The results reject the null hypothesis that the outcome categories can be combined for all pairs of categories ($p < 0.05$). This indicates that patterns of effects are different across latent classes, and leads me to select the 4-class solution. I subsequently

---

[4] Simulation studies indicate that the sample-size adjusted BIC (ABIC) performs better than other likelihood-based and information criterion statistics in determining the number of classes in LCA models (Yang, 2006; Nylund *et al.*, 2006).

Table 5.4 *Relative size of the latent classes and conditional probability of participating in various cultural activities each class*

	latent class			
	1	2	3	4
relative size (estimated model)	0.060	0.596	0.216	0.128
relative size (post-assignment)	0.051	0.611	0.233	0.104
conditional probability of attending:				
a dance performance	0.82	0.03	0.18	0.47
other live performance (pantomime, poetry, comedy, etc.)	0.80	0.04	0.22	0.34
a theatre	0.94	0.03	0.40	0.45
an art exhibition	0.96	0.05	0.50	0.60
a concert	0.94	0.09	0.55	0.68
a movie	0.93	0.17	1.00	0.00
	O	I	ML	LPA

Note: O: Omnivore, I: Inactive, ML: Movie-lover, LPA: Live-performance aficionado.

allocate respondents to the latent class to which they have the highest (or modal) conditional probability of belonging. Some discrepancy between the size of the latent classes originally estimated and the size determined by the modal allocation of respondents emerges. However, as indicated in Table 5.4, this discrepancy is quite small – the largest variation is from 12.8% in the estimated model to 10.4% based on modal allocation for class 4.

Table 5.4 presents the four classes of consumers, their probability of participating in the six activities and the labels used to describe them. The first class contains only 5% of the sample, and its members are very likely to consume all items, including 'high' and 'popular'. The probabilities of consumption range from a low of 0.80 in the case of other live performances, to 0.96 in the case of art exhibitions. This widely voracious group identifies the Chilean *omnivores*. The second cluster comprises the majority of the respondents – 61% of the sample. Its members display a very low probability of engaging in any of the cultural activities considered. The only partial exception is going to the movies, but even for this activity the probability is only 0.17. Therefore, this group will be labelled *inactive*, as they are virtually marginalised from participation in this domain. The third class comprises 23% of the sample, and its members combine a unity probability of going to the movies with a low probability of consuming all other items – giving rise to their characterisation as *movie-lovers*. Finally, the fourth consumer type comprises 10% of the sample. In sharp contrast with the previous class, they have a null probability of going to the movies, and a relatively high probability (lower than omnivores, however) of attending live performances, particularly concerts and art exhibitions. Therefore they will be identified as *live-performance aficionados*.[5]

These results contradict the individualisation argument. Rather than seeing a diversification of tastes into a myriad of individual styles lacking patterned structure, four distinct groups emerge. The findings are more consistent with the 'omnivore–univore' argument, but not without qualifications. While a small group of omnivores exists in Chile, there is no evidence of a cluster of univores. In contrast, we find a large group of inactives. This result departs from the cases of the US and the UK, where a group of univores who only go to the movies is found in this domain (Alderson *et al.*, 2005; Chan and Goldthorpe, 2005).

The distinction between movie-lovers and live-performance aficionados speaks to the homology argument. This predicts the emergence of a cultural elite that favours high culture items, and rejects popular culture ones. The tastes of live-performance aficionados may be an indication of such a cultural elite, if indeed their avoidance of movies could be interpreted as the rejection of a 'popular culture' activity. This is at odds, however, with the evidence presented above. As discussed, movie attendance is highly stratified by income. It is, therefore, inappropriate to identify going to the movies as 'low culture' activity. Even more inappropriate is the identification of movie-lovers with a cultural elite that rejects popular culture, as they do not fully reject live performances. Rather, the consumption patterns of movie-lovers and live-performance aficionados appear to be intermediate locations

---

[5] Both the 3-class and 4-class latent class solution distinguish a large group of inactives and a small group of omnivores. The main difference between these two solutions is that a group displaying moderate consumption of all items in the 3-class solution (and which could appropriately be called 'paucivore') gets divided into movie-lovers (62%) and live-performance aficionados (25%) in the four-class solution.

Table 5.5 *Percentage of respondents within each latent class engaging in other cultural consumption and leisure activities*

	O	ML	LPA	I
using traditional media				
listened to radio in last seven days	98.2	97.6	98.7	93.8
watched TV almost every day	81.4	91.0	89.2	90.4
reading				
read book in last 12 months	78.8	62.4	56.5	29.1
read newspaper almost everyday	62.0	50.0	52.0	32.9
visited library in last 12 months	54.7	35.6	30.8	11.4
attending festivals and fairs in last 12 months				
attended religious festivities	50.4	39.0	51.1	31.7
attended traditional festivities	47.8	28.9	31.8	15.3
attended traditional craft exhibition	76.7	50.5	61.0	22.3
attended street craft fair	89.4	73.5	72.2	43.8
attended food festival	32.6	16.2	25.8	5.5
using new media				
Internet (last 12 months)	80.5	75.1	53.4	26.5
traveling (last 12 months)				
inside Chile	92.9	83.9	73.5	55.5
abroad	22.1	19.9	13.5	7.5

Note: O: Omnivore, I: Inactive, ML: Movie-lover, LPA: Live-performance aficionado. Source: Survey of Cultural Consumption and Time Use (CNCA & INE 2004/5). Restricted to individuals 18+ living in urban areas.

between the hierarchical extremes represented by omnivores and inactives. Movie-lovers and live-performance aficionados may highlight the relevance of different forms of capital – particularly economic against cultural – as a source of symbolic distinctions. Alternatively, they may be expressions of non-stratified differentiation based on factors such as age or gender.

In order to further explore who these four types of cultural consumers are, expanding to other cultural consumption and leisure practices, Table 5.5 reports the proportion of each group who engage in a wide set of activities including: using traditional media (watching TV, listening to radio), reading (reading books, newspapers, going to the library), attending festivals and fairs (attending religious festivities, traditional festivities, traditional craft exhibitions, street craft fairs, food festivals), using new media (using the Internet), and travelling (trips within Chile, trips abroad).

Traditional media activities are quite widespread, showing consistently high engagement rates, with omnivores slightly less likely than others to watch TV. This is in line with Wilensky's (1964, p. 194) finding of a small minority of the elite who isolate themselves from popular culture in the US. In all other activities, there is a clear ranking in which omnivores have the highest participation rates, inactives display the least engagement, and movie-lovers show higher participation rates than live-performance aficionados. The only exception is 'attending festivals and fairs', where live-performance aficionados consistently take the lead. Furthermore, the gap between movie-lovers and live-performance aficionados is wider for the use of Internet. These patterns suggest that live-performance aficionados favour traditional activities, defined by face to face interaction rather than mediated communication. In contrast, movie-lovers appear to embrace new media activities, which imply distance and technological mediation. Furthermore, Table 5.5 suggests that the omnivore lifestyle is not restricted to the cultural items analysed here, but extends to a diverse array of activities.

In sum, the distinction of four groups of cultural consumer provides qualified support for the univore–omnivore argument, but it cannot fully rule out the homology approach. In order to empirically adjudicate between these hypotheses, the stratified nature of these consumer types is now examined.

5.4.2 Bivariate analysis

In what follows I present the overall association of cultural consumption with status and other dimensions of the stratification system. Panel A of Figure 5.2 plots the distribution of consumer types across the 28 categories of the Chilean status scale, and shows that consumer differentiation is highly sensitive to status position. While the proportion of omnivores grows from 0% to 17% across the status hierarchy, the share of the inactives declines from about 90% to about 30%. The share of movie-lovers also rises significantly from about 10% to almost 50% as status increases. In sharp contrast, the proportion of

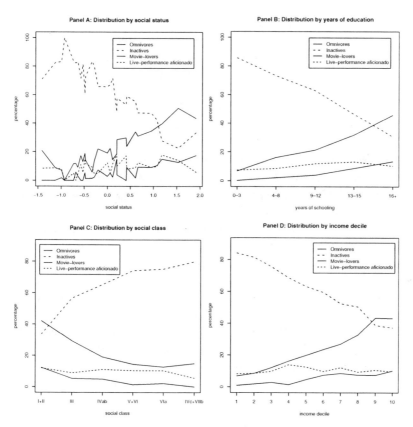

Fig. 5.2 Distribution of types of consumer by status, education, class and income

live-performance aficionados is not highly sensitive to status position. Panels B–D in Figure 5.2 display the bivariate association between type of cultural consumption and education, class and income, respectively. The probability of being an omnivore and a movie-lover consistently increases, and the probability of being an inactive consistently decreases at higher levels of each socioeconomic measure. Patterns are again less clear for the live-performance aficionados: their number does not significantly vary across strata, indicating the weak stratification of this group.

Several findings from the bivariate analysis are noteworthy. First, the association between status and cultural consumption types supports the hypothesis that status position indeed serves as a stratificatory source of cultural consumption. An alternative possibility, tested in the next section, is that this relationship is driven by the strong association between status and other dimensions of inequality such as education, income or social class, combined with a substantive influence of such indicators on cultural consumption.

Second, the probability of being a movie-lover is highly sensitive to all stratification variables, and not only income. This questions the description of movie lovers as low-status univores, or as a philistine economic elite lacking cultural and educational capital. In contrast to the industrialised world, movie attendance – and, indeed, the preference of movies over live performances – appears to serve as a mark of status *selectivity* in Chile.

Third, a remarkable difference exists between omnivores and movie-lovers. While the chances of being a movie-lover substantially grow across the income hierarchy, the probability of being an omnivore grows with status and education, but it is largely insensitive to income. Thus, omnivores do appear to be a cultural elite based on status and education rather than the 'pretensions of mere economic advantage' (Weber, 1968, p. 932). Fourth, being a live-performance aficionado seems to be largely unstratified, pointing to 'horizontal' sources of differentiation. In order to further explore the multidimensional sources of cultural consumption, a multivariate analysis is now presented.

5.4.3 Determinants of cultural consumption: multivariate analysis

The net influence of each socioeconomic factor and demographic controls on cultural consumption is assessed through a multinomial logit model.[6] Results are reported in Table 5.6. First, there are three basic paired comparisons: the determinants of being an omnivore, a movie-lover, or a live-performance aficionado as opposed to being an

---

[6] Valid interpretation of this model is based on the independence of irrelevant alternatives (IIA) assumption. This states that the odds for each specific pair of outcomes do not depend on other outcomes available. The Hausman test (Hausman and McFadden, 1984) indicates that IIA is not violated ($\chi^2_O = -2.88[52]$, $p = 1$, $\chi^2_I = -2.39[51]$, $p = 1$, $\chi^2_{ML} = 9.75[51]$, $p = 1$, $\chi^2_{LPA} = -0.018[52]$, $p = 1$). Also, the substantial correlations between the indicators of socioeconomic advantage could cause multicollinearity. Standard tests indicate that collinearity is not likely to be a problem (largest VIF = 3.42, average VIF across all predictors = 2.12).

Table 5.6 *Multinomial logistic regression of cultural consumption patterns*

	O vs. I		ML vs. I		LPA vs. I	
	$\hat{\beta}$	s.e.	$\hat{\beta}$	s.e.	$\hat{\beta}$	s.e.
constant	−3.049***	0.954	−0.491	0.557	−0.859	0.699
male	0.153	0.224	−0.107	0.129	−0.330*	0.164
age	−0.031**	0.010	−0.026***	0.006	−0.020**	0.007
married/cohab[a]	−0.573*	0.289	−0.515**	0.168	−0.061	0.214
widow/separated	−0.341	0.396	−0.149	0.218	−0.113	0.285
children < 18	−0.241	0.254	−0.264	0.144	−0.064	0.186
status	0.424*	0.215	0.213	0.124	0.199	0.161
education	0.990***	0.200	0.538***	0.110	0.354**	0.135
income	0.271*	0.135	0.544***	0.077	0.129	0.099
class III[b]	−0.391	0.329	−0.136	0.204	−0.483	0.296
class IVab	−0.157	0.320	−0.274	0.211	−0.071	0.282
class V–VI	−1.281	0.675	−0.402	0.295	−0.109	0.365
class VIIab–Ivc	−1.047*	0.518	−0.467	0.265	−0.298	0.342
father's education	0.092	0.112	0.125*	0.063	0.035	0.079

	O vs. ML		O vs. LPA		ML vs. LPA	
	$\hat{\beta}$	s.e.	$\hat{\beta}$	s.e.	$\hat{\beta}$	s.e.
constant	−2.558	0.960	−2.190*	1.081	0.368	0.764
male	0.260	0.226	0.483	0.255	0.223	0.180
age	−0.005	0.010	−0.011	0.011	−0.006	0.008
married/cohab[a]	−0.058	0.291	−0.511	0.330	−0.454	0.235
widow/separated	−0.191	0.400	−0.228	0.451	−0.036	0.313
children < 18	0.023	0.256	−0.178	0.290	−0.200	0.204
status	0.212	0.218	0.225	0.247	0.014	0.176
education	0.452*	0.204	0.636**	0.225	0.183	0.154
income	−0.272*	0.137	0.143	0.154	0.415***	0.109
class III[b]	−0.255	0.326	0.091	0.390	0.347	0.294
class IVab	0.117	0.317	−0.086	0.377	−0.203	0.292
class V–VI	−0.879	0.688	−1.171	0.729	−0.292	0.407
class VIIab–Ivc	−0.579	0.529	−0.748	0.579	−0.169	0.372
father's education	−0.033	0.115	0.057	0.128	0.090	0.089

Note: Pseudo $R^2 = 0.153$, N = 2073 *$p < 0.05$, **$p < 0.01$, ***$p < 0.001$.
[a] singles is reference category, [b] class I+II is reference category.

inactive. Three additional comparisons distinguish between the first three types of cultural consumers (i.e. O, ML and LPA). The twelve regional dummy variables are included in the analysis but are not presented to save space.

I focus on the three basic comparisons, and use the three additional ones as ancillary analysis. Starting with the demographic variables, which provide a glimpse of the 'horizontal' differentiation of cultural consumption, the model shows that younger people are more likely to be omnivores, movie-lovers or live-performance aficionados rather than inactives, but (as indicated by the ancillary regressions) there are not significant age differences among O, ML or LPA. Interesting gender differences emerge: men tend to cluster in the two extremes of the cultural consumption spectrum – omnivores and inactives – while women are more likely to be live-performance aficionados. This is not inconsistent with research indicating that women are higher participators (Bihagen and Katz-Gerro, 2000; Chan and Goldthorpe, 2005), but it specifies a female preference for live performances.[7] There is some variation by marital status: compared to married or cohabiting respondents, singles are less likely to be omnivores or movie-lovers rather than inactives. Having children younger than 18 has an expected negative effect on engaging in any activity, but this effect fails to reach significance, conceivably because the variable does not distinguish number or age of children.

Now I move to the core of the analysis – the stratification of cultural consumption, and particularly the role of status net of other measures of socioeconomic advantage. Status has a substantial effect on the odds of being an omnivore rather than an inactive. The effect of status for the movie-lover–inactive contrast is marginally significant, with $p = 0.08$. In contrast, the odds of being a live-performance aficionado rather than an inactive do not increase with status position. Note also that status does not significantly distinguish omnivores from movie-lovers. This is consistent with the assumption that movie-lovers are not just an economic elite with doubtful social credentials.

Education has a large effect on cultural consumption in any form as opposed to being an inactive, and it also stratifies the cultural consumer types. Education establishes a clear consumption hierarchy,

---

[7] The male parameter for the O v LPA contrast in Table 5.6 is marginally insignificant with $p = 0.059$.

with omnivores at the top, inactives at the bottom, and movie-lovers and live-performance aficionados in an intermediate position. There is no significant educational differences between ML and LPA. How to interpret this substantial influence? Education taps intellectual competence, socialisation influences, and cultural and economic advantage. Given that status and measures of economic advantage are explicitly controlled, I would concur with Chan and Goldthorpe (2007a,c) in interpreting the effect of education as largely capturing the individual 'information processing capacity' (Ganzeboom, 1982). Education trains and signals the individual intellectual ability to process complex information, inducing a preference for cultural activities that demand more complexity – particularly, the intense and wide-ranging omnivore style.[8]

Note also that father's education is largely inconsequential. This variable may identify socialisation influences or information processing capacity not fully materialised in the acquisition of formal schooling, and the influence of intergenerational social mobility (Chan and Goldthorpe, 2007c). I do not attempt to disentangle these influences – indeed the fact that no effect is found suggests that they are not substantively important – but only to provide an additional control to evaluate the net influence of status position.

Income has a substantial net effect on cultural consumption, as would be expected for a developing nation in which economic constraints are still substantial for a large proportion of the population (Inglehart, 1990). However, the pattern of income effects is quite different from that of education. Income has the strongest influence on the probability of being a movie-lover, distinguishing this group from the omnivores, live-performance aficionados and inactives. In fact, higher income significantly *reduces* the chances of being an omnivore versus being a movie-lover. This finding highlights the standing of omnivores as a cultural elite that distinguishes itself by status and education rather than economic capital. Note also that, as is the case with status, the probability of being a live-performance aficionado rather than an omnivore or an inactive is insensitive to income. With the partial

---

[8] The SCCTU does not contain information on genre preference, for instance preference for art movies vs. comedies or classical vs. experimental jazz vs. pop concerts, which would provide a more precise hypothesis of the information processing capacity hypothesis.

exception of education, this group is not responsive to stratification factors.

Before moving to an aggregate evaluation of these effects, a null finding should be mentioned. Once controls for status and other stratification variables are included, the substantial bivariate association between social class and cultural consumption virtually disappears (note that the only significant coefficient is the one capturing the lower likelihood of unskilled manual workers and farm workers (VIIab+IVc), as compared with professionals (I+II), to be omnivores rather than inactives). To interpret this finding, consider that social class captures two dimensions of inequality: on the one hand, economic advantage, and on the other, lifestyle distinctions emerging from a similar position in the occupational structure – the notion of classes as communities. Income should capture the former dimension, and status should be a more valid measure of lifestyle differentiation than class. My results are consistent with this assumption. Indeed, both status and income are needed to remove the influence of class in the multivariate setting (results available from the author upon request). The analysis indicates that status and income have distinct impacts on cultural consumption. To explore these two distinct sources of stratification, Figure 5.3 plots the predicted probability of belonging to each cultural consumer type across status and income levels.

Figure 5.3 displays the probability of being an omnivore, a movie-lover and an inactive across income and status level (the probability of being a live-performance aficionado is not presented because it is not significantly affected by status). The other predictors are set to identify a 41-year-old male, married, with children, whose father completed 9 years of schooling, who is self-employed and earns the sample-average income. These values describe a common demographic profile in current Chilean society. Probabilities are shown across the status range, for individuals in the poorest, median and wealthiest income decile. The slope of the lines quantify the influence of status, and the gaps between lines express differences associated with income. As Panel A of Figure 5.3 indicates, the probability of being inactive significantly declines as status rises. For those with median income, this decline is 18 percentage points (from 0.64 to 0.46). The almost parallel lines across income levels indicate that this decline in the probability of being an inactive is very similar across the income hierarchy. Indeed, the drop across the status range is 17 percentage points for those with

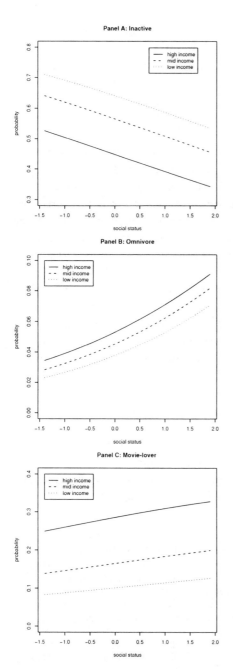

Fig. 5.3 Predicted probabilities of being an inactive, an omnivore or a movie-lover by social status and income

high income, and 19 percentage points for those with low incomes. Income has an impact similar in magnitude to that of status. Examination of the vertical distance between lines indicates that the probability of being an inactive is about 18 percentage points lower for those with high income as compared with those in the bottom income decile, and this influence is constant across the status hierarchy.

The patterns of effect are radically different for omnivore and movie-lovers (Panel B and C of Figure 5.3).[9] Status has a substantial effect on the probability of being an omnivore – there is a 6 percentage-point increase across the status range, which represents a three-fold surge – but the influence of income is negligible, as indicated by the very small vertical distance between the lines. In sharp contrast, income is highly consequential for the chances of being a movie-lover. For someone with a median status score, for instance, the probability of being a movie-lover grows from 0.10 if the person has a low income to 0.28 for high-income respondents. Similar increases are experienced by those with low and high status. Overall, economic resources are crucial determinants of being a movie-lover, but they are irrelevant for omnivorousness, highlighting the multidimensionality in the stratification of cultural consumption.[10]

A related question is about the *fungibility* of status and income. Omnivorousness can be understood as determined by the combination of motivation and economic resources. If motivation is measured by status and economic resources are proxied by income, it is conceivable that the influence of each one of these dimensions varies, depending on the level of the other. Specifically, the motivation emerging from status may be crucial when economic resources are scarce but its

---

[9] Note that the scale for the y-axis varies for the panels of Figure 5.3.

[10] Figure 5.3 plots the probability of belonging to each consumer type across the entire range of status scores for those with low, median and high income. However, there are few respondents characterised by low income and high status, and by high income and low status. As a consequence, the confidence intervals for these respondents' profiles are wider, preventing precise estimation. The main substantive finding conveyed in this graph – the fact that the probability of being an omnivore is largely insensitive to income and more sensitive to status whereas the opposite is true for the probability of being a movie lover – is robust to this issue.

influence may weaken as income becomes more abundant. For those facing budget constraints, status should be 'the difference that makes the difference' in terms of motivating a wider and more intense consumption pattern. As economic restrictions loosen, however, status should lose some of its influence, signalling resource convertibility or fungibility. Alternatively, economic and cultural resources could have a multiplicative impact on cultural consumption. This would result in a growing impact of status as income increases. This is expected if, for instance, higher income would discourage cultural consumption among those with low status (by reducing the pressure to 'prove themselves' via a selective lifestyle), or if having more economic resources significantly encourages intense consumption among high-status individuals, by providing additional resources to afford it (assuming that time is not a major constraint). These alternative hypotheses can be tested by adding an income by status interaction term to the model. The former hypothesis would result in a negative coefficient associated with the interaction term, while the latter would result in a positive interaction.

Table 5.7 presents the model with an interaction between status and income. This term is negative and significant for all comparisons, indicating that the effect of status significantly weakens as income increases for all types of cultural consumer. Given that an interaction term adds to the non-linearities already contained in a multinomial logit model, substantive interpretation requires graphical display. Figure 5.4 shows the probability of being an omnivore, a movie-lover or a live-performance aficionado for the 'modal' individual described above. Results are striking; the probability of being an omnivore increases with status among those with low income, but status does not have any influence for those in the top of the economic hierarchy. This pattern also appears for the live-performance aficionados, but not for the movie lovers. Findings are consistent with the 'fungibility' assumption. Among elite Chileans, status and income appear to become substitutes and their additive effect wanes. Note that this finding may be the result of a low threshold used to define cultural participation – attending an activity once a year makes you a participant – which may not capture important differences in consumption intensity within the elite. Future research with more detailed intensity measures should explore this possibility.

Table 5.7 *Multinomial logistic regression model of cultural consumption pattern with income proxy by status interaction*

	O vs. I		ML vs. I		LPA vs. I	
	$\hat{\beta}$	s.e.	$\hat{\beta}$	s.e.	$\hat{\beta}$	s.e.
constant	−5.877***	1.353	−1.697**	0.619	−1.229	0.749
male	0.151	0.225	−0.107	0.129	−0.332*	0.165
age	−0.029**	0.010	−0.026***	0.006	−0.020**	0.007
married/cohab[a]	−0.565*	0.291	−0.509**	0.169	−0.051	0.215
widow/separated	−0.388	0.398	−0.162	0.219	−0.123	0.286
children < 18	−0.244	0.255	−0.267	0.144	−0.068	0.187
education	0.970***	0.201	0.535***	0.110	0.341*	0.135
income	0.522**	0.168	0.583***	0.083	0.185	0.102
status	0.644**	0.232	0.265*	0.131	0.261	0.163
class III[b]	−0.479	0.329	−0.203	0.206	−0.621*	0.291
class IVab	−0.155	0.319	−0.309	0.210	−0.151	0.285
class V–VI	−1.251	0.667	−0.458	0.296	−0.218	0.368
class VIIab–IVc	−0.961	0.518	−0.480	0.265	−0.333	0.342
father's education	0.091	0.112	0.125*	0.063	0.037	0.079
income × status	−0.471	0.163	−0.181*	0.089	−0.286**	0.113

Note: Pseudo $R^2 = 0.156$, $N = 2073$, *$p < 0.05$, **$p < 0.01$, ***$p < 0.001$
12 regional dummies included in the analysis, coefficients not presented.
[a] singles is reference category, [b] class I+II is reference category.

In sum, the multivariate analysis largely confirms the bivariate findings, except for revealing the irrelevance of social class in delineating cultural consumption styles. Omnivores are an elite distinguished by education and status, rather than by economic resources. In contrast, the movie-lover style is highly stratified by income. This does not mean that movie-lovers are socially excluded philistines – indeed this group has only slightly less educational and status credentials than omnivores. In contrast, the lifestyle centred on live-performances is largely unstratified. These findings indicate that stratification of Chilean cultural consumption cannot be reduced to a unidimensional scale from high- to low-brow, nor to a unidimensional ranking from voracious omnivore to narrowly focused univore. It is true that omnivores and inactives occupy the two extremes of the social hierarchy, but the location of movie-lovers and live-performances aficionados highlights

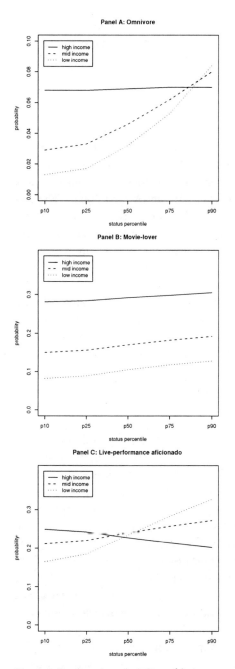

Fig. 5.4 Predicted probability of being an omnivore, a movie-lover or a live-performance aficionado by income and status with income–status interaction

the multidimensional nature of the stratification of cultural consumption, and suggests the relevance non-hierarchical sources of cultural differentiation.

5.5 Conclusions and discussion

This paper has assessed the influence of status position on cultural consumption in contemporary Chilean society. Based on the occupational structure of marriage and cohabitation, a clear status hierarchy emerges in Chile, with professionals in the upper echelons, and agricultural and low service workers at the bottom rungs. The status ranking strongly correlates to standard measures of socioeconomic advantage at the aggregate occupational group level, suggesting the possibility that status is fully determined by socioeconomic position, and therefore lacks any autonomous explanatory power on patterns of individual tastes and behaviour.

In order to determine whether different patterns of cultural consumption, and therefore types of cultural consumers, exist in Chilean society, a latent class analysis of attendance at six types of cultural events was undertaken. The set of events analysed include those conventionally associated with 'high culture' such as dance performances, theatre, and art exhibitions, and others conventionally associated with 'popular culture' such as movies.

To place the Chilean findings in context, a preliminary comparative analysis with Britain, France and the Netherlands was undertaken. The international comparison produces two surprising findings. Firstly, participation in this domain of cultural consumption is not homogeneously lower in Chile, in spite of it being a developing country. Secondly, going to the movies, considered a paradigmatic 'popular culture' activity in the industrialised world, is as stratified as attendance at live performances in Chile. Although further testing with more detailed indicators is needed, these results question the universality of the 'high culture' vs. 'popular culture' distinctions, and suggest the relevance of institutional factors – particularly governmental policy providing subsidised access to specific cultural activities – in determining access to each specific activity.

The results distinguish four groups of cultural consumers in Chile: 60% of the respondents are virtually excluded from participation in this domain; and 5% of them are 'omnivores' who consume the entire range of cultural expressions. Two intermediate groups emerge: the 'movie-lovers' have a unity probability of going to the movies over the last 12 months, but a low probability of attending all other events, whereas the live-performance aficionados display the opposite pattern; null probability of going to the movies, but a substantial probability of attending live-performance activities.

When the determinants of these distinct patterns of consumption are analysed, measures of socioeconomic advantage are found to be quite influential, with education having the strongest effect, particularly on omnivorousness. Status has a substantial positive effect on being an omnivore and a movie-lover even after controlling for education and economic resources. This indicates that status is not merely the symbolic correlate of economic and educational advantage. Higher income induces participation, but not homogeneously across activities. Income is highly determinant of the probability of being a movie-lover, but barely consequential for omnivorousness. Indeed, as income increases, the probability of being an omnivore rather than a movie-lover *decreases*. This finding highlights the multidimensionality of stratification in Chilean society, and it addresses the question about the relative standing of different cultural activities in Chile. Cinema is not a paradigmatic popular culture expression, as it was found to be in the industrialised world, but it is highly stratified by education and status, and particularly by income in Chile. Additionally, the emergence of a live-performance aficionado group highlights that cultural differentiation in Chile is not fully stratified. Although live-performance aficionados are distinguished from omnivores and inactives by education, and from movie-lovers by income, they also appear to embrace a style centred on traditional activities unmediated by technology, largely orthogonal to the stratification system.

Do these findings support a neo-Weberian claim that class and status are two qualitatively different dimensions of stratification, and that cultural consumption, as a key element of lifestyle, should be an expression of status? The answer is a qualified yes. The large and significant influence of status on omnivorousness suggests that the structure of inequality that emerges from patterns of marriage among Chileans is driven by factors other than the mere location in the structure of economic advantage. In other words, this finding is consistent with Weber's claim that 'status groups are stratified according to the principles of their consumption . . . as represented by special "styles of life"' (1946, p. 193). However, the net effect of status is significantly smaller in magnitude than the influence of education. This finding seems sensible for a developing country, where the variance in information-processing capacity that educational attainment identifies is wider than in the industrialised world (Tuijnman, 2001, Table 8). Overall, the findings highlight that cultural consumption is affected by several distinct factors, of which status is only one. The analysis indicates also that the influence of status on omnivorousness is strongest among those with low economic resources, but it declines significantly as income grows. This suggests that cultural and economic resources are fungible in their effect on cultural consumption at the top of the Chilean social hierarchy.

This chapter has introduced a developing country to the international analysis of stratification and cultural consumption. Although more research in other developing nations and in other domains is needed to obtain systematic conclusions, the results presented here are consistent with the omnivorousness hypothesis, and they highlight the relevance of status position as a source of cultural consumption stratification in contemporary societies.

Table 5.8 *Typical occupations within each of the 28 occupational groups in Chile*

Occupational Group	Typical occupations
Professionals in science, engineering and health	Medical doctor, dentist, architect, engineer, chemist, statistician
Professionals in business, law and others	Lawyer, accountant, economist, writer, composer, psychologist, librarian
Professionals in education	College professor, secondary, primary, and special education teacher
Associate professionals in business, law and others	Business assoc. prof., govt. social benefits official, police inspector, commercial designers
Managers in production, operations, and finance	Manager in manufacture, construction, finance, personnel, transportation, hotels
Other associate professionals	Engineer technician, Telecom. technician, computer assistant, aircraft pilot, medical equipment operator, agronomy technician, optician, nurses
Secretaries and numerical clerks	Secretary, data entry operator, stenographer, library clerk, mail carrier, coding clerk
Other clerical workers	Clerical worker nec
Cashiers, tellers, and receptionists	Cashier, teller, receptionist, travel agency clerk
Shop sales workers	Shop sales person, demonstrators, models
Managers in wholesale or retail trade	General manager in wholesale and retail trade
Drivers	Taxi driver, bus driver, crane operator, lifting truck operator
Personal services workers	Childcare provider, nursing home attendant, hairdresser, beautician, valet
Welders, blacksmiths, toolmakers and mechanics	Welder, blacksmith, tool maker, mechanic, potter, printer, motor vehicle mechanic
Service workers	Travel attendant, housekeeper, waiter, bartender, travel guide
Plant and machine operatives	Mining, papermaking, power-producing plant operator, cement, pharm., plastic, food, weaving, electrical machine operator, automated assembly line worker

(*cont.*)

Table 5.8 *(cont.)*

Occupational Group	Typical occupations
Construction workers, plumbers and electricians	Bricklayer, carpenter, plumber, electrician, painter, roofer, miner
Other skilled manual workers	Butcher, baker, wood treater, cabinet maker, weaver, tailor, sewer, shoe maker
Porters, messengers, and doormen	Window and vehicle cleaner, messenger, doorman, garbage collector
Cleaners	Shoe cleaner, office and hotel cleaner, hand launderer
Stall and market salespersons	Stall and market salesperson
Street and door-to-door vendors	Street salesperson, door-to-door vendor, telephone salesperson
Animal producer, forestry and fishery workers	Dairy producer, poultry producer, forestry worker, fishery worker, charcoal burner
Labourer in mining, construction and manufacturing	Unskilled labourer in mining, construction, maintenance, transportation and assembling, freight handler
Subsistence farmers	Subsistence agricultural and fishery worker
Domestic servants	Maid, domestic cleaner
Field croppers, vegetable growers and gardeners	Field crop grower, vegetable grower, tree grower, gardener, mixed-crop grower
Farm labourers	Farm-hands, forestry labourer, fishery labourer

6 Social stratification and cultural participation in Hungary: a post-communist pattern of consumption?

ERZSÉBET BUKODI

6.1 Introduction

Since the collapse of communism in Hungary, major changes have occurred in the level and pattern of cultural consumption. Although the overall amount of leisure time has increased, there has been a significant decline in the amount of time spent attending concerts, theatres and cinemas or visiting museums (Falussy, 2004). In national surveys, the percentage of people who said they have attended a theatre in the year preceding the interview was 36% in 1986, but this had dropped to 23% by 2000 (Bukodi, 2005). Likewise, in the mid 1980s, 42% of Hungarians claimed to have visited a museum at least once over a 12-month period, but in 2000 this figure was only 22%.

In the light of these developments, further enquiry needs to be made into the social bases of cultural participation. This is the main objective of this chapter. More specifically, I investigate the association between individuals' cultural consumption across several different public domains – i.e. attendance at musical events, at theatres and cinemas, and at museums and galleries – and a range of different indicators of social stratification; and, in conclusion, I consider the applicability in the Hungarian case of rival theoretical arguments on the relationship between cultural and social stratification as outlined in Chapter 1.

6.2 In search of the social bases of cultural consumption in Hungary

6.2.1 The role of cultural and economic resources

Cultural participation is thought to be influenced by education in several different ways. Bourdieu (1984) argued that education increases individuals' 'cultural capital' and thus affects their ability to interpret and appropriate different expressions of culture. Others (e.g. Ganzeboom, 1982) have suggested that education is closely associated with individuals' information-processing capacity and thus influences not only the level but also the complexity of the forms of cultural consumption in which they will seek to engage.

In communist societies education played a particularly important role in shaping life chances. Since, under communism, nearly every other agency of social reproduction was eliminated, the educational system, with its legitimising facade of 'meritocracy', became of central importance for distributive processes. In research carried out in the 1980s, Ganzeboom et al. (1990) showed that educational attainment had a direct impact on all other aspects of social inequality – much in line with the thesis of cultural reproduction as a major determinant of social reproduction advanced by Bourdieu. In communist countries even members of less advantaged strata had, in principle, good access to cultural resources. However, their levels of cultural consumption remained relatively low. Drawing on data from five countries (Hungary, Czechoslovakia, Denmark, the Netherlands and the United States) around 1980, Ultee et al. (1993) found that cultural inequalities were in fact highest in the communist states, and especially in Hungary, and that in these countries the association between educational level and cultural participation (going to the theatre, listening to classical music, buying books) was extremely strong. Further, de Graaf (1991) showed that, in Hungary, not only the individual's education but also the spouse's played an important role in the pattern of cultural consumption under communism. In accordance with the 'status maximisation hypothesis', the partner with the higher level of education chiefly determined the cultural behaviour of the family.

In the light of these research results, I expect that, despite regime change, education will still prove to be one of the most powerful predictors of cultural consumption in present-day Hungary. Moreover, cross-national surveys of literacy competency (e.g. OECD, 2000) have found that a significant part of the Hungarian population continues to have serious problems even with basic interpretative skills. In other words, one might say that the information-processing capacity of many people in Hungary, and especially of those with relatively low levels of education, remains comparatively poor. This would then seem likely to adversely affect their propensity to engage in cultural activity of any kind; and, further, marked differences in basic literacy skills could be expected to lead not only to a major division between the culturally active and the inactive but also, among the active, to marked contrasts between those who consume highbrow and lowbrow cultural forms.

One ideological objective of governments in the socialist era was to make different cultural activities available to the broadest audience. In order to achieve this, the costs of cultural participation were kept at an artificially low level, such that individuals' financial resources were found to have no impact, or only a very modest one, on the amount and pattern of cultural consumption (Róbert, 1997). However, after the collapse of communism, former state subsidies were drastically reduced and the 'cultural field' has become much more open to market mechanisms. For instance, in 2003 the average price of a theatre or a cinema ticket was four times higher than in 1996 (Bárdosi *et al.*, 2005),[1] and overall costs to the consumer of cultural and recreational goods increased by 96% between 1996 and 2005. This rate of increase was one of the highest across all European countries (Compendium of Cultural Policies and Trends in Europe, 2007). In line with these unfavourable changes, a recent study (Dudás and Hunyadi, 2005) reports that about half of those who had not attended a theatre or a cinema in the year prior to interview referred to high ticket prices as the main cause of their inactivity. Taking income as a proxy for individuals' economic resources, and taking into account the increasing income inequalities in the period of transformation and then again in the later 1990s (Tóth, 2003), I would expect a marked income effect on the overall level of cultural participation, in addition to that of education.

6.2.2 *The role of social status*

Most research into social stratification under communism has pointed to generally low levels of class formation (Connor, 1988). As Wesolowski (1976) argues, the stratification of communist societies could be better described as a status order deriving from differentiation in education, occupational prestige and income, but one which

---

[1] As regards costs of museum or art gallery attendance, the rate of increase in ticket price was more modest, and in recent years some new state subsidies have been introduced (Dudás and Hunyadi, 2005).

incorporates inconsistencies, especially as regards occupational prestige and income (see also Kolosi, 1984). Consequently, individuals in
high-status positions could not always distinguish themselves by a high
level of material consumption. For them, participation in highbrow
cultural activities would appear to have been especially important and
desirable (Wnuk-Lipinski, 1983). These findings justify a stratification
model in communist Hungary that involves a conflict between culturally defined groups, in particular between individuals at the top and
bottom extremes of the occupational hierarchy, and between groups
that differ in the possession of cultural resources more generally. High-
level professionals, high-ranking administrators and well-trained tech-
nocrats formed the 'knowledge class' of the 1970s and 1980s, and
constituted a status group with its own cultural means of establishing
social closure, in a rather similar way to that suggested by Bourdieu.

Since the collapse of communism, Hungary would appear to have
been moving towards a more Western-type stratification system, where
social class chiefly determines economic inequalities, but where the link
between the amount and variety of cultural resources and status could
still be fairly strong.[2] Although the inconsistencies between education,
occupational prestige and income seem to have been decreasing over
the last decade (Kolosi, 2000), it could be expected that the present-
day counterpart of the old 'intelligentsia' – for example, higher-status
professionals – will still be particularly motivated, and now better
able, to show themselves as 'cultured'; and especially so as to distance themselves from 'people of new money' – for example, from
higher-level managers, business professionals or large employers.[3] At

---

[2] A recent study (Bukodi *et al.*, 2006) shows that in contemporary Hungary
security in the labour market is strongly influenced by social class, defined in
terms of employment relations. In particular, the relative risk of long-term or
recurrent unemployment is significantly higher for individuals holding
working-class, and especially semi- or unskilled, positions. Moreover, the
chances of career advancement and upward mobility are also well predicted by
class position (Bukodi and Róbert, 1999).

[3] Domanski (2000), investigating the basic pattern of stratification in several
post-socialist countries, also found that – in contrast to the communist era –
different mechanisms seem to be responsible for outcomes in economic life and
in the domain of lifestyles and cultural consumption. Private entrepreneurs,
especially those with employees, tend to possess a privileged position in
economic life, but the amount and variety of their cultural consumption is
modest; whereas the high-status intelligentsia appear to follow an 'exclusive'
pattern of cultural participation, engaging chiefly in highbrow activities.

the same time, if modern Hungary is moving closer to a Western pattern of cultural tastes and consumption, it might also be expected that a wider range of cultural participation comprising both highbrow and lowbrow genres – in other words, omnivorousness – will predominate within certain high-status groups; for instance, among younger people or among the new economic elite.

6.2.3 *The role of the family of origin*

Under communism, family background played a crucial role in shaping life-chances and lifestyle and its importance seems not to have diminished after regime change. Kraaykamp and Niewbeerta (2000), analysing highbrow cultural consumption in five former socialist countries, emphasise that parental cultural resources have remained extremely important since the collapse of communism. Transmission of inequality in the cultural domain predominantly takes place through socialisation within the family, and in Eastern and Central Europe this mode of transmission seems to be more marked than in Western societies. In investigating the pattern of intergenerational social mobility in Hungary, Róbert and Bukodi (2004) show that, since the early 1990s, the association between fathers' and children's social class has been increasing. Moreover, Bukodi (1999), analysing trends in educational inequalities after the collapse of communism, shows that parents' education and cultural capital have substantial – and in some cases increasing – impact on children's educational attainment. In the light of these findings, one further expectation arises: that parents' social status will significantly affect cultural consumption in Hungary over and above the influence of the individual's own status.

6.3 Data and analytical strategy

I draw on data from the Way of Life and Time Use Survey carried out in 2000 by the Hungarian Central Statistical Office. This data-set is well suited to the purposes of this study as it contains much factual information on the nature and extent of individuals' consumption in several cultural domains. Face-to-face interviews were carried out with a stratified probability sample of around 10,000 individuals aged between 15 and 85 and living in private households. In the subsequent analyses, I restrict the sample to those aged 20–64 years old, since

Table 6.1 *Percentage of respondents who have taken part in various cultural activities in the past 12 months*

	%
Theatre and cinema	
Theatre	22.6
Cinema	29.8
Music	
Opera/classical music concert	7.8
Pop/rock/jazz concert	23.0
Visual arts	
Museum/art gallery	22.3

the cultural habits of both younger and older groups may well require separate treatment.

As regards cultural consumption, I concentrate on responses obtained from a set of questions covering three cultural domains. Respondents were asked whether or not over the last 12 months they had been (1) to a cinema or (2) to a theatre for any kind of performance; whether or not they had attended (3) an opera or a classical music concert or (4) had been to a pop, rock or jazz concert; and whether or not they had visited (5) a museum or art gallery. Each of these five questions was designed to produce a binary, yes/no, response.

Table 6.1 shows rates of participation in the three domains – labelled as 'theatre and cinema', 'music' and 'visual arts' – as indicated by the responses to the five questions. It should be noted that, in general, levels of participation are not high. Over a 12-month period, 30% of respondents had visited a cinema, but less than 25% had been to a theatre, to a pop, rock or jazz concert, or to a museum or gallery, and only 8% had been to an opera or a classical music concert.

As a basis for studying the social stratification of cultural consumption, some typology of consumers both within and across the three domains is desirable. To begin with, and following the results shown in Table 6.1, I propose types of consumer within each domain as indicated in Table 6.2. I draw here, in part, on 'omnivore–univore' terminology, although without at this stage wishing to imply a commitment to omnivore–univore arguments in all respects.

Table 6.2 *Distribution of respondents in the three*
separate domains of cultural consumption

	%
Theatre and cinema	
Inactives (I)	60.4
Cinema univores (U)	16.6
Exclusive theatre-goers (E)	9.3
Theatre omnivores (O)	13.7
Music	
Inactives (I)	73.3
Pop univores (U)	18.7
Exclusive classical concert goers (E)	3.2
Musical omnivores (O)	4.7
Visual arts	
Inactives (I)	77.4
Museum-goers (A)	22.6

Note: I: inactive; A: active; U: univores; E: exclusives;
O: omnivores.

As can be seen, for each domain alike, those respondents who had
not taken part in any activity over the last 12 months are treated
as 'inactives'. In the case of theatre and cinema, those respondents
who had attended only a cinema are labelled as 'cinema univores',
while those who had visited only a theatre are labelled as 'exclusive
theatre-goers'. Those respondents who had been to both a theatre
and a cinema are then treated as 'theatre omnivores'. Similarly, for
music, those respondents who had attended only a pop, rock or a jazz
concert become 'pop univores'; those who had been only to an opera
or a classical music concert become 'exclusive classical concert goers',
and individuals who had engaged in both activities become 'musical
omnivores'. For the visual arts no further distinction beyond that of
'museum goers' as against 'inactives' can be made.

In each domain inactives are clearly the numerically predominant
type – around three-quarters in the case of music and the visual arts.
Turning to the actives, one can see that, in the case of theatre and
cinema, cinema univores are relatively numerous, as are omnivores,
and exclusive theatre-goers also amount to 9%. However, in the case

Table 6.3 *Goodness-of-fit statistics of log-linear models as applied
to a three-way contingency table cross-classifying types of cultural
participation in different domains*

	L^2	df	BIC
1. M, T, V	7428.10	24	3701.05
2. MT, V	2200.23	15	1920.23
3. MV, T	2864.34	21	2403.01
4. M, TV	2748.99	21	2147.54
5. MT, MV	892.88	12	622.20
6. MT, TV	595.66	12	366.75
7. MV, TV	1166.88	18	849.54
8. MT, MV, TV	59.14	9	−23.35

Note: M: music; T: theatre and cinema; V: visual arts.

of music, while pop univores are also relatively numerous, both omnivores and exclusive classical concert goers appear rather rare.

To move on to a cross-domain typology, I first apply a log-linear analysis to a 4 (theatre and cinema) × 4 (music) × 2 (visual arts) table that cross-classifies the types of consumer shown in Table 6.2.[4] The results of this exercise are reported in Table 6.3. In the light of the BIC statistic, Model 8 fits the observed data best. This means that all two-way associations between types of consumer in the three domains need to be recognised. A four-fold typology of cultural consumers is thus suggested on the lines shown in Table 6.4.

Type 1 is that of inactives – i.e. of individuals who appear not to be engaged in any of the kinds of cultural activities considered here. Half of the sample can be regarded as being culturally inactive in this sense.[5] Type 2 is that of individuals who are cinema univores and/or pop univores, but otherwise inactive, and who account for 17% of the sample. Type 3 covers individuals who are exclusive theatre-goers and/or exclusive classical concert goers, i.e. their defining characteristic is that they do not engage in any form of lowbrow consumption in these

[4] In exploring the pattern of individuals' cross-domain cultural consumption, I also used latent class analysis. This proved unhelpful, as I could achieve a satisfactory fit to the data from the five indicators only with a 5-class model.
[5] A recent study (Bukodi, 2007) of the social stratification of book readership in Hungary also indicates that about half of the population can be considered as inactive in this respect: i.e. they practically never read books.

Table 6.4 *Distribution of respondents by pattern of cultural consumption over the three domains*

| | Types of consumption in | | | | |
	Music	Theatre and cinema	Visual arts	%	%
Type 1: Inactives	I	I	I	50.4	50.4
Type 2: Univores	U	I	I	4.4	
	I	U	I	8.1	
	U	U	I	4.2	16.7
Type 3: Exclusives	E	I	I	0.2	
	I	E	I	3.5	
	E	E	I	0.3	
	I	I	A	3.3	
	I	E	A	1.7	
	E	I	A	0.2	
	E	E	A	0.7	9.9
Type 4: Omnivores	O	I	I	0.1	
	O	U	I	0.1	
	O	E	I	0.1	
	I	O	I	2.3	
	U	O	I	1.8	
	E	O	I	0.3	
	O	O	I	0.3	
	O	I	A	0.3	
	O	U	A	0.3	
	O	E	A	0.7	
	I	O	A	2.2	
	U	O	A	3.0	
	E	O	A	1.2	
	O	O	A	2.7	15.4
	E	U	I	0.2	
	U	E	I	1.0	
	E	U	A	0.1	
	U	E	A	1.2	
	U	I	A	1.6	
	I	U	A	1.9	
	U	U	A	1.6	7.6

Note: I: inactives; A: actives; U: univores; E: exclusives; O: omnivores.

two domains, while they may be either attenders or non-attenders at museums and galleries.[6] Type 3 accounts for 10% of all respondents. Finally, Type 4 is that of individuals who may be regarded as omnivores either in that they have an omnivorous style of consumption in theatre and cinema and/or music,[7] or in that they have an exclusive style of consumption in one domain – including being museum and gallery attenders – but at the same time are cinema and/or pop univores. Such omnivores amount to 23% of the sample.[8]

6.4 Results

6.4.1 *Cultural consumption by social status and social class*

The first question that arises here is whether or not the types of cultural consumer that have been distinguished are stratified by social status and social class.[9] Table 6.5 and Figure 6.1 display the bivariate relationship between consumer type and status. As can be seen, the proportion of omnivores increases with status rather steeply and that of exclusives also rises with status in a more or less linear fashion. The proportion of omnivores is particularly high among senior government officials, general managers,[10] cultural professionals, and professionals in tertiary education, and that of exclusives among welfare and legal

---

[6] Special interest might be thought to attach to those who are exclusive consumers in theatre and in music, and who also attend museums and galleries. But, as can be seen, these individuals represent less than 1% of the total sample.

[7] Again, those who are 'multiple' omnivores – i.e. have an omnivorous style of consumption in the domains of theatre and cinema and of music – might be thought especially interesting but they also are a small minority, less than 3% of the total sample.

[8] The data-set I use makes it possible to investigate the extent to which respondents engage in other spare time activities than those in the cultural domains considered here. Omnivores are more likely than other types of cultural consumer to take part in sports and other outdoor activities, to participate in volunteer activities, or to go out to pubs and restaurants. Details are available upon request.

[9] From the detailed occupational coding that is available in the data-set, respondents can be allocated to the 36-category status scale that is described in Chapter 2. In addition, the survey allows individuals to be allocated to a Hungarian version of the EGP class schema (cf. Goldthorpe, 2007b, vol. II, ch. 5).

[10] Erickson (1996) also notes that employers and managers are especially likely to mix highbrow and lowbrow genres of cultural consumption. She argues that

Table 6.5 *Distribution of types of cultural consumer within status groups (% by row)*

Title	I	U	E	O	N
Legal professionals	4.2	8.3	30.0	57.5	24
Professionals in tertiary-level education	8.3	0.0	26.0	65.7	24
Physicians, pharmacists, natural scientists	18.0	8.0	20.0	54.0	50
Engineers and computer scientists	20.8	15.0	12.5	51.7	120
Cultural and religious professionals	15.9	9.1	6.8	68.2	44
Social science and welfare professionals	16.0	0.0	34.0	50.0	12
Business professionals	25.0	15.3	14.5	45.2	124
General managers	16.3	4.6	13.9	65.1	43
Senior government officials	23.1	0.0	7.7	69.2	13
Professionals in secondary and primary education	12.3	7.4	16.8	63.5	285
High-ranking members of the armed forces	26.9	19.2	11.5	42.3	26
Department managers	31.7	11.0	16.5	40.8	164
General managers of small business enterprises	26.8	24.7	15.5	33.0	97
Health related associate professionals	26.3	15.8	26.3	31.6	19
Cultural and religious associate professionals	12.5	18.7	18.7	50.0	32
Business, legal and financial associate professionals	31.7	16.7	13.1	38.4	419
Technicians and related associate professionals	36.6	15.8	15.8	31.7	246
Office clerks	37.0	15.7	17.6	29.7	414
Production supervisors, site managers	43.3	15.0	15.0	26.7	60
Health and welfare associate professionals	40.9	12.7	14.0	32.3	220
Numerical clerks and other clerical workers	47.4	12.4	8.2	32.0	97
Personal service workers	35.3	25.5	13.7	25.5	51
Public and private security workers and low-ranking members of the armed forces	37.7	31.1	10.7	20.5	122
Sales workers	45.2	22.4	8.3	24.0	491
Communal and other service workers	65.1	16.3	4.6	13.9	43
Health, welfare, cultural service workers	61.4	7.1	12.9	18.6	70

(cont.)

Table 6.5 *(cont.)*

Title	I	U	E	O	N
Hotel and restaurant workers	50.5	23.6	7.1	18.7	182
Skilled handicraft workers	62.7	12.7	10.6	14.1	142
Transport and postal workers	49.3	21.8	3.4	25.3	87
Skilled metal trade workers	62.2	19.5	7.0	11.3	574
Skilled food and other light industry workers	62.6	17.8	7.9	11.7	393
Skilled construction workers	62.1	24.6	5.1	8.2	354
Machine and plant operators	65.2	17.6	6.1	11.0	732
Extraction workers	82.0	9.1	3.2	5.6	339
Routine service workers	72.3	4.3	7.3	6.1	440
General labourers	74.2	17.2	3.4	5.1	291

Note: I: inactives; U: univores; E: exclusives; O: Omnivores.

professionals and, again, professionals in tertiary education. In the case of univores, a more or less curvilinear, though rather weak, relationship shows up; i.e. this type of consumer tends most frequently to be found in the middle ranges of the status order. For instance, the proportion of univores is particularly high among protective service workers, small employers and hotel and restaurant workers. Finally, the proportion of inactives rises sharply, in a linear fashion, as status decreases.

Table 6.6 gives results by class. Fairly clear class gradients show up for inactives, exclusives and omnivores. The proportion of inactives increases across the classes – i.e. is greater in less advantaged classes than in more advantaged ones, although even in the latter, inactives represent far from negligible minorities. In contrast, the proportions of exclusives and omnivores tend to decrease across the classes; exclusives are relatively rare even within the higher salariat, at less than 1 in 5, but decline to only around 1 in 20 among unskilled workers, while omnivores decline from almost half within the higher salariat to less than 1 in 10 among unskilled workers.

> managers in business and governmental organisations, in seeking to exercise their control and coordination functions, need also to maintain social integration and promote effective communication. Thus, there is value for employers and managers in being able to display, in interaction with their subordinates, a relatively wide range of cultural reference.

Table 6.6 *Distribution of types of cultural consumer within classes* *(% by row)*

social class		I	U	E	O	N
I	Upper salariat	24.5	9.4	17.2	48.8	603
II	Lower salariat	28.1	14.0	14.9	43.0	1128
IIIa	Routine non-manuals	37.5	16.4	15.0	31.0	645
IIIb	Routine service	48.7	19.1	8.4	23.8	524
IV	Self-employed	49.5	21.0	7.7	21.8	547
V+VI	Skilled workers	60.2	19.1	7.9	12.8	1499
VII	Unskilled workers	69.1	17.0	5.5	8.4	1898

Note: I: inactives; U: univores; E: exclusives; O: Omnivores.

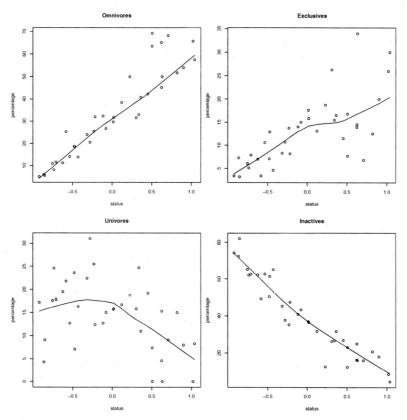

Fig. 6.1 Bivariate association between social status and type of cultural consumer

6.4.2 Multivariate analyses

Moving to a multivariate analysis, I take the types of cross-domain cultural consumer that I have distinguished as forming the dependent variable in a set of logistic regression models, and focus on the effects of the status and class variables that I have already introduced, supplemented by those of individuals' educational qualifications and household income. Socio-demographic variables are also included in the models, to serve primarily as controls. Descriptive statistics of the variables included in the analysis can be found in Table 6.7.

In Table 6.8, I report results for series of contrasts within a multinomial logistic regression analysis.[11] From these results, it may first be noted that some of the socio-demographic variables included as controls do have significant effects on cross-domain cultural consumption. Gender affects the probability of being culturally active rather than inactive but the signs of the coefficients are different in regard to the different types of consumer. Males are more likely than females to be univores rather than inactives, but they are less likely to show either an exclusive or an omnivorous style of consumption rather than being inactives (Table 6.8, first panel). Moreover, where exclusives and omnivores are contrasted with univores (Table 6.8, second panel), the signs of the coefficients for males are negative, implying that the chance of conforming to either of the former types is higher for women than for men. However, in the contrast of omnivores with exclusives (Table 6.8, third panel), the coefficient for males is positive in sign, indicating that men are more likely to show an omnivorous style of cultural consumption than women or, alternatively, that women are more likely to be exclusives than men. Age is significant in regard to the probability of being culturally active rather than inactive in that younger people are more likely than older people to be univores or omnivores. And age is also important in regard to

[11] As well as making the contrast between omnivores and exclusives (Table 6.8, third panel), I also performed a binomial regression analysis where only omnivores were considered, and the dependent variable made a distinction between those with an exclusive style of consumption in one of the three domains and those who have an omnivorous style of consumption in theatre and cinema and/or music (see Table 6.4). As it turned out, in the effects of the stratification variables (income, education, status, father's status, social class), there were no substantial differences between these two types of omnivore, suggesting that in the multivariate analysis I can combine them.

Table 6.7 *Descriptive statistics of covariates (N = 6844)*

	%	
Male (ref: female)	49.0	
Marital status		
single	17.7	
living in partnership (ref.)	67.6	
divorced/widowed	14.7	
Child 0-18 (ref. no child)	42.7	
Residence: Budapest (ref. other)	19.6	
Education		
primary	23.2	
vocational school	29.8	
technical secondary	20.8	
academic secondary	11.2	
lower tertiary (vocational college)	9.2	
higher tertiary (university)	5.7	
Social class		
I (upper salariat)	8.8	
II (lower salariat)	16.5	
IIIa (routine non-manual)	9.4	
IIIb (routine service)	7.7	
IV (self-employed)	8.0	
V+VI (skilled workers)	21.9	
VII (unskilled workers)	27.7	
	mean	s.d.
Age	42.53	12.14
Size of settlement (in 1000)	48.65	44.55
Log-household net income	10.19	0.533
Status	−0.327	0.499
Father's status	−0.531	0.475

cultural exclusiveness in that older people are more likely to be exclusives rather than univores, and more likely to be exclusives rather than omnivores. From the data at my disposal, I cannot tell how far these effects of age should be interpreted as ones of birth cohort or of life-cycle stage. But it can also be seen from Table 6.8 that another life-cycle indicator – marital status – does also have some significant influence on cultural consumption. Singles are more likely to be either univores or omnivores rather than inactives in comparison with their

Table 6.8 *Multinomial logistic regression: type of cultural consumer as dependent variable*

	U vs. I		E vs. I		O vs. I	
	$\hat{\beta}$	s.e.	$\hat{\beta}$	s.e.	$\hat{\beta}$	s.e.
male	0.195*	0.086	−0.519**	0.102	−0.195*	0.084
age	−0.077**	0.004	−0.001	0.005	−0.064**	0.004
living in partnership	−0.802**	0.124	0.023	0.192	−0.670**	0.130
divorced/widowed	−0.792**	0.160	−0.084	0.219	−0.527**	0.158
child 0–18	0.062	0.099	0.192	0.120	0.123	0.097
number of inhabitants	0.002**	0.001	0.001*	0.001	0.001*	0.001
Budapest	0.466**	0.108	−0.174	0.125	0.399**	0.099
vocational school	0.005	0.110	0.556**	0.157	0.649**	0.154
technical secondary	0.046	0.135	1.003**	0.170	1.395**	0.162
academic secondary	0.181	0.158	0.965**	0.192	1.663**	0.174
lower tertiary	0.114	0.224	1.473**	0.232	2.157**	0.209
higher tertiary	0.030	0.298	1.892**	0.285	2.075**	0.258
income	0.738**	0.090	0.688**	0.109	0.954**	0.089
status	0.819**	0.206	0.599*	0.235	0.902**	0.191
father's status	0.194*	0.081	0.240*	0.108	0.567**	0.086
class II	0.441	0.309	0.125	0.182	0.216	0.154
class IIIa	0.568*	0.243	0.254	0.223	0.173	0.192
class IIIb	0.570*	0.272	0.010	0.284	0.301	0.229
class IV	0.888**	0.277	−0.038	0.291	0.250	0.233
class V+VI	0.640*	0.314	0.217	0.292	0.216	0.244
class VII	0.890	0.500	0.008	0.319	0.184	0.262
constant	−5.356**	0.955	−9.026**	1.180	−8.208**	0.949

	E vs. U		O vs. U		O vs. E	
	$\hat{\beta}$	s.e.	$\hat{\beta}$	s.e.	$\hat{\beta}$	s.e.
male	−0.715**	0.118	−0.391**	0.094	0.324**	0.111
age	0.077**	0.006	0.012	0.007	−0.064**	0.005
living in partnership	0.826**	0.199	0.132	0.130	−0.693**	0.193
divorced/widowed	0.708**	0.238	0.265	0.173	−0.443*	0.224
child 0–18	0.129	0.137	0.060	0.108	−0.069	0.128
number of inhabitants	−0.001	0.001	−0.001	0.001	−0.000	0.001
Budapest	−0.640	0.440	−0.066	0.107	0.574	0.326
vocational school	0.550**	0.180	0.643**	0.169	0.093	0.208
technical secondary	0.956**	0.199	1.348**	0.179	0.392	0.216

Table 6.8 *(cont.)*

	E vs. U		O vs. U		O vs. E	
	$\hat{\beta}$	s.e.	$\hat{\beta}$	s.e.	$\hat{\beta}$	s.e.
academic secondary	0.784**	0.224	1.481**	0.194	0.697**	0.233
lower tertiary	1.359**	0.277	2.042**	0.239	0.683**	0.262
higher tertiary	2.162**	0.338	1.844**	0.292	−0.182	0.299
income	−0.049	0.124	0.215*	0.097	0.265*	0.116
status	−0.220	0.267	0.083	0.207	0.303	0.243
father's status	0.046	0.123	0.372**	0.096	0.326**	0.104
class II	−0.315	0.226	−0.224	0.191	0.091	0.171
class IIIa	−0.313	0.278	−0.394	0.235	−0.080	0.227
class IIIb	−0.560	0.349	−0.268	0.269	0.291	0.297
class IV	−0.927**	0.340	−0.637*	0.267	0.289	0.296
class V+VI	−0.522	0.349	−0.524	0.385	−0.001	0.306
class VII	−0.881	0.576	−0.705	0.401	0.175	0.335
constant	−3.669**	1.340	−2.852**	1.049	0.817*	0.261

Note: Log-likelihood = −6615.822, N = 6844, ** $p < 0.01$, * $p < 0.05$.

married (or cohabiting) and their divorced (or widowed) counterparts. But individuals in these latter categories, if active, are more likely than singles to be cultural exclusives. Finally, living in an urban area and in larger settlements, especially Budapest, increases the likelihood of being culturally active rather than inactive, but does not appear to exert any effect on the type of cultural consumption.

In relation to stratification variables, it is apparent from Table 6.8, that education has a fairly systematic effect on cultural participation. The higher the educational level he or she has attained, the more likely an individual is to be a cultural exclusive or omnivore rather than inactive. However, univores do not seem to have higher education than inactives. It is also apparent from Table 6.8 that the probability of individuals being exclusives or omnivores rather than univores increases with educational level. In this respect, the effects of having a tertiary qualification are especially marked. Individuals with a university degree are over 8 times ($e^{2.162}$) more likely than individuals with primary education to be exclusives rather than univores;[12] and

[12] This proves to be especially true for exclusive classical concert attenders. When I restricted the analysis to the domain of music, and ran a multinomial logit model where exclusive and omnivorous classical concert goers constituted the

individuals with a college degree are over 7 times ($e^{2.042}$) more likely
to be omnivores rather than univores. In the contrast between omnivores and exclusives, intermediate levels of education and lower tertiary degrees would appear to increase the probability of individuals
belonging to the former rather than the latter type.

Income also proves to have pervasive effects on cultural consumption. Higher income significantly increases the probability of being an
actual cultural consumer of any kind rather than inactive.[13] Further,
the chances of culturally active individuals being omnivores rather
than univores increase with income, as also – and perhaps more significantly for the Hungarian case – do the chances of individuals being
omnivores rather than exclusives.

Coming now to the effects of social status on cultural consumption,
the results shown in Table 6.8 are somewhat less straightforward than
in the case of education and income. It can be seen that individuals'
status, like their income and their education, has a significant, positive
effect on the probability of their being culturally active – especially as
omnivores or univores – rather than inactive. But, focusing on actives,
individuals' own status does not then appear to have any clear influence in differentiating among types of cultural consumer – despite the
pattern revealed in this regard in the bivariate analysis of Table 6.5
and Figure 6.1. However, it can further be seen that father's status
does have significant effects. Not only do the chances of individuals
being cultural consumers of any type rather than inactive rise with
father's status, but so too do the chances of their being cultural omnivores rather than univores, and their chances of being omnivores rather
than cultural exclusives.[14]

Finally, Table 6.8 shows that the effects of social class are rather
slight, contrary to the impression that might be created by Table 6.6.

dependent categories, with pop/rock univores as reference, individuals with a
university degree were around 25 times ($e^{3.227}$) more likely to be placed in the
exclusive category than were individuals with a basic education. (The results
are available upon request.)

[13] When I repeated this analysis for the three cultural domains separately, the
coefficient for income turned out to be largest for theatre and cinema and
smallest for the visual arts. This can be readily explained in terms of the
differences in the costs involved – i.e. admission prices for museums and art
galleries are somewhat lower than for theatres, cinemas or concerts. (The
results are available upon request.)

[14] It may be added that even if father's status is dropped from the analysis, the
effects of respondent's own status remain insignificant in the contrasts in the
second and third panels of Table 6.8.

With status, education and income controlled, class has some significant effect on the chances of being a univore rather than inactive, but it has no significant effect as regards cultural omnivorousness or exclusiveness as against inactivity. More specifically, members of intermediate classes – those of routine non-manual and service workers, small employers and self-employed workers and skilled workers – are more likely than members of the higher salariat to show a univorous style of consumption rather than to be inactive. And also as compared to the higher salariat, small employers and self-employed workers seem more likely to be univores than either exclusives or omnivores.

6.4.3 The magnitude of education, income and status effects

In present-day Hungary, education, income, individuals' own and their parental status all have significant effects on cultural consumption in some way. But how strong are these effects in relation to each other? To address this question, let us take a hypothetical person and calculate under an appropriate version of our regression models: first, the probability of her being culturally active – in other words, the probability of her being a cultural consumer of any type (Figure 6.2); and, second, and supposing that she is active, the probability of her being an omnivore (Figure 6.3). More specifically, let us examine pairwise the strength in these respects of the effects of education, income and status in the case of a hypothetical women who is 35 years old, married, and living in a relatively small settlement (where the number of inhabitants is less than the mean of the sample excluding Budapest).

Let me first show the probability of our hypothetical woman being culturally active, if I set her status and education[15] at different values, fix the net income per capita in her household as being 25,000 Hungarian forints, and take her father as being a skilled construction worker. The slopes of the lines in Panel A of Figure 6.2 depict the strength of the status effect within each educational category. The first point to be noted is that at all three educational levels, our hypothetical woman is more likely to be active as her status increases. If she

---

[15] In this exercise I collapsed the six schooling categories previously used into three: primary and vocational school, ('low'), technical and academic secondary ('intermediate') and lower and higher tertiary ('high').

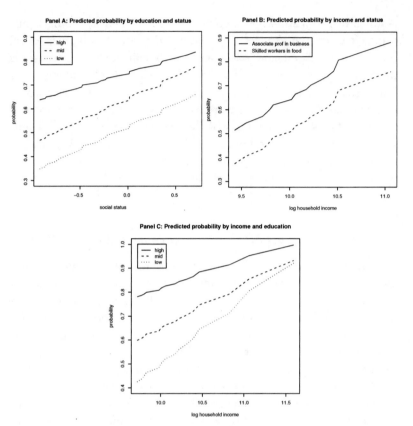

Fig. 6.2 Predicted probability of being culturally active
For Panel A, per capita household income is fixed as 25,000 HUF. For Panel B, education is fixed as secondary. For Panel C, status is fixed as associate professional in business, law and finance. For all panels, other covariates are fixed as follows: women, aged 35, lives in a small settlement, father is a skilled construction worker. The children dummy is dropped.

has only primary or lower vocational education, her propensity to engage in cultural activity of any kind increases by about 30% across the whole range of status. The rate of increase is fairly similar for intermediate level education, and for higher education is only a little lower, at about 20%. This suggests that there are no major differences in status effects between persons at various levels of education, and that status may provide an additional motivation for being culturally active, more or less irrespective of the amount of cultural resources one

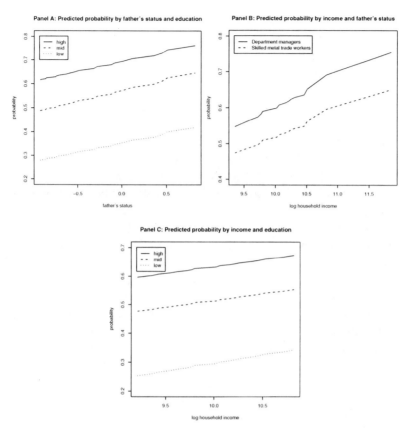

Fig. 6.3 Predicted probability of being an omnivore

For Panel A, per capita household income is fixed as 25,000 HUF. For Panel B, education is fixed as secondary. For Panel C, father's status is fixed as skilled metal trade worker. For all panels, other covariates are fixed as follows: woman, aged 35, lives in a small settlement, father being a skilled construction worker. The following parameters are dropped from the model: children dummy, respondent's own class and status.

possesses.[16] The strength of education effects appear to be quite similar – see the vertical distance between lines. At the bottom end of the

---

[16] In order to examine this question in a more rigorous way, I included in the regression model education-by-status interaction terms. These terms proved to be insignificant in all cases.

status order, the maximum education effect is about 30%, while at the
top end of status order it is smaller at around 20%.

The next question concerns the relative importance of income and
status on the probability of our hypothetical woman being culturally
active. In this case, I set her income and social status at different values and fix her educational attainment at secondary level (Panel B
of Figure 6.2). It is apparent that the income effect is very strong,
irrespective of status level. Other things being equal, the probability
of this woman taking part in any kind of cultural activity increases
by around 40% over the whole range of income, whether she is
taken to be a business associate professional or a skilled light industry
worker. Furthermore, the effect of income is especially marked at the
top end of the range, implying that a relatively high level of financial resources can promote cultural consumption even at lower status
levels.

Finally, Panel C of Figure 6.2 shows the magnitude of the income
effect in relation to education. It is apparent that if our hypothetical woman has a low level of schooling, the probability of her being
culturally active increases enormously, by around 50%, across the
whole range of income. However, if she has a tertiary degree, the rise
is more modest, at only about 12%. In other words, the indication
is that where cultural resources are scarce, a higher level of income is
required in order to promote cultural activity.[17]

In relation to the chances of our hypothetical woman conforming to
one or other type of cultural consumer, Figure 6.3 shows the predicted
probabilities of her being found as an omnivore rather than as a univore
or exclusive. Since, as could be seen in Table 6.8, the probability of
individuals being omnivores is significantly affected by their father's
status rather than by their own, I calculate the same probabilities as in
Figure 6.2 but replace the variable of own status with that of father's
status. From Panel A of Figure 6.3, it is apparent that the probability of
our hypothetical woman being an omnivore is strongly influenced by
educational level – falling by around 35% between low- and high-level
education. At the same time, the probability of her being an omnivore
also rises with her father's status, in a more or less linear fashion

[17] I included education-by-income interaction terms in the regression. The
coefficient for the interaction term for low education and income was
significant (at level of $p < 0.05$) and positive in its sign. Details are available
upon request.

and at roughly the same rate for each of the three educational levels considered, with the difference over the whole parental status range amounting to some 15–20 percentage points. Further, if we assume that our hypothetical woman has a degree, then the probability of her being an omnivore rather than one of the two other types of consumer is in fact already quite high (60%) even if she ranks low on the status scale.

The magnitude of the income effect relative to that of status is clearly less strong than that of education (Panel B of Figure 6.3). Considering our hypothetical women where her father is taken to be a department manager, the probability of her being found as an omnivore is around 55% if she ranks low on the income scale, and about 75% if she ranks high. For her counterpart with a skilled metal trade worker as father, the rate of increase is more or less the same at around 18 percentage points over the entire range of income. As with the probability of being culturally active, the effect of income is especially strong at the top of the range, irrespective of our hypothetical woman's parental status.

Finally, as regards the relative importance of the effects of income and education, it is apparent (Panel C of Figure 6.3) that income effects are less pronounced in this regard than they were for the likelihood of our hypothetical woman being culturally active. The probability of her being an omnivore, rather than a univore or an exclusive, increases only by about 10% across the whole range of income, irrespective of the educational level attributed to her.

To sum up, education and income can be regarded as the two chief bases of the social stratification of cultural consumption in contemporary Hungarian society. Income has a very strong impact on the probability of being culturally active, suggesting that a lack of financial resources may make it practically impossible for many individuals to engage in cultural activity of any kind. The effect of education is also pronounced in this respect, but it proves to be an even more salient stratifying force as regards the likelihood of individuals being omnivores rather than other types of cultural consumer. This suggests that fairly substantial cultural resources are required in order to have the capacity and also perhaps the motivation to mix different genres of cultural consumption. However, it should also be emphasised that status is still an important factor. Within each income and educational level, status has a clear and relatively large effect on the probability of being culturally active rather than inactive; and parental status systematically influences the probability of being an omnivore rather than a univore or an exclusive.

6.4.4 *The influence of parental status*

This last finding is one of particular interest, and calls for further attention, so far as underlying mechanisms are concerned. At least three possibilities can be suggested. First, it may be that upwardly mobile individuals (whose own social status is higher than their father's) might be eager to engage in the consumption of legitimate culture in order to demonstrate that they have good taste and that they have appropriated modes of sophisticated culture in accordance with what is expected of people in their position. This may be referred to as the status maximisation hypothesis (Ganzeboom, 1982). Second, childhood socialisation could be the crucial determinant of cultural consumption. One would then expect that upwardly mobile people would be less culturally active than their immobile counterparts (who are intergenerationally stable in their high status positions) because they have been endowed with fewer cultural resources in their family of origin. The downwardly mobile (who achieve a lower status compared to that of their father) are in turn expected to insist on the consumption pattern they have been accustomed to in their childhood and will therefore be more inclined to consume high culture than their immobile counterparts. This could be labelled the socialisation hypothesis (van Eijck, 1999). Third, a somewhat modified version of this latter hypothesis suggests that the upwardly and downwardly mobile not only retain the cultural practices in which they were socialised but also acquire new forms from their current social milieu (Chan and Goldthorpe, 2007c). As a result, they are likely to be culturally eclectic and tend to switch between different cultural genres according to the social context and the people with whom they are in everyday interaction. This might be called the culture-switching hypothesis.

As an example of different combinations of individuals' own and fathers' status, let me first take a hypothetical woman with tertiary education who is a primary or secondary school teacher, and calculate the probability of her conforming to one or other of the four types of cultural consumer that I have identified, depending on her father's status score. It is apparent from the first panel of Table 6.9 that the

Table 6.9 *Examples of predicted probabilities of cultural activities by father's social status*

sex	education	occupation	father's occupation	mobility	I	U	E	O
F	tertiary	teaching prof.	skilled metal trade worker	upward	0.2430	0.0945	0.1150	0.5475
			teaching prof.	stable	0.1006	0.0834	0.1311	0.6849
			physican	downward	0.0213	0.0805	0.2119	0.6863
M	primary or vocational	skilled metal trade worker	general labourer	upward	0.6528	0.1865	0.0495	0.1112
			skilled metal trade worker	stable	0.6347	0.1890	0.0418	0.1045
			technicans & related prof.	downward	0.6382	0.1850	0.0510	0.1258

Note: I: inactives; U: univores; E: exclusives; O: omnivores. Other covariates in the model: age: 35, marital status: living in partnership, living in a relatively small settlement (where the number of inhabitants is less than the mean of the sample excluding Budapest), income: 25,000 HUF.

probability of this woman being an omnivore varies quite considerably according to the status of her father – ranging from 0.55 if he was a skilled metal trade worker (in other words, if his daughter was upwardly mobile), to 0.69 if he was a physician (i.e. if his daughter was downwardly mobile); and, as regards the probability of her being an exclusive, a similar pattern emerges. Likewise, with the probability of our hypothetical woman being an inactive, consistent results are revealed: the higher her father's status, the lower her risk of falling into this category. Only the probability of her being a univore seems to be unaffected by parental status. These findings are then broadly consistent with the socialisation hypothesis rather than with the status maximisation hypothesis, although there are also features that seem to some extent to support the culture-switching hypothesis. For example the relatively high probability of our hypothetical woman, if downwardly mobile, to be an omnivore could be taken to indicate that she combines cultural practices of her childhood with participation in more popular genres.[18]

However, if we consider another hypothetical person, a male skilled metal trade worker with primary or vocational education (see Table 6.9), it is apparent that his pattern of cultural consumption is not, or is only very slightly, affected by parental status. One would then suggest a possible explanation that – despite perhaps relatively high parental status – the lack of educational and financial resources makes it difficult for a low-status person to take part in cultural activity of any kind.

6.5 Conclusions

In this chapter I have investigated the social stratification of public forms of cultural consumption in Hungary across three different domains: music, theatre and cinema, and the visual arts. An obvious focus of sociological interest is on the extent of continuity or change in the sources and emergent patterns of this stratification as between the present day and the former communist period.

---

[18] Moreover, if our hypothetical primary or secondary school teacher is upwardly mobile, she also appears to have a fairly high probability of being culturally inactive. This result suggests an interesting variant of the culture-switching hypothesis: namely, that an alternative to cultural switching in the context of the cross-pressuring relationships that may result from social mobility is a simple withdrawal from problematic activities (cf. Chan and Goldthorpe, 2007c).

As regards the sources of stratification, education, as expected, continues to exert a powerful influence on cultural consumption just as it did under communism. In general, the higher the educational level that individuals have attained – and thus, one may suppose, the greater their cultural resources – the higher the probability of their being culturally active rather than inactive. Moreover, level of education is, overall, the most important variable distinguishing different types of cultural consumer, and in particular in distinguishing omnivores from either univores or exclusives.

However, and again as expected, a major change from the communist era occurs in that cultural consumption is now also strongly affected by income. The higher the individuals' income – or, in other words, the greater their economic resources – the higher the probability of their engaging in cultural activity of some kind or other. Furthermore, the probability of culturally active individuals being omnivores rather than univores or exclusives – that is, having a relatively wide range of cultural consumption – also increases with income. In other words, in contemporary Hungary, in contrast with the situation under communism, economic resources, or constraints, have assumed a large importance in the patterning of cultural consumption.

Finally, status, which would appear to have been a major stratifying factor in cultural consumption under communism, still continues to exert an effect, and one which is clearly more important than class. While there are indications that in post-communist Hungary class stratification is becoming in some respects more consequential, this cannot be thought to be the case with cultural consumption. At the same time, though, the effects of status are not as pervasive or as straightforward as might have been expected. The probability of an individual being a cultural consumer of any type rather than inactive does rise with his or her status, and in a more or less linear fashion. But the individual's own status does not have any significant effect in differentiating among types of cultural consumer. What does, however, appear as a significant influence in this regard is father's status. The higher his or her father's status, the higher the probability of an individual being not only culturally active but also an omnivore rather than a univore or an exclusive. Moreover, for individuals whose own status is different from that of their father, I find evidence favouring the socialisation hypothesis, at least for those at the higher levels of the status hierarchy. That is to say, intergenerationally mobile people tend to follow the cultural practices into which they were socialised in their childhood. This finding is, in fact, consistent with other indications previously noted that in post-communist Hungary the direct intra-familial transmission of inequalities persists and is perhaps becoming a yet more powerful process than before.

How then does the stratification of cultural consumption in present-day Hungary that emerges from these effects of education, income and status relate to the more general arguments in this regard that have wide currency in the sociological literature and that were outlined in Chapter 1? First of all, the findings reported must call into question the individualisation argument. Whatever the applicability of this argument to the more economically advanced 'consumer societies' of the Western world, it would seem to have little relevance to the Hungarian case. In Hungary cultural consumption has a clear social basis, and the most salient dividing line within its stratification has to be seen as that between the culturally active and the culturally inactive. As regards the forms of cultural consumption covered in this chapter, inactives account for about half of the Hungarian adult population, and in an earlier publication (Bukodi, 2007), focusing on book readership, I have shown that a similar proportion can also be classified as inactive in that respect, i.e. as being virtual non-readers. Inactives in theatre and cinema, music and the visual arts tend – in the same way as non-readers – to be individuals with relatively low levels of income, education and status. They are more likely than others to be lacking in the resources and perhaps also the motivation to engage at all extensively in cultural consumption. Furthermore, the analyses I have presented bring out how, among the culturally active, differences in income, education and status also characterise different types of cultural consumer.

However, while cultural consumption in post-communist Hungary is in these ways socially stratified, the effects of income, education and status should not be seen as overwhelmingly strong. This serves to throw doubt on the applicability of homology arguments. Thus, on the one hand, the culturally inactive cannot be simply equated with the 'socially excluded' in contemporary Hungary or even with lower social strata more generally. Their numbers alone rule out any such interpretation, and inactives are far from being uniformly disprivileged. They can in fact be shown to constitute quite substantial minorities even within higher-status groups and more advantaged classes. For instance, the proportion of those who do not engage in any of the forms of cultural activity considered here amounts to around 25% among business professionals and 20% among engineers and computer specialists. It could then be the case that insofar as members of these groups seek to express and confirm their social status through consumption, many do so by pursuing relatively high levels of consumption of a material rather than a cultural kind.

On the other hand, those cultural consumers who have been labelled as exclusives, and who could perhaps be regarded as forming some kind of cultural elite, could not at the same time be regarded as a social elite, as homology arguments would require. Although having a university degree appears as an important factor in being an exclusive – as is being an older woman – exclusives are not significantly different from univores in their income or in their own or their parental status. Also, while being comparable to omnivores in their own status, they in fact fall significantly below them in income and parental status. Given these characteristics, one may speculate that exclusives represent, at least in some part, the remains of the 'intelligentsia' of the communist era, who seek still to maintain the pattern of high cultural consumption into which they were socialised, even though in the new Hungary they no longer enjoy particularly privileged economic or status positions.

Finally, then, what conclusions may be drawn regarding the applicability of omnivore–univore arguments, which have been underwritten in the foregoing at least as regards terminology? One qualification is clearly necessary concerning univores. In omnivore–univore arguments, univorous cultural consumption, in the sense of consumption limited to more popular cultural forms, is usually associated with membership of lower social strata. However, in the analyses presented above, univores – that is, those men and women whose cultural activity is essentially limited to going to the cinema or attending pop, rock or jazz concerts – are not most likely to be found among those with the lowest levels of income and status. Although univores have similar educational levels to inactives, they have significantly higher income and status, and tend to be most predominant in intermediate classes. In other words, it would seem that in Hungary, univores are to some extent displaced 'upwards' by the unusually large numbers of the culturally inactive.

However, the findings reported in this chapter are for the most part supportive of the idea that in modern societies the pattern of cultural consumption most typical for members of higher social strata is one of an omnivorous kind. In present-day Hungarian society cultural omnivores – those who engage in both highbrow and lowbrow cultural activities – tend to have higher incomes and status and to be better educated than the culturally inactive, and further to have higher incomes, better education and higher parental status than univores or exclusives. In addition, omnivores tend to be more youthful in comparison with inactives, on the one hand, and exclusives, on the other. What is then suggested is the emergence in post-communist Hungary of new social strata whose members come from relatively advantaged backgrounds, who enjoy relatively high levels of both cultural and economic resources, and who seek to make the cultural omnivorousness in which they are able to engage – rather than exclusiveness – an important marker of the high status that they wish to maintain.

7 | Status, class and culture in the Netherlands

GERBERT KRAAYKAMP, KOEN VAN EIJCK
AND WOUT ULTEE

7.1 Introduction

Cultural consumption in present-day highly industrialised societies is a leisure activity with a distinct social base. People's tastes and lifestyles are not pre-given and do not develop in a vacuum. Socialisation, starting in the family of origin, strongly stamps cultural preferences and activities (Bourdieu, 1984). Later on, the schools a person attends are likely to affect taste in cultural matters (Ganzeboom, 1982). Yet, even in adult life cultural consumption is not fixed. Theatre-going and museum visits are fuelled by significant others such as friends and, most notably, a person's spouse or partner (van Berkel and de Graaf, 1995).[1]

Many research findings speak in favour of the social roots of cultural lifestyles. This, however, does not mean that there is agreement on which concrete social phenomena should be taken into consideration when explaining cultural tastes and activities. Findings from sample surveys indicate that cultural consumption is affected by parental schooling levels and aspects of family socialisation (Mohr and DiMaggio, 1995; van Eijck, 1997; Nagel and Ganzeboom, 2002), level and type of education (DiMaggio and Mukhtar, 2004; van de Werfhorst and Kraaykamp, 2001), occupational class (Katz-Gerro, 2002; Chan and Goldthorpe, 2005), income (DiMaggio and Useem, 1978; O'Hagan, 1996), social network (Erickson, 1996; Warde and Tampubolon, 2002), and cultural preferences and background characteristics of the partner (Upright, 2004).

All of these determinants of cultural consumption are in some way related to issues of class and status. One of the current controversies surrounding cultural tastes and activities is the question of whether status or class is a more influential characteristic. Both parties in the

---

[1] Hereafter we shall use the term partner to refer to spouse or partner.

debate take status and class as referring to a person's occupation. According to Bourdieu (1984), a person's leisure is commensurate to a person's job. Thus, manual workers who use their muscles are more interested in activities contesting physical strength, whereas persons in intellectually demanding jobs are more likely to participate in activities testing information-processing capabilities. But leisure is not a mere symptom of one's position in the labour market. It is also, if not primarily, a *signal* (Veblen, 1994; Weber, 1968; Chan and Goldthorpe, 2004; van Eijck and Mommaas, 2004). Society at large confers a certain amount of honour to specific occupations and leisure activities. Persons with similarly honourable lifestyles tend to interact with one another, as indicated by marriage patterns and the composition of friendship networks. In the current study, using information from the Netherlands gathered between 1992 and 2003, we investigate the extent to which cultural consumption is indeed affected by a person's social class or status.

Explanations by either class or status do not fully cover hypotheses about the social origins of cultural consumption. In this paper, we therefore take into account two additional features of possible participants of highbrow culture. Firstly, it makes sense to assume that resources relevant for enjoying cultural products are measured more accurately by a person's educational attainment than by measures of occupational position. Cultural consumption is an effective means of status affirmation in part because it requires highly valued cultural resources necessary to digest and enjoy cultural stimuli. Earlier research has consistently demonstrated the large impact of educational attainment on these cultural resources, and thereby on cultural consumption (e.g. van de Werfhorst and Kraaykamp, 2001; Chan and Goldthorpe, 2005). A proper estimate of the effects of class versus status therefore requires the inclusion of education into statistical models. Incorporation of education factors out the cognitive aspects from class and status.

Secondly, we include characteristics of a person's network. In this paper, these are the education, status and class of a person's partner. We have two reasons for including partner's characteristics. On the one hand, status predominantly relies upon whom one associates with (Weber, 1968). We therefore include a direct measure of the status position of the partner, who is generally the most important person in one's life. On the other hand, it is likely that cultural socialisation continues into adulthood. A culturally competent partner might introduce a person into the field of highbrow culture, making cultural consumption more rewarding. Earlier research has convincingly demonstrated that partner's characteristics affect cultural participation (van Berkel and de Graaf, 1995; Upright, 2004).

7.2 Theoretical background

7.2.1 Status and class

Claims to honour are effective whenever people are able to monopolise access to specific occupations, forms of property and types of education (Scott, 1996). This implies a close link between the economic domain of class and the social domain of status. As Weber (1968) put it: 'The social order is of course conditioned by the economic order to a high degree, and in its turn reacts upon it.' In fact, 'today the class situation is by far the predominant factor [in status group formation], for of course the possibility of a style of life expected for members of a status group is usually conditioned economically'. As such, class and status are analytically distinct, but empirically closely entwined.

According to Scott (1996), distinguishing between class and status is indeed fundamental to any viable investigation of social stratification. Whereas the terms of status, honour or prestige have been around for at least some thousand years, the word class emerged with the industrial revolution and initially only referred to a person's position in the system of production. During the nineteenth century, however, the term class absorbed much of what was originally referred to as status, i.e. a hierarchy of superiority and inferiority. Through the expressions higher, middle and lower classes, the term class took on characteristics of a vertical hierarchy as well, especially in the United States.[2] It is therefore a relevant question whether class differences, conceived of as a perhaps partial ordering ranging from superior to subordinate classes, are empirically sufficiently distinct from a status hierarchy to enable a simultaneous comparison of class and status effects on cultural

---

[2] Income is an example of a continuous yardstick to measure the standing of diverse occupations. In sociological research, interval scales such as Duncan's (1961) SEI or the ISEI developed by Ganzeboom *et al.* (1992) have become very popular, and statistically convenient, tools for students of stratification.

consumption. Even if class is purely economical and status a matter of honour, the fact that class and status both involve occupation creates a relationship between the two characteristics of a person, regardless of the different ontological roots of the concepts.

Looking at sources of status other than occupation and property, such as 'descent' or 'birth', it might be argued that these are likely to have lost their impact since Weber's days. Without eradicating them completely, the rise of meritocracy did away with these resources as a guarantee for obtaining honourable positions. Subsequently, stratification more or less takes the form of a hierarchy of social classes within which the various status groups are located. The classes that form a modern society are therefore likely to have certain status characteristics, even where traditional status ideas have disappeared (Scott, 1996). Thus, it is likely that aspects of class have become the most important status markers. According to Lamont (1992), we may be witnessing a convergence of status markers towards signs of economic success and spending power at the cost of intellectual qualities or moral dignity. Economic capital then tends to become the most generalised basis for status claims at the cost of cultural capital and moral virtues.

Notwithstanding these hypotheses, status honour, according to Weber (1985), stands in sharp opposition to the pretensions of sheer property. Weber also holds that money and entrepreneurship are not in themselves status qualifications, although they may bring honour. And the lack of property is not in itself a status disqualification, although it may be a reason for it (Weber, 1968). In other words, class is measured 'objectively', while status groups are measured 'subjectively' through honour. This does not in itself make status groups weaker than classes. The reverse might well be true, as classes only have a potential to foster ties, whereas status groups refer to actual groups or communities (Morrison, 1995). The presence of status groups implies a reciprocal recognition of group members and an awareness of common positions and interests (Hughes *et al.*, 1995). In that sense, status groups are perhaps more 'real' than classes, at least in people's heads – and networks.

Another reason why status may remain relevant independent of class lies in what Pakulski and Waters (1996) call the 'death of class' thesis. This holds that the impact of class is disappearing in present-day, highly industrialised societies. As a consequence, the relation between class on the one hand and just about everything else, including status, on the other, should weaken. In a similar vein, it has been argued that the sphere of consumption has become increasingly autonomous (Baudrillard, 2000), that consumption (status) rather than production (class) determines people's identities (Offe, 1985), and that class consciousness is giving way to a greater sense of individual responsibility (Beck, 1992). Nevertheless, given the paramount importance of consumption as a means of status achievement and status display, we argue that class and status are closely related, today perhaps even more so than ever before. The demise of class consciousness, which does appear to have taken place, does not imply that class differences in practices have lost their significance as well, as Bottero and Prandy (2004) found for the UK.

When it comes to class and its consequences, however, the Netherlands provides an interesting case, as it was never a significant 'class society'. Industrialisation began late in the country, and manufacturing never gained the prominence it did in neighbouring countries. Also, early on, banking, transportation, insurance and other services were relatively important sectors of employment. In addition, no unified labour movement developed. There were separate unions for Catholics, Protestants and Socialists (with the Catholics and Socialists merging in the 1970s). This split was prompted by the division of the Netherlands into three religious–political 'pillars', and until the 1960s people tended to spend their leisure time and seek company within these groups (Ultee *et al.*, 1992). As a result, class in the Netherlands is a less prominent dividing force than in other comparable Western countries. The limited role of class in the Netherlands may imply two things for our current analyses. On the one hand, it can be hypothesised that class effects will be smaller in the Netherlands than in most other countries. On the other hand, the marginal independent role of class might make it more difficult to distinguish between class and status effects in the Netherlands.

7.2.2 Cultural consumption: highbrow and lowbrow

In the current study, we examine the effects of class and status position on cultural consumption. When considering cultural consumption, it is important to acknowledge that going to the theatre, classical music concerts or museums are typically regarded as highbrow activities (Bourdieu, 1984). Gans (1999) describes highbrow culture as those activities for which the audience is dominated by cultural professionals, mostly from the middle class. This association with cultural professionals can be understood with reference to information theory which states that cultural competencies are essential for enjoying and valuing cultural expressions. As highbrow culture is often complex, innovative and/or experimental, specific competencies are needed to enjoy and comprehend it. Several scholars, however, also argue that aspects of prestige and honour are associated with the consumption of highbrow culture (Bourdieu, 1984; DiMaggio, 1994). The act of consuming cultural events may be perceived as a group-specific token to signal a certain status position to the outside world (Kraaykamp, 2002). In that respect, decisions on cultural choices often seem to reflect status considerations. Social differentiation in cultural tastes exists because there is mutual agreement on aesthetic standards and values within classes or social groups (Bourdieu, 1984; Gans, 1999). As such, consumption need not even be deliberately or consciously conspicuous to carry distinctive value.

We will also consider popular culture participation by analysing status and class effects on attending pop concerts. By studying this activity, we will be able to test whether the relation between the social and the cultural domains is one of homology, as posited by Bourdieu (1984), or whether a conceptualisation in terms of omnivores and univores is more appropriate, as suggested by Peterson (Peterson, 1992; Peterson and Kern, 1996). We will examine class and status effects on specific cultural activities as well as on patterns of cultural consumption by distinguishing four types of cultural consumer: omnivores, highbrows, univores and inactives. If homology provides the best description of taste patterns, we would expect negative effects of class or status on attending pop concerts, indicating that popular culture is mainly enjoyed by the lower socio-economic strata, while status considerations among members of the higher strata would keep them from participating in such activities. In that case, the number of people combining highbrow and lowbrow cultural activities would be small, and class and status effects should indicate a position for these few omnivores that is somewhere between the highbrows and the univores. If, on the other hand, Peterson's (1992) omnivore–univore distinction offers a more accurate depiction of the patterning of cultural tastes, then the effects of class or status on attending pop concerts should be absent, if not positive. This would indicate that members from the higher social strata are at least as likely as those from the lower strata to engage in popular culture. Through appreciating popular culture alongside highbrow activities, members of the higher strata are thought to demonstrate their openness to a wide range of cultural products (e.g. Peterson and Kern, 1996). This would imply a class or status position of the omnivores that is close to that of the highbrow cultural elite.

Previous research has shown that cultural omnivorousness is indeed positively related to socio-economic status (Peterson and Simkus, 1992; van Eijck, 2001; López-Sintas and Katz-Gerro, 2005). The omnivore taste pattern, signalling inclusive cultural competence, seems to be a characteristic of members of the higher social strata, who are most likely to have the ability to participate in a broad range of socio-cultural worlds (Emmison, 2003). Their willingness to do so further depends on age and gender, as omnivores, compared with highbrows, are more likely to be young and male (van Eijck, 2001). Since cultural omnivores and highbrows are both expected to be members of higher socio-economic strata (see Peterson and Rossman, 2007), it is important to look at patterns of consumption of multiple cultural activities. For example, it is likely that people who are popular culture univores have a lower socio-economic status than people who engage in both popular *and* highbrow culture. But does this imply that highbrow 'snobs' also hold a status position that differs from that of the omnivores because they do not engage in popular culture? Or are other socio-demographic indicators more relevant for distinguishing between these two types of cultural consumer? The latter might be the case if the 'status value' of popular culture depends on the cultural taste pattern of which it is a part, i.e. whether or not it is combined with highbrow culture.

For highbrow, popular and omnivore cultural consumption, we expect status effects to be stronger than class effects. One reason is the limited relevance of class in the Netherlands mentioned above. An additional reason for this expectation lies in the fact that highbrow culture in the Netherlands is heavily subsidised by the state and therefore not necessarily more expensive than popular culture participation. Therefore, cultural consumption in general might be a means of conveying social status rather than of expressing class. It is a way of demonstrating to which social group one belongs and from which other groups one wants to distance oneself, given a certain amount of cultural, economic and social resources.

7.2.3 Educational attainment and cultural consumption

The impact of educational attainment on cultural consumption has been well established. A consistent finding in empirical studies is that the better educated are more culturally active than the less well educated (Ganzeboom, 1982; Kraaykamp and Niewbeerta, 2000; van Eijck and Mommaas, 2004). There are two explanations for this (Gans, 1999). Firstly, school can be regarded as a selection device that separates the cognitively talented students from the less talented students. If it is true that highbrow cultural activities are to a large extent more difficult activities requiring complex information processing (Ganzeboom, 1982), it is likely that students with higher levels of education will participate relatively often in highbrow activities. Secondly, school levels differ with respect to the attention given to culture as part of the curriculum. At higher levels of education, more time is spent on acquainting students with highbrow culture through, for example, reading literature, visiting exhibitions, or discussing architecture, sculptures or paintings (Nagel and Ganzeboom, 2002; Kraaykamp, 2003). Thus, the better educated, after leaving school, would possess more cultural resources which makes their consumption of highbrow culture more rewarding and pleasant.

As mentioned above, however, the better educated today are more active in the majority of all outdoor leisure activities, including sports and popular cultural activities (Peterson and Kern, 1996; Social and Cultural Planning Bureau, 2001). It may therefore be held that intellectual ability seems to be invested in doing and appreciating lots of different activities, rather than in concentrating on difficult or highbrow culture alone. Thus, cultural competencies are a necessary but not a sufficient condition for participating in highbrow culture (van Eijck and Mommaas, 2004). On the other hand, we do see status differentiation between so-called brow-levels. Although the upper strata in the Netherlands are overrepresented among people who play soccer, their overrepresentation is even greater in tennis and golf (van der Meulen *et al.*, 2005). If people participate in supposedly lowbrow activities such as sports, some sports seem to be more distinctive than others.

Overall, we can expect education to affect cultural activity in most areas, so the better educated are likely to be overrepresented among highbrow participants as well as among popular culture participants and the omnivores.

7.2.4 *Partner influences and cultural consumption*

Cultural participation is typically not engaged in individually. Taking into account the impact and presence of significant others improves the quality of explanatory models. For example, Warde and Tampubolon (2002) demonstrate that the size and diversity of a person's social network positively affects the scope of people's leisure activities. Furthermore, de Graaf and Ganzeboom (1990), using diagonal reference models, establish that the relative impact of a partner's educational attainment on cultural consumption was 33%, as compared to 48% for own education and 19% for parental education. Kalmijn and Bernasco (2001) find that partners spend most of their leisure time together, especially when it comes to activities that are labelled as 'entertainment', which includes cultural participation outside the home. For example, some 90% of respondents indicate that, if they go to a theatre or a cinema, they 'always' or 'mostly' do so with their partner. Similar numbers are found for activities typically undertaken in a domestic context, such as watching TV, reading or listening to music. Looking at the effects of partner's arts socialisation and educational attainment, Upright (2004) also finds strong partner effects, especially for men and especially for partner's schooling level. Upright (2004) concludes that arts attendance of many married men and women is predicted as strongly by their partner's educational attainment and arts socialisation as by their own. Even more striking, such effects are evident for the probability of partners attending arts events *either* jointly *or* alone. Thus, the impact of the partner is not only a result of the obvious fact that partners often provide company for cultural activities, but partners also seem to contribute to a person's cultural socialisation through their cultural resources: their knowledge of, and interest in, the arts. In addition, we argue that a partner may contribute to a family's economic resources, which makes cultural consumption more feasible. Thus, we have reason to expect that partner characteristics will contribute to the explanation of participation in arts events and that controlling for these characteristics will lead to a better estimate of the net effects of one's own class and status.[3]

7.3 Data and measurement

7.3.1 *Family Survey Dutch Population 1992–2003*

We use data collected in the Family Survey of Dutch Population (FSDP) of 1992, 1998, 2000, 2003. These surveys were organised and conducted by the Department of Sociology at Nijmegen University.[4] Response rates for the four surveys were 43%, 47%, 41%, and 53% respectively. In the Netherlands, response rates are rarely over 50%. Since the interviews of the FSDP are lengthy (more than an hour) and both partners have to be interviewed, these response rates are satisfactory. The four FSDP surveys are to a large extent representative of the adult Dutch population.[5]

Primary respondents and their partners were questioned using a face-to-face computer-assisted interview and an additional written questionnaire. Respondents in all four surveys were selected from a random sample of the non-institutionalised Dutch population between 18 and 70 years of age. In the interviews, a complete educational history, occupational career, and family history of both partners were collected with retrospective structured questioning. While one partner answered the written questionnaire, the interviewer conducted an interview with the other, and vice versa. The formulation of the questions and the format of the surveys are highly comparable over time. The data not only contain information on occupational positions, social background and family structure, but also include several questions on cultural participation outside the home. For our purpose, we select respondents with

---

[3] This expectation holds even if the causality runs the other way. That is, if people choose partners partly on account of their cultural taste, background characteristics of the partner may explain class or status effects to the extent that such effects are mediated by these partner characteristics.

[4] The chief investigators for the 1992 survey are Wout Ultee and Harry Ganzeboom, and the chief investigators for the other three surveys are Nan Dirk de Graaf, Paul de Graaf, Gerbert Kraaykamp and Wout Ultee.

[5] In the FSDP only the young (18 to 24 year-olds) and people with a lower vocational training are slightly underrepresented. As we use here information on couples and apply multi-variate correlational techniques we do not think this has affected the results of our study.

valid scores on all relevant variables. We also exclude single respondents since we are interested in partner effects on cultural behaviour. Finally, we employ the information on both partners as if they were independently sampled. Certainly, this means that the standard errors are underestimated. Analyses based solely on primary respondents, however, did not lead to different results. Thus, in our analyses we use information on 5,639 individuals from 2,874 couples.[6]

7.3.2 Measurements

Cultural consumption is measured using four indicators: attending classical concerts, attending pop concerts, attending theatre and visiting museums. Due to differences in measurement across the four waves of the FSDP, the responses to the four cultural activities are dichotomised, with 0 indicating not attending and 1 attending. In addition, the exact question wordings sometimes differ between surveys. To enhance comparability, the distinction between 'serious' and 'popular' theatres is disregarded for the 1998 and 2000 survey, as this distinction was not made in 1992 and 2003. Similarly, in measuring museum visits, historical and art museums are treated as one category for the 1992, 1998 and 2000 data. Attending pop concerts is not available in the 2003 survey, which restricts our analyses when using this dependent variable to 3,975 cases.

To test the omnivore–univore argument, we have constructed a new variable with four categories. Respondents who did not participate in any of the four cultural activities are assigned to the category of *inactives*, 'I', (17.5%). Those who attended pop concerts but none of the other activities are labelled *univores*, 'U', (4.8%). Those who attended classical concerts, theatres or museums, but not pop concerts, are labelled *highbrows*, 'H' (46.6%). Finally, those combining pop concerts with at least one of the other, more highbrow, cultural activities are assigned to the category of *omnivore*, 'O' (31.1%). Because the

---

[6] From 1992 we have 1,283 respondents in 688 couples, from 1998 1,451 respondents in 731 couples, from 2000 1,241 respondents in 622 couples, and from 2003 1,664 respondents in 833 couples; a total of 5,639 respondents from 2,874 couples. Note that in 109 cases some relevant information to employ a person as primary respondent is missing. This explains why we do not have information on 5,748 respondents from the 2,874 couples.

number of cultural indicators that is available to us is limited, we prefer this straightforward classification method to more empirical ways for determining clusters of cultural consumer.[7] Note that the analyses pertaining to pattern of taste employ the 1992, 1998 and 2000 FSDP data only.

Several alternative constructions of this typology have been tested. In the 1998 and 2000 surveys we can distinguish between art museums and historical museums, and between drama and cabaret/comedy. A factor analysis on the resulting total of six items converged to a two-factor solution with a popular dimension (referring to pop concerts) and an elitist dimension (including all other five activities). This solution makes sense in the Dutch case. Almost all museums are elitist in the nature of their collection, and in the way their exhibitions are presented, given their goal of knowledge enhancement. In the case of theatre-going the situation is more debatable. Several more popular plays are performed in theatres and cabaret has been attracting larger audiences during the last decade. However, there is hardly any difference in the social composition of the audience of serious and popular theatre. For example, during the second half of the 1990s the better educated in the Netherlands were about twice as likely as the less well educated to attend serious plays, but more than three times as likely as the less well educated to attend popular plays or cabaret performances (Social and Cultural Planning Bureau, 2001). Theatre attendance is not popular among members of lower social strata, even if the productions put on stage are aiming at a broad audience. Since the inclusion of popular theatre as a pop activity in our typology hardly affects the results of the multinomial logistic regression (see Table 7.6 below) but would result in a serious loss of cases, we choose the typology described above.

In order to construct a *status* scale, we use the method proposed by Chan and Goldthorpe (2004). To estimate social status scores, they study the pattern of friendship choice of incumbents of 31 occupational groups. For the Netherlands, we identify 26 occupational groups by combining appropriate four digit occupational categories of Statistics Netherlands.[8] Status scores are assigned to respondents on the basis of

[7] In an exploratory factor analysis all four cultural activities positively loaded on the same factor.
[8] For a more detailed discussion of the construction of the Dutch status order, see Chapter 2 of this volume.

their current occupation or, if they are not working, their last occupation, and range from −1.75 to 1.90. This status score correlates well with respondents' own education ($r = 0.53$) and with their father's education ($r = 0.27$). It is also strongly correlated ($r = 0.83$) with the often used standard international socio-economic index (ISEI) (Ganzeboom *et al.*, 1992). As for social class position, we use the well-known EGP-scheme (Goldthorpe, 1997), distinguishing seven classes: higher professional (class I), lower professional (II), routine non-manual (III), self-employed/farmers (IV), supervising manual (V), skilled manual (VI), unskilled manual (VII).

Initially, we planned to compare class and status effects on cultural behaviour simultaneously. It turns out, however, that class and status are very closely intertwined in Dutch society. Our data show that multiple Rs of class and status are around 0.82. A regression of status on class shows adjusted R^2 of 66.3% in 1992, 66.6% in 1998, 70.3% in 2000 and 69.7% in 2003. We have checked whether this strong relationship was a peculiarity of the FSDP data, but this was found not to be the case. A comparison of the associations between status and class from the 1970s onwards employing 27 data files indicates that the mean adjusted R^2 is 65.9% for men and 60.3% for women.[9] It thus seems that class and status cannot be empirically separated in Dutch society. In analytic terms, this means that class and status cause multicollinearity problems in the regression models. Our strategy therefore has changed into a separate modelling of the effects.

In addition to class and status of both respondents and partners, we also include the following variables: their educational attainment, employment status and household income. A person's highest level of education is measured in 10 categories, ranging from (1) primary school (not finished) to (10) PhD. We recode this into the number of years required to obtain a degree at that level. Accordingly, years of schooling for respondents and partners ranged from 5 to 21 (centred at 10). Employment status is coded 0 for not working and 1 for working. Household income is converted from euro to Dutch guilders, and subsequently divided by 1,000 for presentation purposes. We centred it at 4,000 guilders (i.e. 1,815 euro). A major drawback of our income

---

[9] We would like to thank Dr. Ruud Luijkx of Tilburg University for providing us with this information. Exploring multicollinearity in the FSDP data shows VIF values of 3.3 for respondent's status. VIF values above 2.5 for 4 out of 6 class dummies. In logistic regression values above 2.5 may be a cause for concern.

measure was that it was asked differently in all four surveys. So the effects of household income should be interpreted with care.

We employ several controls. For gender, men is the reference category. Degree of urbanisation is available on a five-point scale ranging from urban (1) to rural (5). A person's birth year is a continuous variable with values between 1915 and 1985. It is centred at 1950. To control for family restrictions in cultural participation, we have two variables measuring the number of children under the age of 4 and between the ages of 4 and 12 respectively. Possible variation due to differences in the questionnaires is dealt with by controlling for survey year (1992–2003), with 1992 chosen as the reference year. A respondent's background is measured using father's education and father's occupational status. The educational level of the father is measured as years of schooling, which ranges from 6 to 21. For presentation purpose, it is centred at 10. Father's occupational status is measured using the same status scale we apply to the primary respondents and their partners (ranging from −1.75 to 1.90). A description of all variables is presented in Table 7.1.

7.4 Descriptive results

Before we start analysing class and status effects on cultural participation, we offer a description of cultural differentiation. Panels A and C of Figure 7.1 display class and status variation respectively in visiting museums, attending theatre, and attending classical and pop concerts. They show that both class and status are strongly related to highbrow cultural participation. People from the higher classes, especially professionals, stand out in their cultural interests; over 70% of all professionals in our surveys visit museums and theatre at least once a year, and about 40% attend classical concerts. This is in strong contrast to the lower classes, where highbrow culture is much less popular. Among the working class, only 12% attend classical concerts and 40% go to museums and theatres. The picture is more or less identical if we replace occupational classes by a categorisation of status groups (in seven levels). For all three activities, there is a more or less monotonic relation. People at higher status levels participate in highbrow activities more often than people at lower status levels. It is, however, remarkable that participation is almost equal at the three lowest status levels; differentiation occurs mainly in the higher social strata. For

Table 7.1 *Descriptive statistics*

	mean	s.d.	min	max
dependent variables				
visiting classical concerts	0.26	0.44	0	1
visiting museums	0.59	0.49	0	1
visiting theatre	0.58	0.49	0	1
visiting pop concerts	0.36	0.48	0	1
control variables				
women	1.50	0.50	1	2
urbanisation (1 = urban, 5 = rural)	3.12	1.31	1	5
birth year (1950 = 0)	4.77	12.30	−35	34
number of children < 4 years of age	0.26	0.56	0	3
number of children 4–12 years of age	0.44	0.78	0	4
year of survey (1992 = 0)	6.55	4.02	0	11
education father in years (10 = 0)	−0.32	3.61	−4	11
father's status score	−0.15	0.81	−1.75	1.90
respondent characteristics				
education in years (10 = 0)	2.35	3.52	−5	11
employment status (1 = paid work)	0.71	0.45	0	1
status score	0.16	0.85	−1.75	1.90
class I	0.11	0.31	0	1
class II	0.29	0.45	0	1
class III	0.27	0.44	0	1
class IV	0.05	0.21	0	1
class V	0.02	0.14	0	1
class VI	0.09	0.29	0	1
class VII	0.17	0.38	0	1
partner characteristics				
status score	0.16	0.85	−1.75	1.90
class I	0.11	0.32	0	1
class II	0.29	0.45	0	1
class III	0.27	0.44	0	1
class IV	0.05	0.21	0	1
class V	0.02	0.14	0	1
class VI	0.09	0.29	0	1
class VII	0.17	0.38	0	1
education in years (10 = 0)	2.32	3.54	−5	11
household income /1,000 (4 = 0)	1.40	2.69	−3.95	16.00

Source: Family Survey Dutch Population 1992–2003; N = 5,639 (with pop concerts N = 3,975).

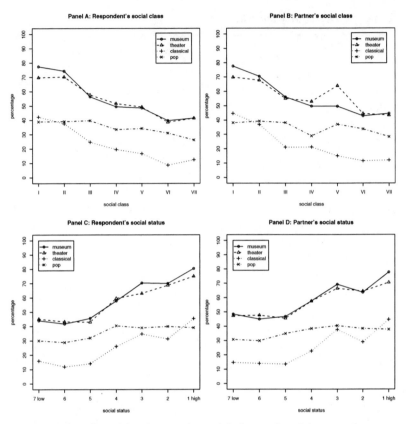

Fig. 7.1 Cultural participation rate by social class and social status of respondent and partner

attending pop concerts, social differentiation is less obvious. Although at lower status levels and among the lower classes attendance rates at pop concerts are somewhat lower, the differences with the higher groups are only about 10%. Nevertheless, going to a pop concert is not a lower-class activity. This result is more in line with Peterson's omnivore–univore conceptualisation of cultural patterns than with the more traditional 'snob vs. slob' perspective.

Panels B and D of Figure 7.1 show cultural differentiation in relation to partner's class and status, demonstrating that partner characteristics are important. The associations here are very similar to those pertaining to respondents' own class and status. Respondents with a partner who is a higher professional are most culturally active, whereas

people with a lower-class partner are markedly less likely to participate. Again, the differences are smaller for pop concerts but the direction of the association is the same.

Overall, it seems that substantial class and status effects on cultural
participation exist. In addition, effects of class and status are largely
similar, as was expected given their strong correlation.

7.5 Results

7.5.1 Effects of class and status on four cultural activities

As indicated earlier, due to the high correlation between status and
class, it turns out to be impossible to enter both variables simultaneously into a logistic regression model. Because of this multicollinearity
problem, we turn to a comparison of models using status with models
using class. Our research strategy regarding the analysis of individual
cultural items is as follows. For visiting museums, attending theatre,
and attending classical and pop concerts, we estimate four logistic
regression models. In models 1 and 2, respectively, the status position and the class position of a respondent are introduced. We control
for gender, urbanisation, birth year, family situation, year of survey,
employment status and family background. In addition to status and
class effects, we are also interested in the direct effects of years of
education. In models 3 and 4, information on the partner and the
household's financial situation is included. Partner's status (model 3)
and class position (model 4) are added, together with partner's years
of education and household income at the time of the survey.[10]

The results in models 1 and 2 of Table 7.2 on visiting museums
show some expected results.[11] Women go to museums more often than

[10] The coefficient for the controls in the models 1 and 2 differ slightly. We
therefore chose to discuss the effects of model 1 only.
[11] In addition to the analyses presented in Tables 7.2 to 7.5, we also tested for
interaction effects of status with both income and education. Theoretically, it
might be that status will only motivate cultural participation if people have
sufficient cultural (education) or material (income) resources. This was not the
case, as the status effects were independent of education and income in all but
one case. We only found a significant interaction of -0.52 for income and
status in the model for pop concerts. As this effect goes in the other direction
than we hypothesised, and as all other interactions were insignificant, we will
not comment on it further.

Table 7.2 Regression of visiting museums on individual and partner's class and status position

	model 1		model 2		model 3		model 4	
	$\hat{\beta}$	s.e.	$\hat{\beta}$	s.e.	$\hat{\beta}$	s.e.	$\hat{\beta}$	s.e.
female	0.423***	0.064	0.420***	0.069	0.338***	0.065	0.344***	0.076
urbanisation	−0.157***	0.024	−0.154***	0.024	−0.148***	0.024	−0.144***	0.024
birth year (1950 = 0)	−0.043***	0.003	−0.042***	0.003	−0.044***	0.003	−0.044***	0.003
number of children < 4	−0.253***	0.057	−0.249***	0.057	−0.258***	0.058	−0.247***	0.058
number of children 4–12	0.039	0.039	0.044	0.039	0.032	0.040	0.039	0.040
year of survey (1992 = 0)	0.054***	0.008	0.055***	0.008	0.045***	0.008	0.046***	0.008
education father in years (10 = 0)	0.032**	0.011	0.030**	0.011	0.019	0.011	0.018	0.011
father's status score	0.119**	0.044	0.113**	0.044	0.083	0.044	0.075	0.045
education in years (10 = 0)	0.163***	0.011	0.157***	0.011	0.131***	0.011	0.125***	0.011
employment status (1 = paid work)	0.283***	0.078	0.278***	0.078	0.187*	0.081	0.204*	0.081
respondent's status score	0.337***	0.041			0.255***	0.042		
respondent's class II[a]			−0.069	0.117			−0.036	0.120
respondent's class III			−0.480***	0.123			−0.389**	0.126
respondent's class IV			−0.794***	0.169			−0.684***	0.172

	b	SE	b	SE	b	SE	b	SE
respondent's class V			−0.612**	0.222			−0.395	0.224
respondent's class VI			−0.822***	0.144			−0.611***	0.147
respondent's class VII			−0.846***	0.132			−0.645***	0.136
partner's status score					0.119**	0.042		
partner's class II[a]							−0.216	0.120
partner's class III							−0.382**	0.127
partner's class IV							−0.671***	0.174
partner's class V							−0.551*	0.229
partner's class VI							−0.509***	0.147
partner's class VII							−0.431**	0.136
education partner in years (10 = 0)					0.077***	0.011	0.072***	0.011
household income /1,000 (4 = 0)					0.066***	0.016	0.060***	0.016
constant	−0.416*	0.162	0.057	0.187	−0.366*	0.165	0.330	0.228
variance explained	0.220		0.225		0.247		0.254	

Source: Family Survey Dutch Population 1992–2003; N = 5,639; [a] class I as reference.

Table 7.3 *Regression of attending theatre on individual and partner's class and status position*

	model 1		model 2		model 3		model 4	
	$\hat{\beta}$	s.e.	$\hat{\beta}$	s.e.	$\hat{\beta}$	s.e.	$\hat{\beta}$	s.e.
female	0.568***	0.062	0.558***	0.066	0.496***	0.063	0.532***	0.072
urbanisation	−0.092***	0.023	−0.089***	0.023	−0.079***	0.023	−0.076**	0.023
birth year (1950 = 0)	−0.019***	0.003	−0.018***	0.003	−0.019***	0.003	−0.018***	0.003
number of children < 4	−0.300***	0.055	−0.299***	0.055	−0.290***	0.055	−0.295***	0.056
number of children 4–12	−0.053	0.037	−0.051	0.037	−0.055	0.038	−0.057	0.038
year of survey (1992 = 0)	−0.013	0.007	−0.012	0.008	−0.027***	0.008	−0.026***	0.008
education father in years (10 = 0)	0.014	0.010	0.012	0.010	0.002	0.010	−0.001	0.010
father's status score	0.025	0.042	0.017	0.042	−0.008	0.042	−0.017	0.043
education in years (10 = 0)	0.112***	0.010	0.106***	0.010	0.084***	0.011	0.080***	0.011
employment status (1 = paid work)	0.428***	0.074	0.414***	0.075	0.307***	0.077	0.301***	0.077
respondent's status score	0.282***	0.040			0.200***	0.041		
respondent's class II[a]			−0.023	0.107			0.026	0.109
respondent's class III			−0.356**	0.114			−0.244*	0.117
respondent's class IV			−0.372*	0.161			−0.248	0.165

	Model 1 b	Model 1 SE	Model 2 b	Model 2 SE	Model 3 b	Model 3 SE	Model 4 b	Model 4 SE
respondent's class V			−0.427*	0.213			−0.204	0.216
respondent's class VI			−0.727***	0.136			−0.499**	0.139
respondent's class VII			−0.740***	0.124			−0.514***	0.128
partner's status score					0.107**	0.041		
partner's class II[a]							0.092	0.109
partner's class III							0.004	0.117
partner's class IV							−0.264	0.165
partner's class V							0.412	0.230
partner's class VI							−0.360*	0.138
partner's class VII							−0.232	0.127
education partner in years (10 = 0)					0.045***	0.011	0.040***	0.011
household income /1,000 (4 = 0)					0.093***	0.015	0.085***	0.015
constant	−0.524***	0.155	−0.140	0.177	−0.445***	0.157	−0.180	0.213
variance explained	0.130		0.135		0.154		0.162	

Source: Family Survey Dutch Population 1992–2003; N = 5,639; [a] class I as reference.

Table 7.4 *Regression of attending classical concerts on individual and partner's class and status position*

	model 1		model 2		model 3		model 4	
	$\hat{\beta}$	s.e.	$\hat{\beta}$	s.e.	$\hat{\beta}$	s.e.	$\hat{\beta}$	s.e.
female	0.633***	0.072	0.623***	0.076	0.505***	0.074	0.483***	0.083
urbanisation	−0.175***	0.026	−0.170***	0.027	−0.161***	0.027	−0.157***	0.027
birth year (1950 = 0)	−0.056***	0.004	−0.056***	0.004	−0.058***	0.004	−0.057***	0.004
number of children < 4	−0.150*	0.071	−0.140*	0.071	−0.151*	0.072	−0.143*	0.073
number of children 4–12	−0.123**	0.046	−0.120**	0.046	−0.137**	0.047	−0.136**	0.047
year of survey (1992 = 0)	0.004	0.009	0.005	0.009	−0.012	0.009	−0.008	0.010
education father in years (10 = 0)	0.078***	0.011	0.076***	0.011	0.059***	0.011	0.058***	0.011
father's status score	0.037	0.048	0.023	0.048	−0.010	0.049	−0.028	0.049
education in years (10 = 0)	0.168***	0.013	0.158***	0.013	0.123***	0.013	0.112***	0.013
employment status (1 = paid work)	0.361***	0.089	0.353***	0.089	0.233*	0.092	0.240*	0.093
respondent's status score	0.274***	0.048			0.157**	0.050		
respondent's class II[a]			−0.126	0.105			−0.069	0.108
respondent's class III			−0.356**	0.120			−0.214	0.124
respondent's class IV			−0.659***	0.191			−0.529*	0.195

respondent's class V			−0.527	0.270			−0.189	0.275
respondent's class VI			−1.080***	0.188			−0.768***	0.192
respondent's class VII			−0.951***	0.150			−0.641***	0.154
partner's status score					0.214***	0.050		
partner's class II[a]							−0.087	0.107
partner's class III							−0.378**	0.123
partner's class IV							−0.408*	0.188
partner's class V							−0.645*	0.289
partner's class VI							−0.761***	0.177
partner's class VII							−0.619***	0.150
education partner in years (10 = 0)					0.083***	0.013	0.075***	0.013
household income /1,000 (4 = 0)					0.087***	0.014	0.076***	0.014
constant	−2.000***	0.184	−1.52***	0.201	−1.918***	0.189	−1.224***	0.239
variance explained	0.234		0.243		0.274		0.284	

Source: Family Survey Dutch Population 1992-2003; $N = 5,639$; [a]class I as reference.

Table 7.5 *Regression of attending pop concerts on individual and partner's class and status position*

	model 1		model 2		model 3		model 4	
	$\hat{\beta}$	s.e.	$\hat{\beta}$	s.e.	$\hat{\beta}$	s.e.	$\hat{\beta}$	s.e.
female	-0.123	0.078	-0.198*	0.084	-0.158*	0.079	-0.242**	0.090
urbanisation	-0.156***	0.029	-0.153***	0.029	-0.150***	0.029	-0.147***	0.029
birth year (1950 = 0)	0.072***	0.004	0.072***	0.004	0.074***	0.004	0.075***	0.004
number of children < 4	-0.227***	0.068	-0.229***	0.068	-0.213**	0.068	-0.219***	0.068
number of children 4–12	-0.127**	0.044	-0.127**	0.044	-0.118***	0.044	-0.119***	0.045
year of survey (1992 = 0)	-0.042***	0.012	-0.041***	0.012	-0.054***	0.012	-0.052***	0.012
education father in years (10 = 0)	0.026*	0.012	0.024*	0.012	0.022	0.012	0.020	0.012
father's status score	-0.072	0.053	-0.085	0.053	-0.080	0.053	-0.092	0.053
education in years (10 = 0)	0.014	0.013	0.010	0.013	0.004	0.014	0.001	0.014
employment status (1 = paid work)	0.398***	0.097	0.391***	0.098	0.311**	0.100	0.318***	0.100
respondent's status score	0.079	0.051			0.042	0.052		
respondent's class II[a]			0.009	0.123			0.035	0.124
respondent's class III			0.106	0.139			0.161	0.140

	b	s.e.	b	s.e.	b	s.e.	b	s.e.
respondent's class IV			0.043	0.200			0.087	0.202
respondent's class V			−0.054	0.284			0.039	0.287
respondent's class VI			−0.417*	0.174			−0.300	0.177
respondent's class VII			−0.307*	0.157			−0.199	0.160
partner's status score					0.006	0.051		
partner's class II[a]							0.014	0.125
partner's class III							−0.053	0.141
partner's class IV							−0.166	0.207
partner's class V							0.210	0.287
partner's class VI							−0.065	0.175
partner's class VII							−0.192	0.158
education partner in years (10 = 0)					−0.001	0.013	−0.008	0.013
household income /1,000 (4 = 0)					0.071***	0.018	0.061	0.018
constant	−0.247	0.199	−0.067	0.223	−0.170	0.200	0.027	0.262
variance explained	0.195		0.200		0.199		0.205	

Source: Family Survey Dutch Population 1992-2003; N = 3,975; [a] class I as reference.

men ($e^{0.423} = 1.53$), and people from younger birth cohorts are less likely to visit museums than people from older birth cohorts ($e^{-0.043} = 0.96$). A supply side effect is found regarding degree of urbanisation; as museums are located mostly in major cities, inhabitants of these cities are far more likely to have visited museums. Having young children restricts museum visits (a 22% reduction of the odds for each pre-school child), but when these children are over the age of 4, they no longer affect the likelihood of museum visits. In line with figures from Statistics Netherlands (www.statline.nl), year of survey has a positive effect, as the number of museum visitors has increased between 1992 and 2003. Family background also matters. A father who is highly educated and holds a higher status position certainly contributes to socialising into highbrow culture. Each additional year of father's schooling is associated with a 3% increase in the odds of visiting museums.

Model 1 further shows that paid employment increases the odds of museum visits ($e^{0.283} = 1.33$). Class (model 2) and status (model 1) both have the expected effects. A higher-class position cultivates a person's cultural behaviour; the odds of a higher professional visiting museums are 2.33 times higher than those of an unskilled manual worker. Remarkably, class differences are mostly found contrasting professionals with the other classes. Classes IV to VII hardly differ from one another in their likelihood of visiting a museum. We also find large status effects on museum visiting ($\hat{\beta} = 0.337$); an increase of one status point raises the odds of being a museum visitor by 40%. Note that, comparing the models for class and status, the explained variance is somewhat higher in the model including class (22.0% v 22.5%). This difference probably has to do with the internal homogeneity of classes and the number of classes in the model. A model that divides status into seven categories, however, still does slightly worse in predicting museum visits than the model using class. Nevertheless, comparing maximum effects of class and status shows a somewhat different picture. For class, the largest difference is found between class I and VII (a difference of 2.33 times in odds), whereas for status the difference between the highest and lowest position is 3.42 ($e^{3.65 \times 0.337} = 3.42$). Obviously, using 26 status groups allows for a more fine-grained measurement than a division into seven classes. In addition, educational attainment is a strong predictor for museum visits; every year of education raises the odds of having visited a museum during the last 12 months by 18%. Comparing the effects of education to those of class or status shows that education is most influential.

Introducing partner characteristics in models 3 and 4 clearly improves our explanatory models. First, both class and status of the partner contribute to the explanation of museum visiting. Compared to a partner from class I, a working class partner halves the chance to visit a museum. In the case of status, the same picture emerges ($\hat{\beta} = 0.119$). Note that these effects are net of respondent's own class/status. The effects of respondent's class and status position are partly interpreted by introducing partner aspects; the status effect by 24% and the class effect by up to 35% (for class V). Second, models 3 and 4 also demonstrate the effects of a partner's education and household income; particularly that higher income raises the odds of museum visits. Since successive Dutch governments have subsidised museums substantially, this is contrary to our expectation. The effect of partners' educational attainment is also noteworthy; each additional year that a partner is trained gives 8% higher odds of being a museum visitor. This amounts to almost half the effect size of respondents' own education. Adding the partner effects also renders the effects of father's education and father's status insignificant.

Table 7.3 displays the results for attending theatre. This activity is clearly less elitist than museum visits or, as we will see later, attending classical concerts; the proportion of explained variance of the models is smaller and the effects of the stratification variables are substantially lower. The effects of the control variables, however, resemble those for museum visits: women, people from urban communities and those without young children are more likely to be theatre-goers. Moreover, individuals from younger birth cohorts are less inclined to go to the theatre than individuals from older birth cohorts; with each additional year, the odds reduce by 2%. Surprisingly, no significant effects of family background on theatre-going can be found.

Models 1 and 2 further show that class and status have the expected effects. Theatre-going is more common among the higher classes and the higher-status groups; the odds of an unskilled manual worker going to the theatre are less than half ($e^{-0.740} = 0.48$) those of a professional in class I. And each additional status point is associated with a 33% increase in the odds of theatre-going. Again, the model introducing class has a slightly higher R^2 than the model for status. However, comparing maximum effects again reveals that the largest class difference, found for class I versus class VII, is 2.10 ($e^{0.740} = 2.10$), whereas the difference between the highest and the lowest status position is 2.80 ($e^{3.65 \times 0.282} = 2.80$). It is remarkable that the odds of the employed going to the theatre are 53% higher compared with the non-employed. Again, education proves to be the most important predictor for theatre visits: the odds for people with the highest level of education are six times higher ($e^{16 \times 0.112} = 6.00$) than for those with the lowest level of education.

In relation to attending theatre, partner characteristics are also relevant (models 3 and 4). Partner features mediate 29% of the respondent's own status effect. It must be noted, however, that a partner's class and status position only have modest effects on theatre-going; each additional status point (of the partner) is associated with an 11% increase in the odds of attending theatre and the parameters for partner's class are mostly not significant. It appears that theatre-going is also an elitist activity in a financial sense. Comparing the highest and lowest income groups, the odds increase by over sixfold ($e^{19.95 \times 0.09} = 6.39$). Again, this result contradicts our expectation. Evidently, theatre-going is a more expensive activity than presumed earlier.

The results in Table 7.4 (on attending classical concerts) are very similar to those of Table 7.2 (on visiting museums). Women, people living in large cities, and members from older birth cohorts attend classical concerts relatively often. But in Table 7.4 the parameters of children are different. Each child aged 0–3 is associated with a 12% reduction in the odds of going to classical concerts, and for each child aged 4–12, the odds reduce by 14%. Family background is influential as well; the maximum difference in father's years of schooling is associated with a threefold difference in the odds of going to classical concerts ($e^{15 \times 0.078} = 3.22$).

In models 1 and 2, class and status are included and their effects very much resemble those found for museums and the theatre. A high class and status position is associated with a higher chance of attending classical concerts. Again, for class the largest differences are found contrasting the professionals with all other classes. Every point increase in status raises the odds of attending classical concerts by 32%. Once more, the models with class show a slightly higher adjusted explained variance than the models with status. Looking at maximum effects comparing class I and class VI, we see an odds ratio of 2.94, while the difference between the highest and lowest status position amounts to an odds ratio of 2.72 ($e^{3.65 \times 0.274} = 2.72$). One could say that class and status effects here are almost equal in their impact. Education again had the largest effect on attending classical concerts; each additional year of schooling is associated with an 18% higher increase in the odds.

Models 3 and 4 again show considerable partner effects on attending classical concerts. Partner features account for 43% of the individual status effects. Each additional status point of a partner is associated with a 24% increase in the odds of visiting classical concerts. The odds of people with a professional partner are 114% higher than those whose partner is a skilled blue-collar worker. As expected, partner's education and household income are also relevant. Each additional year of education of a partner increases the odds of attending classical concerts by 9%. Household income also determines concert-going; comparing the highest and lowest income groups, their odds ratio is over five ($e^{19.95 \times 0.087} = 5.67$).

In Table 7.5, the effects for attending pop concerts are shown. People from more urban areas and people without children are more likely to go to pop concerts. As expected, it is mostly people from the younger birth cohorts (perhaps reflecting an age effect) who find pop concerts appealing. The results further show that attending pop concerts is indeed relatively independent of a person's socio-economic background. Stratification effects are almost non-existent. The effects of respondent's and partner's status are not statistically significant. For class in model 2 the manual workers of classes VI and VII stand out. Compared with the salariat, manual workers actually have lower odds (52% and 36% respectively) of going to pop concerts.

7.5.2 Effects of class and status on patterns of cultural consumption

The analyses reported in Section 7.5.1 demonstrate that highbrow activities are closely related to both class and status while going to pop concerts is largely not socially stratified. Put differently, these results also suggest that participation in popular culture, measured as going to pop concerts, does not rule out participation in highbrow culture. It therefore makes sense to look more closely at possible patterning of

Table 7.6 *Frequencies of overlapping audiences*

	participation in other activities			
	classical	museums	theatres	pop
classical concerts	100.0	85.9	84.8	38.3
museums	38.0	100.0	72.1	39.2
theatres	38.0	73.0	100.0	43.6
pop concerts	30.8	66.3	73.6	100.0

cultural tastes. Table 7.6 shows the extent to which participation in the four activities overlap with each other.

The first row of Table 7.6 shows that visitors of classical concerts are very active in the other three domains: 86% of them visit museums, 85% go to theatre and 38% go to pop concerts. Joint participation rates are somewhat lower in the other three rows. But still 38% of museum visitors and the same proportion of theatre-goers also attend classical concerts. Of those who go to pop concerts, 66% are museum-visitors, 74% are theatre-goers, and a smaller but still substantial 31% attend classical concerts. These numbers do indicate a great degree of overlap between the audiences of highbrow and popular arts.

As explained above, we have constructed a fourfold typology of cultural consumers: omnivores, inactives, univores and highbrows. Given the available indicators (3 for highbrow, 1 for popular), it is to be expected that patterns that include elements of highbrow culture will be most prevalent (in this sample). Indeed, the largest types are the highbrow (46.6%), and the omnivores (31.3%). Given that pop concert goers also show a good deal of enthusiasm for museums and the theatre, it is not surprising that the univores comprise only 4.8% of our sample. The inactives make up the remaining 17.5%. This fourfold typology is then used as a dependent variable in a multinomial logistic analysis.[12]

---

[12] Note that if we make the distinction between popular and serious theatre, and treat the former as a popular rather than a highbrow activity, then the distribution of the four types of cultural consumer will change as follows: highbrows (15.9%), omnivores (58%), univores (12.8%) and inactives (13.3%). The share of inactives has changed because the 1992 FDSP data is disregarded. There is no information in that survey that will allow us to make the distinction between popular and serious theatre.

Table 7.7 presents the results of a multinomial logistic regression analysis where the fourfold typology of cultural consumer is the dependent variable. Class is no longer included in the model, as the results for class and status were shown to be very similar in Tables 7.2 to 7.5. We will therefore focus on the effects of status of the respondents and their partners. Table 7.7 includes the same set of control and stratification variables as model 3 of Tables 7.2 to 7.5. We choose the omnivores as the reference category.

Looking at the first column, it can be seen that females ($e^{-0.345} = 0.71$) and younger people ($e^{-0.028} = 0.97$) are less likely to be inactives rather than omnivores. The opposite is true for people who live in more rural communities ($e^{0.195} = 1.22$), and people with young children ($e^{0.377} = 1.46$). The effects of education, employment and social status on the odds of being an inactive rather than an omnivore are all significantly negative. The difference between the highest and the lowest level of schooling implies an odds ratio of 5.63. For respondents' status, the maximum effect amounts to an odds ratio of 2.49, indicating that people from higher-status groups are more likely to be culturally active. The effect of partner's status is, however, not significant. Other characteristics of the partner do matter; a less well educated partner and a lower household income increase the odds of being an inactive.

If we compare the univores with the omnivores, we see that coming from a more rural area raises the odds of being a univore. Here, supply side effects may be the explanation; pop concerts are found over virtually all the country, whereas highbrow culture is mostly located in urban areas. Birth year has a positive effect; each additional year (i.e. younger people) increases the odds of being a univore rather than an omnivore by 7%. Respondents' education and social status affect the likelihood of being a univore rather than an omnivore negatively. The maximum effect for education implies an odds ratio of 6.30, which is again larger than the maximum status effect of 3.45. Partners with a higher level of schooling and a higher household income also increase the likelihood of being an omnivore. Clearly, omnivores come from more advantaged socio-economic strata than univores.

Most crucial is whether status effects are present if we compare the omnivores to the highbrows. Both of these taste patterns include highbrow culture, but the omnivore pattern is argued to be on the rise as a new way to signal status, while the numbers of highbrow

Table 7.7 *Multinomial regression of omnivorousness versus non-participation, univore pop attendance*

	I vs. O		U vs. O		H vs. O	
	$\hat{\beta}$	s.e.	$\hat{\beta}$	s.e.	$\hat{\beta}$	s.e.
female	−0.345**	0.120	−0.245	0.179	0.291***	0.087
degree urbanisation (1 = urban, 5 = rural)	0.195***	0.042	0.213***	0.065	0.171***	0.032
birth year (1950 = 0)	−0.028***	0.006	0.070***	0.011	−0.078***	0.005
number of children < 4 years of age	0.377***	0.098	−0.047	0.141	0.110	0.079
number of children 4–12 years of age	0.106	0.067	0.073	0.100	0.137**	0.050
year of survey (1992 = 0)	−0.022	0.016	−0.009	0.027	0.089***	0.013
education father in years (10 = 0)	−0.028	0.019	−0.005	0.029	−0.021	0.013
father's status score	−0.020	0.078	−0.057	0.121	0.106	0.058
education in years (10 = 0)	−0.108***	0.019	−0.115***	0.032	0.021	0.015
employment status (1 = paid work)	−0.441**	0.142	0.149	0.246	−0.235*	0.109
respondent's status score	−0.250***	0.073	−0.339**	0.114	−0.026	0.057
partner's status score	−0.088	0.073	−0.204	0.112	−0.014	0.057
education partner in years (10 = 0)	−0.065***	0.019	−0.064*	0.031	0.017	0.015
household income /1.000 (4 = 0)	−0.240***	0.037	−0.172**	0.059	−0.061***	0.019
constant	0.132	0.293	−2.421***	0.469	−0.614**	0.224

Variance explained (Nagelkerke) = 0.3220. *Source:* Family Survey Dutch Population 1992–2000; N = 3,975.

exclusivists are thought to be diminishing. But do these two taste groups actually differ in status, or should they be seen as two segments of the upper social strata, as suggested by van Eijck (2001) and vander Stichele and Laermans (2006)? In column 3 of Table 7.7, we see no effects of education or of status of both the respondents and their partners on the odds of being a highbrow 'snob' rather than an omnivore. But net of other effects, higher household income actually reduces the odds of being a highbrow rather than an omnivore. The control variables further indicate that omnivores are more likely to be male, living in urban areas, younger and without children aged 4–12.

The results shown in Table 7.7 suggest that there is no status difference between cultural omnivores and highbrow 'snobs'. In terms of status and education, the omnivores differ most markedly from the univores. Clearly, going to pop concerts in itself does not signal a lower status; only going to pop concerts without also attending highbrow cultural events does so. This ambivalent status of popular culture participation probably explains why we found no impact of status in Table 7.5. Engaging in popular culture as a highbrow participant does not seem to harm one's status, indicating that the omnivore taste patterns is by all means respectable, and even preferred among younger generations with ample economic resources who live in urban areas with generous cultural infrastructure.

7.6 Conclusion and discussion

In the Netherlands, status seems a relevant predictor for differentiation in highbrow cultural consumption, but it is not more important than class. We address questions on the role of class and status on highbrow and popular cultural participation, both separately and combined, employing representative data on 5,639 individuals from 2,874 couples. Unfortunately, it turns out to be impossible to empirically distinguish class and status in the Netherlands. As a result, the controversy of whether it is class or status that is most relevant in determining taste cannot be resolved by confronting them directly in a single model. It is clear, though, that status and class are both influential in explaining differentiation in cultural participation, even when aspects of cognitive competence and income are controlled for. It thus seems that these remaining effects of class and status should be interpreted in terms of status seeking rather than information-processing skills. This, we believe, is an interesting conclusion and a substantive addition to previous studies on cultural consumption.

There are four additional results that should be stressed. First, it must be emphasised that the most important predictor of highbrow cultural behaviour is educational attainment. For visiting museums, attending classical concerts, and visiting theatre plays, schooling effects are up to four times as strong as the effects of status or class. Schooling effects remain highly significant even after we have been controlled for presence of children, supply-side effects, and class or status. Thus, for the Netherlands, it may be stated that the differentiation in highbrow cultural behaviour is best explained by aspects of cultural skills and competencies. Bear in mind, however, that these abilities might also be seen as tokens of prestige, especially in a meritocratic society where class distinctions are not strongly felt.

Second, we find that partner characteristics are important in explaining highbrow cultural participation. Household income, which in part depends on one's partner, is a relevant variable. Moreover, partner's educational attainment matters. A highly educated partner not only provides company when participating in cultural participation, he or she is also likely to socialise the respondent into highbrow culture. In that case, we may interpret partner effects as learning effects. But a partner's status or class position adds to our understanding of participation in highbrow culture as well. People with a high-class or high-status partner are more likely to be culturally active. Note that these effects were established after controlling not only for own status or class and educational attainment, but also for household income and partner's educational attainment. It underscores that highbrow cultural participation is a social activity that is affected by the social characteristics of significant others.

Third, the effects of class and status are strongest for highbrow activities. These are still very much socially stratified, thus contradicting bold arguments that class or status has become irrelevant for taste formation. The only item in our study that is not significantly affected by class or status is the attendance of pop concerts. This type of popular cultural behaviour is not, or is no longer, shunned by members from the upper social strata. Taken together, these findings already point towards a patterning of cultural behaviour that is more in line with the omnivore–univore argument than with either the homology or the sweeping individualisation arguments.

Finally, this last point is further substantiated by our study of participation patterns. Status clearly distinguishes between cultural omnivores on the one hand, and inactives or univores on the other, but no status or education differences are found between highbrows and omnivores. Omnivores and highbrows do, however, differ significantly in terms of age, gender, place of residence, employment status and income. On the basis of these characteristics, they can be distinguished quite well within the higher-status groups. Partner status does not affect any of the contrasts between the various participation patterns. This might indicate that partners tend to affect each other's highbrow cultural participation, but do not affect the actual patterning of a cultural taste. Alternatively, an omnivorous taste pattern may be more prevalent among people whose partners are a source of 'status inconsistency'. In that case, omnivorousness might be positively related to marital heterogamy, just like a person's own social mobility contributes to an omnivorous taste pattern (van Eijck, 1999). Partner's education, however, remains significant for distinguishing between participation patterns with and without highbrow culture. Our research of participation patterns again demonstrated that highbrow cultural participation is always positively related to status. The status connotations of popular culture participation depend on whether or not it is combined with highbrow elements. Engaging only in pop culture indicates the lowest status position, but incorporating pop culture into a pattern that also encompasses highbrow elements does not imply a lower status at all. It rather seems to signal a youthful, urban openness or tolerance that might be increasingly prevalent and appreciated among higher status groups.

8 Social stratification of cultural consumption across three domains: music; theatre, dance and cinema; and the visual arts

TAK WING CHAN AND JOHN H. GOLDTHORPE

8.1 Introduction

In Chapter 1 of this volume, we have outlined three widely discussed arguments concerning the social stratification of cultural consumption: that is, what we have labelled as the 'homology', the 'individualisation' and the 'omnivore–univore' arguments. In our own previous work (Chan and Goldthorpe, 2005, 2007d,e) we have examined the validity of these arguments in the light of analyses of cultural consumption in England in three different domains: that is, in music, in theatre, dance and cinema, and in the visual arts. Through this work we have sought to make some advance on previous research in two main ways.

First, we have recognised that insofar as the focus of interest *is* on cultural consumption, then this must be studied as directly as possible, and that patterns of consumption cannot be reliably inferred from data that amount to no more than individuals' expressions of their cultural tastes and preferences. Reliance on the latter may well give an exaggerated or distorted idea of the extent of consumption (cf. Chan and Goldthorpe, 2007b).[1] We have based our own analyses on data from the Arts in England Survey, carried out in 2001 (for further details see Skelton *et al.*, 2002), which involved face-to-face interviews with a national sample of persons aged 16 and over, and

---

[1] It seems often to be overlooked that Bourdieu's work (1984) relies far more on respondents' expressions of their taste than on their reports of their actual 'cultural practices' – although Bourdieu regularly elides the distinction. Such reports may of course themselves give an exaggerated account of consumption, although checks against attendance figures, etc. are then possible. Insofar as we can make such checks in the British case, we find no indication of any gross distortion in our survey data. There may, of course, be good grounds for studying taste per se but it would seem important that these should always be spelled out.

which aimed to assess the extent of their attendance at cultural events and their participation in cultural activities, very broadly understood. The degree to which activities within particular domains are differentiated in this survey is often not as great as we would wish but this is more than compensated for by its comprehensive coverage and by the range of socio-demographic information that was also collected.

Secondly, as regards social stratification, we have urged the need for a more considered approach to its conceptualisation and measurement on the lines already indicated in Chapter 1. Thus, throughout our work we have applied separate measures of class and status understood in a Weberian sense – and further of education and income – so that assessments can be made of their relative importance in regard to cultural consumption through appropriate multivariate analyses, and also so that pointers may be gained to the actual social processes or mechanisms that underlie the statistically demonstrated effects of these variables.

In each of the three domains in which we have analysed cultural consumption, we have proceeded in the following three-step way.

(i) From the Arts in England survey, we have derived indicators of cultural consumption, using data on whether or not individuals had participated in a particular kind of cultural activity in the twelve months preceding the survey (or, in the case of listening to different genres of music, in the preceding four weeks). We have concentrated on individuals aged 20–64, since preliminary analyses suggested that the cultural consumption of both younger and older persons would require separate treatment.

(ii) In each domain, we have taken our indicators of cultural activity as input to latent class measurement models: that is, we have sought to capture the association that exists between different kinds of cultural consumption through identifying a limited number of underlying *patterns of consumption* within the domain in question that can in turn serve as the basis for distinguishing different *types of consumer*.

(iii) We have then investigated the social characteristics of different types of consumer in each domain, first through simple bivariate analyses, in which we consider their distribution by class and status, and then, more importantly, through multivariate, logistic regression analyses. In this latter case, we examine simultaneously the effects of class, status and other stratification variables on the chances of individuals approximating one type of consumer rather than another, while controlling demographic variables such as age, sex, marital status, family composition and region of residence.

Overall, our findings provide little support for, and indeed run generally counter to, both the homology and the individualisation arguments. It turns out that in each domain we consider a rather simple latent class model gives a good fit to our data. That is to say, consumption, rather than expressing a great diversity of styles, as the individualisation argument would imply, shows a quite strong patterning that can in fact be adequately represented by distinguishing just two or three types of consumer – which in turn prove to be socially differentiated to a greater or lesser degree.[2] Moreover, while it might sometimes be possible to equate one of these types of consumer with the 'mass consumer' postulated by the homology argument, in no case can we identify the counterpart 'elite consumer' who engages actively in 'high' culture while shunning 'low' or 'popular' forms. The elite consumer does, we would suppose, exist but is so minoritarian as not to show up in any national survey of normal size. And certainly the number of individuals involved would seem by far too small to allow any plausible equation with, for example, Bourdieu's 'dominant class'.

The types of consumer that emerge from our analyses would in fact appear generally more consistent with the omnivore–univore argument – at all events, sufficiently so for us to have adopted this terminology, with some reservations and consequent refinements, in the presentation of our results. In Table 8.1 we show the distribution of the types of consumer that we distinguish within each domain.

In the case of music, univores, the numerically preponderant type, consume pop and rock but largely, if not entirely, to the exclusion of

---

[2] This is not to deny that a diversity of styles may exist *within* the various different forms of cultural consumption that we distinguish – as, say, within the consumption of popular music or, for that matter, classical music. But it is important to note that while we cannot with the data at our disposal capture such diversity, this does *not* undermine the typology that we have established. For example, *whatever* kind of popular music they may favour, those whom we have labelled as univores in the domain of music still have the low propensity that we indicate to consume classical music, opera or operetta or jazz; and whatever style of classicial music omnivores may favour, they are still omnivorous in the sense of consuming both classical and popular forms.

Table 8.1 *Distribution of respondents by latent classes within the three cultural domains (N = 3819)*

Music		Theatre		Visual Arts	
Univores	70.4	Univores	64.2	Inactives	58.2
Omnivore – listeners	19.1	Omnivores	35.8	Paucivores	37.1
Omnivores	10.4			Omnivores	4.7

other kinds of music (some possible 'crossover' effects are suggested). In contrast, omnivores have relatively high levels of consumption of classical music, of opera and operetta, of jazz *and also* of pop and rock, whether 'live' or via various media. But we need then to distinguish a further type of consumer, whom we label as 'omnivore-listeners', who are also wide-ranging in their musical consumption but via media only: that is, who are largely non-attenders at concerts and other musical events. With theatre, dance and cinema, univores, again the majority, tend to be cinema-goers only, or, one could say, are another kind of non-attender so far as live performances are concerned. Omnivores, on the other hand, have a relatively high frequency of attendance at plays, musical comedies and pantomimes, and at ballet and other dance performances *as well as* at cinemas. Finally, though, with the visual arts, the numerically most important type that we identify is not some kind of univore but rather the virtual *non*-consumer or culturally inactive individual, at least so far as consumption in institutional settings is concerned.[3] And while in this domain we do once more find omnivores, who make relatively frequent visits to museums and galleries, to special arts exhibitions and events, and also to craft fairs and cultural festivals, they represent only a quite small minority. Further, we have here again to recognise another, far more numerous, type of consumer that also compromises the omnivore–univore dichotomy.

[3] We have no data available to us on 'home' consumption of the visual arts, nor on the consumption of 'street art' in the form of advertisements, graffiti etc. If such consumption could be taken into account, it is possible that some 'inactives' would appear as univores in this regard. However, our own view would be that an appreciation of art in the home (cf. Halle, 1993; Painter, 2002) and in the street is more likely to be correlated with, than disassociated from, the consumption of art in institutional settings (see further Chan and Goldthorpe, 2007e,b). In any event, in what follows we treat inactives in the visual arts together with univores in the two other domains we consider.

These are consumers whom we label as 'paucivores' in that their participation in the visual arts, while clearly more than univorous – they attend museums, galleries and less *avant garde* kinds of exhibition – still falls some way below that of omnivores in its level and its range alike.

As regards the social stratification of these types of consumer, our findings again give broad, but not unqualified, support to the omnivore–univore argument. In particular, omnivores – as this argument would require – are drawn disproportionately from higher strata, however understood; and univores, and also 'inactives' in the visual arts, are drawn disproportionately from lower strata. But it has at the same time to be noted that neither the differentiation of 'true' omnivores from omnivore-listeners in music nor that of omnivores from paucivores in the visual arts is all that marked; and further that even within the most advantaged social classes or highest ranking status groups univores, or inactives, still represent at least fairly substantial minorities. In other words, while the forms of cultural consumption that we have examined are quite clearly socially stratified – that is, on something like omnivore–univore rather than elite–mass lines – the *strength* of this stratification should not be exaggerated.

Finally, though, we can also report that our results in this connection do rather strongly confirm our own Weberian expectation that in so far as cultural consumption *is* socially stratified, this will be on the basis of status rather than of class. From our multivariate analyses in each of the domains we study it emerges that individuals' chances of being one type of consumer rather than another – and in particular, omnivores rather than univores or inactives – are far more strongly influenced by their status than by their class, with the latter only rarely having significant effects.[4] Income effects, too, are quite limited. In contrast, educational level proves to be a consistent and important influence on cultural consumption in addition to status, and in some cases outweighs the latter. However, the question arises, and is taken up further in our

---

[4] We further show that such results are not the merely artefactual outcome of measuring status on an interval scale while class is represented as categorical. The importance of status remains even when treated simply in terms of the four major bands distinguished within our scale. Moreover, we show elsewhere (Chan and Goldthorpe, 2007a) that in other respects – for example, economic life-chances and political partisanship – it is class rather than status that is the dominant stratifying force.

concluding section, of whether, in this context, education is in fact best understood as operating as a stratification variable.

In sum, in treating separately three different cultural domains, our previous work has shown that, contrary to the individualisation argument, cultural consumption remains, in England at least, quite strongly patterned and in significant respects socially stratified, most notably by status; and that, further, as regards the form of this stratification, the homology argument has clearly less to commend it than does the omnivore–univore argument. At the same time, though, various difficulties with this latter argument are also revealed in moving from the domain of music – in which it was originally developed – to other domains, and especially, perhaps, to that of the visual arts.

It would, then, seem a logical continuation of the line of enquiry that we have so far pursued to move on to a cross-domain approach: that is, to examine individuals' cultural consumption in its totality – or at least across the three major domains that we have so far considered separately – and the nature of its patterning and of its stratification at this overall level. In this way, new perspectives may be gained on the main theoretical issues with which we have been concerned, and on the omnivore–univore argument in particular. Whether or not this argument holds good in regard to individuals' total cultural consumption is in fact in some degree independent of its validity in specific domains. Thus, even if the omnivore–univore division may appear inappropriate in certain cases, such as the visual arts, it could still be found of relevance when an overview of cultural consumption is taken – as referring, say, to a general 'cultural voraciousness'. Or, conversely, even if the division quite often shows up when the focus is on particular domains – where omnivorousness takes the form of 'taste eclecticism' – it might still not apply overall, and if only because a 'universal', cross-domain omnivorousness might be difficult to sustain, even for members of higher social strata, on account of financial or of time constraints (see e.g. Linder, 1970).[5]

In taking up these issues in an English context, some advantage may be derived from the very 'middling' position that, in comparative perspective, England would appear to hold as regards both national

---

[5] Little previous research would appear to have been carried out into the issues that here arise. One exception is López-Sintas and Katz-Gerro (2005), although the range of cultural consumption they were able to cover was relatively limited.

cultural policy and general levels of cultural consumption: i.e. there
is little reason to view England as being in any sense an extreme or
special case. In England state responsibility for cultural policy and for
financial support for the arts – which is probably around the average
level for economically advanced societies – is more fully recognised
than, say, in the US. However, the state largely operates via quasi-
public institutions, notably the Arts Councils, that are at 'arm's length'
from government, in contrast with the situation in many continental
European countries where cultural policy and funding are the direct
responsibility of a government ministry. Whether or not as a reflection
of this, cultural consumption in England would then seem also to
be at an intermediate level. While such comparisons as can be made
suggest generally higher cultural consumption in England than in the
US, Eurobarometer data would indicate that, with the main exception
of theatre-going, England is either at or somewhat below the European
average – showing, for example, lower attendance at classical music
concerts and opera than Austria or Germany and at cinemas, dance
performances and museums and galleries than most Nordic countries.[6]

8.2 Data and analytical strategy

We continue to use the data of the Arts in England Survey, as previously: that is, we work with an analytical sample of 3,819 men and
women out of the original 6,042 respondents, following restriction to
the age-range of 20–64 and the omission of cases where information
was lacking on variables of key interest to us.

   We also rely on the same indicators of cultural consumption as previously. In the case of music, we take results from questions – requiring a
'yes/no' answer – on whether in the twelve months preceding interview
respondents had attended a classical concert, an opera or operetta, a
jazz concert or a pop or rock concert; and, further, whether over the
preceding four weeks they had listened through any medium (radio,
TV, records, CDs, tapes etc.) to these same four genres of music. For
theatre, dance and cinema (henceforth 'theatre'), we take results from
similar questions on whether in the preceding twelve months respondents had attended a play, a musical comedy or a pantomime, a ballet

---

[6] The Eurobarometer data that we refer to were collected in August to September
2001 and March to April 2003.

or some other form of dance performance, or a cinema; and for the visual arts on whether in the same period respondents had visited a museum or gallery, an exhibition of art, photography or sculpture, a craft exhibition, an event involving video or electronic art or a cultural festival.[7]

As already described, latent class analyses drawing on these indicators in each domain enable us to identify the patterns of consumption and in turn the types of consumer that are reported in Table 8.1. In seeking to follow a cross-domain approach, it might then be thought a natural step to apply latent class analyses once again to all our indicators taken together. However, since there are in total 19 indicators (8 for music, 6 for theatre and 5 for the visual arts), the underlying contingency table with 2^{19} cells would be impossibly sparse even with a sample many times larger than that available to us.[8] Thus, the strategy that we follow is based on retaining the types of consumer in different domains that are shown in Table 8.1, and asking, first of all, about the pattern and extent of the cross-domain association that exists among these types.

We first apply loglinear analysis to a 3 × 2 × 3 table cross-classifying our respondents' latent class membership in the three domains, as shown in Table 8.1.[9] The results of this analysis are reported in Table 8.2. As can be seen, all two-way associations have to be included before a fitting model is obtained (though there is no need for a three-way term). That is to say, a significant degree of association exists between patterns of consumption from one domain to another.[10] Given

---

[7] We include attendance at cultural festivals as an indicator of consumption in the visual arts in the light of evidence that the visual arts – understood as including crafts – tend to figure prominently in their programmes. However, the results of our analyses are little changed if we exclude this item.

[8] We have also tried using modally assigned latent class membership in the three domains as indicators in a further round of latent class analysis. But this strategy proved unhelpful as we ran out of degrees of freedom before achieving a satisfactory fit with the data.

[9] This contingency table is available upon request.

[10] There is also some indication that the strongest association occurs between consumption in theatre, dance and cinema and in the visual arts. This emerges from the comparison of models 5, 6 and 7 in Table 8.2 with model 8. By removing the TV term from model 8 and thus turning it into model 6, G^2 is increased by 341.5 for 2 degrees of freedom. This is a much bigger increase in deviance per degree of freedom than that which is found if model 8 is compared with either model 5 or model 7.

Table 8.2 *Goodness-of-fit statistics of loglinear models as applied to a three-way contingency table cross-classifying cultural participation in (1) music, (2) theatre, dance and cinema, and (3) the visual arts*

model	G^2	df	p
1. M,T,V	1225.94	12	0.000
2. MT,V	883.53	10	0.000
3. M,TV	673.57	10	0.000
4. MV,T	691.77	8	0.000
5. MV,TV	139.40	6	0.000
6. MT,MV	349.36	6	0.000
7. MT,TV	331.16	8	0.000
8. MV,TV,MT	7.86	4	0.097

Note: M: music, T: theatre, dance and cinema, V: visual arts.

such cross-domain association, a fairly simple typology of levels of overall cultural consumption does then suggest itself of the lines that we set out in Table 8.3.

At level 1, the lowest level, are those individuals who are univores in the domains of music and theatre and inactives in the visual arts. That is to say, the cultural consumption of these men and women, who account for around two-fifths of our total sample, tends to be limited to listening to pop and rock music and going to the cinema. At level 2 are then those individuals, just over one-fifth of the sample, who, while having somewhat higher levels of consumption than those at level 1, are still not – fully – omnivorous in any of the three domains covered. As can be seen, they divide almost equally into those who are univores in music and theatre but paucivores in the visual arts and those who are omnivore-listeners in music but univores in theatre and either inactives or paucivores in the visual arts. At level 3 come those individuals, approaching a third of the total sample, who are omnivores in one or other of our three domains. The majority turn out in fact to be omnivores in theatre – in which domain omnivorousness is most common – while at the same time, it may be noted, being often only univores in music. And finally at level 4, the highest level of consumption, we have those individuals, just a tenth of the sample, who are omnivores in two or, very exceptionally, in all three domains.

Table 8.3 *Distribution of respondents across levels of cultural participation over all three domains*

overall level of participation	music	theatre	visual arts	%	%
	types of consumers in				
1 lowest level	U	U	I	39.0	39.0
2 Omnivore in no domain	U	U	P	11.1	22.0
	OL	U	I	5.8	
	OL	U	P	5.1	
3 Omnivore in one domain	OL	O	P	4.7	29.0
	OL	U	O	0.4	
	O	U	P	1.4	
	OL	O	I	2.2	
	U	O	P	9.8	
	U	U	O	0.3	
	O	U	I	0.9	
	U	O	I	9.2	
4 Omnivore in two or three domains	O	O	P	5.1	10.0
	OL	O	O	0.9	
	O	U	O	0.1	
	U	O	O	1.1	
	O	O	I	0.9	
	O	O	O	1.9	

Note: Music: O = Omnivore, OL = Omnivore-listener, U = Univore; Theatre, dance & cinema: O = Omnivore, U = Univore; Visual arts: O = Omnivore, P = Paucivore, I = Inactive.

Half, it can be seen, are omnivores in music and in theatre while being paucivores in the visual arts.

Already from these results we can then make some observations regarding the omnivore–univore argument at the level of cross-domain cultural consumption. On the one hand, the applicability of this argument is supported by the fact that univorous and omnivorous patterns of consumption do show some degree of persistence from one domain to another. This effect is most apparent with the two-fifths of our sample who are placed at level 1 – at all events if inactivity in the visual arts can be treated as in some sense equivalent to univorousness in music and theatre. But, on the other hand, individuals at level 2 are not readily seen as either univores or omnivores; and, further, cross-domain omnivorousness – or omnivorousness as general cultural voracity – is not all that marked. Nearly two-fifths of the sample, that is, those individuals placed at levels 3 or 4, are omnivores in at least one domain, yet of these only a quarter are omnivores in at least two domains, that is, are placed at level 4 rather than level 3, and with less than 5% being omnivores in all three domains. At this stage, therefore, perhaps the most we can conclude is that while the omnivore–univore argument would still appear more apt to the social reality that we are examining than either the homology or individualisation arguments, a cross-domain approach confirms our previous view that patterns of cultural consumption in present-day societies will tend to be rather too complex to be adequately captured in omnivore–univore terms alone.

We now move on to the analysis of the social correlates of cultural consumption at the four cross-domain levels that we have identified.

8.3 Cross-domain cultural consumption by class and status

To repeat, our findings on cultural consumption in music, theatre and the visual arts considered separately show that the stratification of this consumption does not occur on elite–mass lines but does, at least in some large part, follow the omnivore–univore distinction. It is then of interest to ask whether, insofar as univorous and omnivorous tendencies are also revealed in cross-domain cultural consumption, they are stratified in a similar way.

In Table 8.4 we show the distribution of respondents to the Arts in England survey by their level of cross-domain cultural consumption within each of the seven classes of the UK National Statistics Socio-Economic Classification.[11] As can be seen, class differences are quite marked and rather clearly patterned. The proportion of respondents at level 1 – i.e. those whose cultural consumption tends to be limited to listening to pop and rock music and going to the cinema – increases steadily from around a sixth in Class 1 to more than three-fifths in Class 7. Conversely, the proportion of respondents at level 3, who are omnivores in one of the domains we consider, steadily decreases across

---

[11] This classification can be regarded as a new, updated version of the Goldthorpe class schema (see Rose *et al.*, 2005; Office for National Statistics, 2005). The seven 'analytical' classes of NS-SEC here used correspond fairly closely to those of the seven-class version of the original schema.

Table 8.4 *Distribution of respondents by level of cross-domain cultural participation within social class*

	level of cultural consumption			
	1	2	3	4
1 Higher managers and professionals	16.8	22.8	40.2	20.3
2 Lower managers and professionals	24.1	20.9	37.8	17.1
3 Intermediate employees	38.7	22.0	32.4	7.0
4 Small employers and own-account workers	44.7	23.3	22.6	9.5
5 Lower supervisors and technicians	49.3	25.6	22.6	2.5
6 Semi-routine workers	55.5	19.5	21.5	3.6
7 Routine workers	61.3	23.1	13.3	2.3

the classes, as too, with only minor irregularities, does the proportion at level 4, who are omnivores in two or in all three domains. In fact, if we consider respondents at levels 3 and 4 together, we find essentially the reverse situation to that we noted with level 1 respondents. Over three-fifths of members of Class 1 are at level 3 or 4 – or, in other words, display some form of omnivorousness – while this is the case with less than a sixth of members of Class 7.

Turning to stratification by status, we show in the graphical form of Figure 8.1 data analogous to those of Table 8.4 but with consumption level now being related to our status scale, as described in Chapter 2. Here again fairly systematic stratification is in evidence. It can be seen that although respondents at level 2 are fairly evenly distributed by status (as indeed by class, as Table 8.4 reveals), the proportion at level 1 decreases more or less linearly as status rises, while the reverse is the case with the proportion at level 3, and the proportion at level 4 increases with status more steeply in something approximating a curvilinear fashion. More detailed examination of these data reveals that if we consider the four major bands of our status scale (see Chapter 2, pp. 28–56 above), only one of the seven groups in the highest band has more than 25% of its members at level 1 – and that the five highest-ranking groups have in fact more members at level 4 than at level 1. In contrast, in the two lower bands of the scale only one of the thirteen groups covered has clearly below half of its members at level 1 and only three show more than 5% at level 4.[12]

[12] The data of Figure 8.1 in tabular form are available from the authors on request.

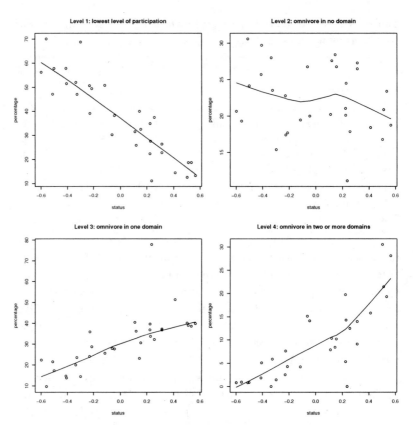

Fig. 8.1 Bivariate association between social status and level of cross-domain cultural participation

We can therefore conclude that univorous and omnivorous tendencies in cross-domain cultural consumption are socially stratified in essentially the same ways as we have found in consumption within particular domains. Members of less advantaged classes and lower-ranking status groups are more likely to follow the highly restricted pattern of consumption represented by level 1; and members of more advantaged classes and higher-ranking status groups are more likely to show omnivorousness at least in one domain as represented by consumption at levels 3 and 4. Indeed, a comparison of the results set out above with those reported in our previous papers on particular domains would suggest that the stratification of cultural consumption is in fact more marked and more regular when a cross-domain view is taken. However, in order to consider this possibility further and also in order to address the major issue of the relative importance of class and status as the bases of the stratification in question, we need to move on to analyses of a more sophisticated kind.

8.4 Cross-domain cultural consumption: multivariate analyses

As well as providing data on individuals' participation in a wide range of cultural activities and also information that allows for the construction of the stratification variables used in the previous section, the Arts in England Survey is also well suited to our purposes in that it further contains information on respondents' education and income and on a number of their socio-demographic characteristics. In proceeding now to a multivariate analysis, we take the four levels of cross-domain cultural consumption that we have distinguished as the dependent variable in a multinomial logistic regression model, and focus our explanatory interest on the class and status variables that we have already introduced, supplemented by those of respondents' educational qualifications and personal income. We also include socio-demographic variables in the model, which, though of some interest in themselves, are intended here primarily to serve as controls.[13]

In Table 8.5 we show the results we obtain from our model. In the first three columns of the table these results refer to effects on the chances (log odds) of individuals being found at each of the three higher levels of cultural consumption rather than at level 1 – i.e. that in which such consumption tends to be limited to pop and rock music and cinema-going; and then in the remaining three columns they refer, respectively, to effects on the chances of individuals being found at levels 3 and 4 rather than at level 2 and at level 4 rather than at level 3.

As regards the socio-demographic variables that we include, age has the most consistently significant effects. Older people are more likely to be found at higher levels of consumption than are younger people, except for a reverse tendency in the case of being at level 3 rather than at level 2. From the data we have available, we cannot tell whether or how far this generally positive effect of age on cultural consumption

---

[13] Descriptive statistics of all the variables involved in the analysis are given in our earlier papers and are also available from the authors on request.

should be interpreted as one of period, of birth cohort or of life-cycle stage. But it can also be seen from Table 8.5 that another life-cycle indicator – having a child below the age of four – does often have a significantly negative effect on cultural consumption: that is, as regards the chances of being found at levels 3 or 4 rather than at level 1 or at level 2. Finally, there is a gender effect in that women are also more likely to be at levels 3 and 4 rather at level 1 or 2, although men are more likely to be at level 2 than at level 1. These results are in fact broadly in line with those that we have reported in our studies of particular domains. However, it may also be noted that while in our earlier analyses living outside London did in some instances prove to have a negative effect on cultural consumption, most strongly in the visual arts, regional effects on cross-domain consumption can be effectively discounted.

Turning now to the stratification variables included in the analysis, we can first of all note further confirmation of our Weberian expectation that it is status rather than class that underlies the stratification of cultural consumption. Despite the clear bivariate association between class and level of cross-domain consumption that is shown up in Table 8.4, it can be seen from Table 8.5 that once status is included in the analysis, class effects become largely non-significant. In contrast, level of cultural consumption is found to increase significantly with status in all contrasts except that between levels 2 and 3. In particular, status has strong effects on the relative chances of individuals being found at level 4 – that is, on their chances of being omnivores in at least two of the three domains we consider. In the extreme contrast, an increase of one standard deviation in status turns out to raise the odds of being at level 4 rather than at level 1 by around 84%.[14] We could in fact say that the dominance of status over class as shown in Table 8.5 is yet clearer than when we examine consumption in our three domains separately (cf. the corresponding tables in Chan and Goldthorpe, 2005, 2007d,e), and the importance is thus further underlined of treating class and status as qualitatively differing forms of stratification rather than inadvertently blurring the distinction between them or seeking, as in the manner of Bourdieu, to transcend it.

---

[14] With the standard deviation of our status score being 0.365, we have
$$e^{(0.365 \times 1.675)} - 1 = 0.84.$$

Table 8.5 *Multinomial logit model: level of cultural participation as the dependent variable*

	2 vs. 1		3 vs. 1		4 vs. 1		3 vs. 2		4 vs. 2		4 vs. 3	
	$\hat{\beta}$	s.e.	$\hat{\beta}$	s.e.	$\hat{\beta}$	s.e.	$\hat{\beta}$	s.e.	$\hat{\beta}$	s.e.	$\hat{\beta}$	s.e.
female[a]	-0.253*	0.110	0.487**	0.109	0.497**	0.154	0.741**	0.116	0.751**	0.156	0.010	0.146
married[b]	0.007	0.133	0.212	0.130	-0.196	0.192	0.205	0.143	-0.203	0.196	-0.408*	0.185
sep/div/wid	-0.004	0.164	0.122	0.162	0.150	0.232	0.126	0.179	0.154	0.238	0.028	0.226
age	0.031**	0.005	0.018**	0.005	0.054**	0.007	-0.013*	0.005	0.023**	0.007	0.036**	0.007
child (0–4)[c]	0.002	0.131	-0.546**	0.129	-0.661**	0.223	-0.548**	0.142	-0.663**	0.227	-0.115	0.220
child (5–10)	0.070	0.123	0.166	0.114	-0.107	0.192	0.096	0.127	-0.177	0.197	-0.274	0.186
child (11–15)	-0.101	0.129	-0.016	0.120	-0.069	0.196	0.084	0.136	0.032	0.202	-0.052	0.190
The North[d]	-0.191	0.155	-0.373*	0.149	-0.280	0.211	-0.181	0.156	-0.089	0.211	0.093	0.199
Midlands	-0.219	0.155	-0.288	0.148	-0.412	0.211	-0.069	0.155	-0.193	0.211	-0.124	0.197
South East	-0.241	0.178	-0.025	0.164	0.108	0.224	0.216	0.174	0.349	0.226	0.133	0.205
South West	0.106	0.186	-0.159	0.183	-0.182	0.266	-0.265	0.189	-0.288	0.264	-0.023	0.251
income	0.008	0.006	0.029**	0.006	0.029**	0.008	0.021**	0.006	0.021**	0.007	-0.000	0.007
CSE/others[e]	0.439**	0.150	0.325*	0.164	1.005**	0.325	-0.114	0.186	0.566	0.335	0.680*	0.338
O-levels	0.563**	0.139	0.848**	0.141	1.326**	0.283	0.286	0.161	0.764**	0.291	0.478	0.290
A-levels	0.806**	0.174	1.388**	0.166	2.069**	0.306	0.582**	0.185	1.263**	0.314	0.680*	0.306

	coef	SE	coef	SE	coef	SE	coef	SE	coef	SE	coef	SE
sub-degree	0.877**	0.199	1.135**	0.192	2.427**	0.308	0.258	0.205	1.550**	0.313	1.292**	0.305
degree	1.384**	0.196	1.670**	0.190	3.231**	0.303	0.286	0.192	1.847**	0.301	1.561**	0.294
class 2[f]	0.032	0.190	0.078	0.173	0.152	0.209	0.046	0.162	0.120	0.195	0.074	0.174
class 3	0.010	0.222	−0.141	0.204	−0.374	0.284	−0.151	0.206	−0.384	0.281	−0.233	0.261
class 4	0.035	0.265	−0.210	0.255	0.300	0.335	−0.244	0.261	0.266	0.332	0.510	0.316
class 5	0.309	0.273	0.067	0.262	−0.292	0.457	−0.242	0.272	−0.601	0.457	−0.359	0.445
class 6	0.026	0.257	−0.150	0.241	−0.168	0.363	−0.176	0.251	−0.194	0.364	−0.018	0.347
class 7	0.198	0.278	−0.446	0.276	−0.160	0.451	−0.644*	0.288	−0.358	0.453	0.286	0.446
status	0.800**	0.223	0.849**	0.213	1.675**	0.318	0.049	0.228	0.876**	0.321	0.827**	0.306
constant	−2.245**	0.369	−2.335**	0.355	−5.801**	0.529	−0.089	0.373	−3.555**	0.531	−3.466**	0.504

Note: $* p < 0.05$, $** p < 0.01$; [a] male is the reference category; [b] single is the reference category, sep/div/wid stands for separated, divorced or widowed; [c] no children is the reference category; [d] London is the reference category; [e] no qualifications is the reference category; [f] class 1 is the reference category.

The effect of education on cross-domain cultural consumption is also of evident importance. Having higher-level educational qualifications significantly increases individuals' chances of being found at consumption levels 2, 3 or 4 rather than at level 1, and at levels 3 and 4 rather than at level 2. In the extreme contrast, individuals with degree-level qualifications are around 25 times more likely ($e^{3.231} = 25.30$) to be found at level 4 rather than at level 1 than are individuals with no qualifications. However, it may also be noted that education – like status – does not have a significant effect on the chances of individuals being at level 3 rather than at level 2; and, further, that while status, as we have seen, has a strong effect on the chances of being at level 4 rather than at level 3, educational attainment is of clear importance in this regard only in the case of post-secondary qualifications.

Finally, income can also be seen to have a positive influence on cross-domain cultural consumption, although in rather specific ways: that is, in significantly increasing the chances of individuals being found at levels 3 or 4 rather than at level 1 or level 2, although not on their chances of being at level 2 rather than at level 1 or at level 4 rather than at level 3. The effects of income, where they do occur, would appear weaker than those of status or education: for example, an increase of one standard deviation in income raises the chances of an individual being at either level 3 or level 4 rather than at level 1 by about 37%.[15] None the less, the results shown in Table 8.5 still stand in some contrast to those of our domain-specific analyses where income appeared as clearly less important, having a positive effect on the chances of being an omnivore rather than a univore only in the case of theatre and not in those of music or the visual arts.[16]

In general, then, we might say that cross-domain cultural consumption is primarily stratified by status and education, with income in a secondary role. However, the findings of our multivariate analysis are perhaps of greatest value and interest not in what they tell us about the overall importance of status, education and income, but rather – following the different contrasts that are made in Table 8.5 – about the particular ways in which these variables are important to a greater or a lesser degree. For this information can provide us with at least

[15] With the standard deviation of income being 10.863, we have
$e^{(10.863 \times 0.029)} - 1 = 0.37$.

[16] Income did, however, also have a slight and just significant positive effect on the chances of being a paucivore in the visual arts rather than an inactive.

some clues as to what may be the social processes or mechanisms that underlie the statistical results that we have obtained.

8.5 Theoretical considerations

We have shown that cross-domain cultural consumption in its pattern and its stratification tends broadly, though not in all respects, to follow the omnivore–univore lines that we have earlier found in consumption within particular domains. This similarity is most apparent in the case of those individuals who are placed at level 1 in our typology of cross-domain consumption in which univorousness in music and theatre go together with inactivity in the visual arts. However, the cultural consumption of individuals at level 2 seems not to fit well with an omnivore–univore dichotomy; and, further, the tendency for omnivorousness to extend across domains, though present, is not especially strong. As we have noted, of those respondents, two-fifths of the total, who are omnivores in at least one of the three domains we consider, only a quarter (or a tenth of the sample as a whole) are omnivores in two or all three domains – that is to say, are placed at level 4 in our typology rather than at level 3.

These results would thus underline a point that we have already made in our studies of particular domains: that in seeking a better understanding of patterns of cultural consumption and their stratification in modern societies, we need to recognise a situation of greater complexity than has often been supposed. The omnivore–univore argument has, at all events, the merit of challenging the rather simplistic 'matching' of social stratification and level and style of cultural consumption that is essential to versions of the homology argument. And, in so doing, it also calls into question, if more implicitly than explicitly, the 'over-socialised' conception of the actor on which the latter tend to rely – most extremely in Bourdieusian appeals to the exigencies of the *habitus* (cf. Coulangeon, 2003) – without making the unwarranted shift to the other extreme of accepting the apparently unconstrained cultural choices, and ones reflecting entirely personal rather than any socially grounded motivations, that are integral to versions of the individualisation argument.

What would then seem the most promising way to move ahead theoretically is to try to provide an explanation for the broadly, if qualified, omnivore–univore pattern of cross-domain cultural consumption we have documented that derives from a conception of actors as subject to differing kinds and degrees of constraint yet as still possessing degrees of freedom within which some range of choice is possible. In what follows, we aim to make a start in this direction. We do not claim to do more than to set out the elements of an explanation of the kind in question; but, we hope, we do so in a way that will encourage both empirical testing and further theoretical development.

Cultural consumption, as a form of social action, can be treated as the outcome of individuals' pursuing certain of their ends as best they can with the means available to them. As regards means, we would think primarily in terms of the extent of individuals' economic and cultural resources and in turn of the constraints that they face and the capacities that they can exploit. On the basis of the data used in the analyses that we have presented, we can take economic resources as being proxied by income; and we can take cultural resources as being proxied by education – in fact, in two different ways: first, in respect of individuals' basic information-processing capacity that has been emphasised by proponents of 'empirical aesthetics' as a key factor in cultural consumption (Moles, 1971; Berlyne, 1974); and second, in respect of individuals' degree of familiarity with and knowledge of different cultural forms and the modes of their appreciation.[17]

As regards the ends of cultural consumption, we would recognise that these are likely to be to an important degree *intrinsic*. That is to say, cultural consumption is a form of social action that can be readily engaged in 'for its own sake' – for the satisfactions that follow directly from the exercise of the resources and capacities for such consumption that individuals possess. However, our empirical findings clearly show that status – though not class – exerts a significant and often strong positive effect on level of cultural consumption over and above that of economic and also of cultural resources as indicated by income and education. This would therefore lead us to regard such

[17] For our present purposes, we need not enter into the issue of how far information-processing capacity should be regarded as innate or acquired, nor in turn into that of whether it is more likely to be a cause or consequence of educational attainment. We use the term 'cultural resources' rather than Bourdieu's 'cultural capital' to avoid any suggestion of commitment to his conceptualisation of 'forms of capital' or his theory of social reproduction (see further Goldthorpe, 2007a). A promising line of research into the effects of education in creating cultural resources is that which takes into account field, as well as level, of education (see e.g. van de Werfhorst and Kraaykamp, 2001).

consumption as being also undertaken out of concerns over status: that is to say, we would treat such concerns as a source of motivation for cultural consumption in addition to, or apart from, the intrinsic satisfactions that may be gained. While such motivation may focus on deliberate status enhancement or 'climbing', or on status demarcation with exclusionary intent, as emphasised by Bourdieu and his followers, we need not suppose that this is always or even typically the case.[18] The more extensive cultural consumption that would appear to follow from higher status is after all omnivorous rather than elitist in character. What is more generally involved, we would suggest, is a desire to express a lifestyle, associated with a particular status level, that seeks in some degree to give value to more than merely material consumption and preoccupations – and a desire that may then be to some extent reinforced by the normative expectations of 'significant others' in social networks of family, friends or colleagues at this same status level. As DiMaggio (1987) has observed, in modern societies shared cultural consumption is perhaps more important than shared material living standards in providing a basis for everyday social interaction and thus for a sense of 'belonging' in particular social circles (cf. also Chan and Goldthorpe, 2007c; López-Sintas and Katz-Gerro, 2005).

How, then, can such an approach be followed in seeking to account for the empirical regularities in cross-domain cultural consumption that we have demonstrated? We may begin with what we would see as the basic contrast that emerges from our types of cultural consumer: that between individuals at level 1 and those at levels 3 and 4; or, that is, between individuals whose consumption is essentially limited to pop and rock music and the cinema and those who are omnivorous in at least one cultural domain. As we have already noted, the relevant contrasts in Table 8.5 show that higher income, higher education and higher status *all* make independent contributions to increasing the chances of individuals being at level 3 or level 4 rather that at

[18] We recognise that some interpreters of Bourdieu, for example Holt (1997), would take him to argue that what are in effect exclusionary consumption practices come about not through deliberately strategic manoeuvering by individuals but simply through their disinterested pursuit of their tastes. However, others, for example Jenkins (2002, p. 87), point to evident confusion and contradiction in Bourdieu on this issue. Jenkins notes that Bourdieu readily refers to actors' interests, in regard among other things to status, and then observes that 'it is very difficult to imagine how an "interest" can be anything other than something which actors *consciously* pursue'.

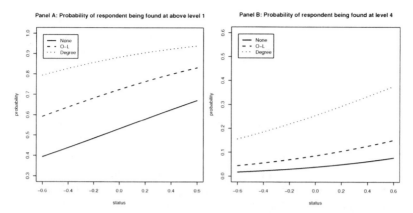

Fig. 8.2 Probability of a hypothetical respondent being found at above level 1 (Panel A) and at level 4 (Panel B) by educational qualifications and status
Note: Other covariates fixed as follows: Woman graduate, aged forty, living in London, with no children, and earning £25,000 p.a.

level 1. Or, in terms of the preceding paragraphs, we could then say that individuals' cultural consumption tends to increase – to become less univorous and more omnivorous – as greater economic and cultural resources reduce constraints on, and increase capacities for, such consumption, and as status provides motivation to consume at a higher level.

It should though be added here that it is tertiary education that appears as the strongest prophylactic against low cultural consumption. In other words, insofar as individuals have the capacities for cultural consumption that such education can be taken to indicate, there is a rather strong propensity for them to put these capacities to more than minimal use, and regardless of other factors. To illustrate, we show in Panel A of Figure 8.2 the predicted probabilities, under our logistic regression model, of being above level 1 for a hypothetical person, defined as a woman aged 40 with no children, living in London and earning £25,000 p.a. (as of 2001), as we vary her education and her status. As can be seen, if we assume that this woman has a degree, then while her probability of having a level of cultural consumption above the minimum in our typology does still increase with her status, this probability is in fact already quite high, at over 80%, even if she ranks low on our status scale.

Turning next to individuals at level 2, the situation here is evidently less straightforward. These are men and women whose cultural consumption appears to be not well captured by the omnivore–univore distinction. Although clearly more than univores (as earlier noted, they are most often omnivore-listeners to music and/or paucivores in the visual arts), they are still less than fully omnivorous in any of the three domains we consider. We can, however, here usefully return to certain more detailed points emerging from the results of Table 8.5. It may be recalled that while the chances of individuals being found at level 2 rather than at level 1 increase with education and status but not with income, just the reverse pattern of effects operates on their chances being found at level 3 rather than at level 2: that is, these chances increase with income but not with either education or status.

Following the theoretical approach that we have outlined, we are then led to regard individuals at level 2 as having a pattern of cultural consumption that is inferior to what it would otherwise be on account primarily of a lack of economic resources and of resulting constraints – maybe ones following from various contingent and relatively short-term changes in their life situations. These individuals are comparable to those at level 3 in their capacities for cultural consumption deriving from their cultural resources and also in their status motivation to engage in such consumption; but in their economic resources they are more comparable to individuals at level 1.[19] In other words, men and women at level 2 could be seen as being *potential* consumers at level 3, that is, as being potentially omnivorous in one domain or another, should some improvement in their economic circumstances allow, just as, conversely, men and women at level 3 could 'fall' to level 2 should their economic circumstances for some reason deteriorate. The – testable – prediction thus follows that mobility over time between levels 2 and 3 should be relatively high. If viewed in this perspective, the level 2 pattern of consumption, it should then be noted, is no longer so anomalous in regard to the omnivore–univore argument as it might initially appear: it becomes in fact a quite conceivable pattern of consumption within the context of this argument.

---

[19] In the level 3 versus level 2 contrast, having children under age 5 also has a significant negative effect on cultural consumption, as it does in several other contrasts.

Finally, we come to individuals at level 4 and, thus, to the question of propensities for 'universal' omnivorousness which, as we have shown, although present, are not especially strong. How are we to explain why only a quite small minority of the individuals we study are omnivorous in more than one cultural domain? To begin with in this regard, it would seem necessary to recognise that some limits to cross-domain omnivorousness must be expected to result from purely personal tastes and characteristics, including perhaps physical ones. Thus, some people are simply 'not musical' (e.g. are tone deaf) or lack visual sense (e.g. are colour blind). However, following the approach that we have outlined, we may take matters somewhat further. In this regard, we would focus on the last column of Table 8.5, where the chances of being at level 4 are contrasted with those of being at level 3. What is here shown is a pattern of effects interestingly different from that found in other contrasts. While status is again important, income is in this case non-significant and, further, education effects are only irregularly significant up to the tertiary level when, however, they too become strong.

What we would therefore suggest is, first of all, that the only rather weak tendency for omnivorousness in one cultural domain to be associated with omnivorousness in another is not primarily the result of constraints, as might prima facie be thought likely. Although income certainly counts in increasing the chances of individuals being omnivorous in one domain – that is, being at level 3 rather than at levels 1 or 2 of our typology – economic constraints, at least as proxied by income, do not appear to affect the chances of individuals being at level 4 rather than at level 3. It is possible that time constraints may play a larger part in restricting omnivorousness. But while we cannot measure such constraints directly, it is relevant to note that having children under age 5, which exerts a negative effect on cultural consumption in most other contrasts, is also, like income, non-significant as regards the chances of being found at level 4 rather than at level 3.[20] Of greater importance in this case, we would therefore argue,

[20] It should also be kept in mind in this regard that our requirements for omnivorousness in a particular domain are not all that demanding: that is, individuals are counted as consuming a particular cultural form if they have done so once in the last twelve months (or once in the last four weeks in the case of listening to different kinds of music via media).

are capacities and motivation. A tendency for cross-domain omnivo-rousness would appear to be most strongly promoted when a relatively high level of cultural resources and thus capacity for cultural consump-tion, as indicated by tertiary education, comes together with a relatively high level of status and thus – following our theoretical expectations – an associated lifestyle, the expression of which provides additional motivation for such consumption.

At least to illustrate the argument, we may revert to our hypothetical woman, as previously defined, and show, in Panel B of Figure 8.2, the predicted probabilities under our regression model of her being found at level 4 when again we vary her education and status. As can be seen, if we suppose that she has no or only secondary educational qualifications, her probability of being at level 4 rises only rather slowly with her status. But if we suppose that she has a degree then the increase with status is clearly more marked, reaching around 35% at the highest status levels.[21] In considering individuals' chances of being found at above level 1, we concluded that a powerful effect was exerted by a high level of cultural resources alone; having a capacity for consumption above the minimal level would appear almost sufficient in itself to ensure that such consumption in fact occurs. However, as regards the chances of being found at level 4, the strongest effect results from a high level of cultural resources *coexisting with* high status; cross-domain omnivorousness seems most likely where status provides extra motivation, over and above intrinsic satisfaction, for the use of such resources.

8.6 Conclusions

In this chapter we have considered the social stratification of cultural consumption across three different domains: music, theatre, dance and cinema, and the visual arts. In earlier work focusing on each of these domains separately, we were able to show that, contrary to the individualisation argument, consumption was in fact strongly patterned and socially stratified; and further that, contrary to the

---

[21] As noted only 10% of the total sample are at level 4. The suggestion of a status–education interaction effect in Figure 8.2 may be found surprising in view of the fact that no such interaction term is included in our logistic regression model. However, although log-odds are linear in the predictor, probabilities are not.

homology argument, both its pattern and stratification were on – broadly – 'omnivore–univore' rather than 'elite–mass' lines. The central question from which our present analyses start out is therefore that of whether, or how far, the omnivore–univore argument is still supported if a cross-domain approach is taken.

As regards the pattern of cross-domain cultural consumption, our main finding is that some tendency does exist for omnivorous or univorous consumption to be associated from one cultural domain to another, which in turn allows us to construct a fairly straightforward fourfold typology of cross-domain consumers. At the same time, though, we recognise that univorousness, or perhaps cultural inactivity, is more likely to be associated across domains than is omnivorousness. Two-fifths of our national sample are at level 1 in our typology – that is, are univores in music and in theatre while being inactive in the visual arts. But, as well as more than a fifth being at level 2, and thus not readily characterised as omnivores or univores, only one tenth are at level 4, that is, are omnivores in two or three domains, despite almost a third of the sample being at level 3 or, that is, omnivores in one domain.

As regards the stratification of cross-domain cultural consumption on the pattern represented by our typology, we find that this is also broadly in line with the expectations of the omnivore–univore argument, and that the degree of stratification is, if anything, rather more marked than within individual domains. Omnivorous tendencies are again positively associated with status – rather than with class, following our own Weberian expectations; educational attainment is again of fairly general importance in promoting omnivorousness – although perhaps not, or not only, as a stratification variable; and the effects of income on level of cultural consumption, if more specific than those of status and education, are still more often significant than when domains are considered singly. However, while these results are of evident interest, we would still wish to return to a point that we have also emphasised in the light of our previous analyses: that is, that while cultural consumption is without question socially stratified, this stratification is of a less clear and straightforward kind than seems often to have been supposed in earlier literature, and especially in that inspired by versions of the homology argument.

As well, then, as regarding the omnivore–univore argument as being on empirical grounds generally more apt than its rivals to the understanding of the pattern and stratification of cultural consumption in contemporary societies, we would further regard it as at least implicitly suggestive of a more appropriate theoretical orientation. While rejecting the idea of 'high' and 'low' forms of cultural consumption being maintained in a direct homologous relationship with the stratification order, through distinctive and exigent forms of socialisation, it also rejects the idea of cultural consumption as now having become quite disassociated from any social structural grounding that it may once have possessed. Or, one could say, the omnivore–univore argument points to the importance of avoiding the error of – in Warde's nice phrase (1997, p. 8) – a too dramatic shift of emphasis 'from *habitus* to freedom'.

To end with, we have therefore sought to outline a theoretical approach to the explanation of empirical findings of the kind that we have presented that pursues this insight. We treat cultural consumption as a form of social action, and actors as being capable in this, as in other respects, of making meaningful choices, although subject always of course to constraints. As regards cultural consumption, we see constraints and likewise individual capacities as being determined primarily by economic and cultural resources, while status is viewed as a key source of motivation. As well as being engaged in for its intrinsic rewards – for its own sake – cultural consumption is a way of expressing an aspect of a valued lifestyle associated with a particular status level and also thus a potential source of normative approval and acceptance on the part of others at this level. Following this approach, and with reference to our empirical findings, we can then say that in general individuals' cultural consumption increases – that, in terms of our typology, they become less univorous and more omnivorous – as greater economic and cultural resources reduce constraints on and increase capacities for such consumption and as higher status provides a greater motivation to consume. Moreover, we can at the same time suggest explanations for the seeming deviations from the omnivore–univore patterns of cultural consumption that we have revealed. Thus, individuals at level 2 in our typology can be understood as being potential omnivores in at least one domain who are, however, restricted in their cultural consumption by economic constraints though perhaps only for the time being. In contrast, the limited number of individuals at level 4 rather than at level 3 – i.e. the limited number of those omnivorous not just in one but in two or more domains – would appear not to result from economic constraints at least, but rather from the fact that cross-domain omnivorousness is promoted only when a high level of cultural resources and of status-linked motivation for such consumption coincide.

The theoretical approach that we propose is, we would repeat, here presented in a still very elementary fashion. It is, though, we would hope, capable of being applied in relation to other empirical results on the stratification of cultural consumption with both critique and, if thought appropriate, further development in mind.

9 | Conclusion

TAK WING CHAN

In this concluding chapter, I shall draw on the results reported in the six national chapters and ask if they collectively provide some coherent answers to the research questions set out in Chapter 1. Let me begin by restating the nature of our comparative enterprise. Unlike cross-national comparative research on social mobility, educational inequality, or other more established topics, social stratification of cultural consumption is still a relatively underdeveloped field. This means that the data sets that are available to us, and measures of cultural consumption contained therein, are not as standardised as we would have liked. As a result, we could not have carried out exactly the same analysis in all six nations. Instead, we have sought to achieve cross-national comparability by addressing the same set of research questions, and to do so within a shared conceptual framework.

We have two main goals. Our first goal is to further our knowledge of the social stratification of cultural consumption in contemporary societies. In particular, we wish to evaluate three competing sets of arguments which purport to describe how cultural consumption is, or is not, mapped onto the stratification order. Following Warde *et al.* (2000), we have labelled these as 'homology' arguments, 'individualisation' arguments and 'omnivore–univore' arguments respectively. Our second goal is to bring cultural consumption research closer to mainstream stratification research. This means specifying more carefully the manner in which cultural consumption is stratified. In this regard, we are especially interested in exploring the relevance of Max Weber's distinction between social class and social status. Our expectation is that cultural consumption, as an aspect of lifestyle, would be stratified primarily by social status rather than by social class. More generally, though, our objective is to seek a better understanding of how inequalities in cultural consumption arise and how they are sustained in contemporary societies. So how far have we met our objectives? What have we learned from this comparative study?

9.1 The three arguments evaluated

9.1.1 *Individualisation arguments*

Of the three arguments outlined in Chapter 1, individualisation arguments are least supported by empirical evidence. In four of our six countries, namely Chile, England, France and the US, we have carried out latent class analysis, or cognate data reduction techniques such as multiple correspondence analysis and cluster analysis, in order to identify types of cultural consumer.[1] In each of these cases, far from there being a myriad of styles of cultural consumption, as implied by individualisation arguments, we have observed a few well-defined types of cultural consumer instead. In other words, cultural consumption is still very patterned in these four countries.

As for Hungary and the Netherlands, it turns out that the indicators of cultural consumption that are available do not lend themselves to latent class analysis.[2] As a result, our Hungarian and Dutch colleagues have resorted to more direct classification procedures that are not based on any statistical model. However, when regression analyses are carried out, irrespective of whether it is individual cultural genre or latent class membership that serves as the dependent variable, it is clear that, in all six countries, cultural consumption is differentiated by gender, age and other socio-demographic variables, *and* stratified by education, income and social status. Many of these statistical associations are quite substantial in magnitude. Overall, then, our results are incongruent with the views, articulated by Beck (1992), Giddens (1991), Bauman (1988) and others, that cultural consumption has lost its moorings in the social structure. On the contrary, cultural consumption in contemporary societies remains socially

[1] In the case of England, results of latent class analysis that are referred to in Chapter 8 were first reported in previously published papers (see Chan and Goldthorpe, 2005, 2007d,e).
[2] In the Dutch case, only four indicators are available. In the Hungarian case, there are five indicators. But it would take a five latent class model to achieve a good fit with the data. So no effective data reduction could be achieved by latent class models. See note 4 of Chapter 6.

structured and stratified along lines that are mostly expected if not fully understood.

9.1.2 Homology arguments

As for homology arguments which postulate a close, one-to-one mapping between the cultural hierarchy and the social hierarchy (Gans, 1999; Bourdieu, 1984), our results are somewhat mixed but on the whole negative. In the four countries where latent class or cluster analysis has been carried out, there is no evidence that a cultural elite exists. That is, there is no sizeable social group which would consume highbrow culture while shunning popular culture.[3] Instead, the general pattern is that those who consume highbrow culture also consume popular culture. In some instances, they are, in fact, even *more* avid consumers of popular culture than those who do not consume highbrow culture. Furthermore, while the consumption of highbrow culture is more common among the socially advantaged, it should be stressed that a non-negligible minority, indeed sometimes a large minority, of the most advantaged groups do *not* consume highbrow culture.

In the two countries where typologies of cultural consumer are derived by 'direct' classification, cultural elites can indeed be found. In the case of Hungary, Erzsébet Bukodi reports that about 10% of her sample are cultural exclusives. But she also stresses that 'this cultural elite could not . . . be regarded as a social elite, as homology arguments would require'. Compared with cultural omnivores, the exclusives *cannot* claim any superiority in terms of education, social status or income. Indeed, even though the exclusives tend to be better educated than the univores, the former do *not* have higher status or income than the latter. This leads Bukodi to speculate that the 'exclusives represent . . . the remains of the "intelligentsia" of the communist era, who seek still to maintain the pattern of high cultural consumption into which they were socialised, even though in the new Hungary they no longer enjoy particularly privileged economic or status positions'. Clearly, then, the cultural exclusives are very far from being the 'dominant class' in Hungary.

---

[3] There is no denying that there are individuals who restrict their cultural consumption to highbrow genres only. But they typically amount to no more than 2 or 3% of the population and thus are not readily identifiable in sample surveys.

In the case of the Netherlands, Gerbert Kraaykamp, Koen van Eijck and Wout Ultee report four types of cultural consumers, which they label as highbrows (47% of the sample), omnivores (31%), univores (5%) and inactives (18%) respectively. As almost half of their sample are highbrow-only consumers, it must be said that the size of the Dutch cultural elite is very large (some might say implausibly large). But it should be noted that this typology is constructed on the basis of three highbrow genres (i.e. classical concert, museum and theatre) and just one popular genre (i.e. pop concert). Thus, the extent of popular culture consumption in the Netherlands is probably underestimated. Indeed, the relative size of the four cultural types proves to be extremely sensitive to the choice of indicators. As Kraaykamp *et al.* acknowledge in note 12 of Chapter 7, had they made a distinction between 'popular' and 'serious' theatre, and treated the former as a popular genre, the relative size of the highbrows would drop from 47% to 16%, while that of the omnivores would rise from 31% to 58%. Finally, the highbrows in the Netherlands, as they are currently defined, are not better educated than the omnivores, nor could they claim to have higher social status. In fact, the highbrows tend to have *lower* household income than the omnivores (see Table 7.7). Thus, as with their Hungarian counterpart, the Dutch cultural elite cannot, in any case, be regarded as a social elite, and homology arguments have to be discounted in the Dutch context as well.

9.1.3 Omnivore–univore arguments

By comparison to homology or individualisation arguments, omnivore–univore arguments, with revisions, have received the strongest empirical support. Thus, in all six countries, more advantaged social groups, defined in terms of education, income, social class or social status, do tend to have a broader range in their cultural consumption, comprising not just highbrow genres, but also middlebrow and lowbrow genres. In contrast, the cultural consumption of less advantaged social groups tend to be restricted to middlebrow or lowbrow genres. This result can be seen directly from the solutions of latent class or cluster analysis (and accompanying regression analysis) that are reported for Chile, England, France and the US. But support for omnivore–univore arguments can also be seen indirectly in the other two cases. For example, in the Netherlands, Kraaykamp *et al.*

have carried out separate regressions for individual cultural activities, and they show that while there are clear educational and status (or class) gradients for consumption of highbrow genres, going to pop concerts is *not* a socially stratified activity (see Tables 7.2–7.5). In other words, whilst people with more education or higher social status are more likely to consume highbrow culture, they are just as likely as others to consume popular culture. This result is consistent with omnivore–univore arguments.

In a recent review article, Peterson (2005, p. 261) notes that omnivore–univore arguments have been tested in eleven countries which, with two exceptions, are all found in North America or Western Europe. Furthermore, the two exceptions, Australia and Israel, are culturally similar to North American or Western European countries. Thus, he calls for comparable research to be carried out in countries with different cultural traditions. Against the background of this call, the Chilean and Hungarian chapters of this collection are of particular interest.

For example, Florencia Torche points out that the income gini coefficient of Chile is 0.571, making it the 11th most unequal country in the world. The comparable figure for Hungary is much lower at 0.269 (United Nations, 2005, p. 270). But this still represents a sharp rise in economic inequality since 1989,[4] which is especially salient given the withdrawal of previously generous state subsidies of cultural activities under communism. Would cultural consumption take on an even greater symbolic significance when economic inequality is large or rising sharply? Would the relationship between culture and stratification assume a different form under these circumstances?

It turns out that, with minor revisions, omnivore–univore arguments apply to Chile and Hungary as much as they do to other countries. The revision required in the Hungarian case concerns the group of cultural exclusives, which I have already discussed in Section 9.1.2 above. As for Chile, the revision that is called for concerns a type of cultural consumer which we have labelled as paucivores. Paucivores and cultural inactives are two new groups that have been reported in this collection, to which we now turn.

---

[4] Kattuman and Redmond (2001), for example, report that the gini coefficient for Hungary was about 0.20 in the late 1980s.

It should be noted that while cultural omnivores are indeed found among socially advantaged groups, their counterparts among less advantaged groups are often cultural *inactives* rather than (or sometimes in addition to) cultural univores. Inactives are reported in all six countries, though their relative size is quite variable, depending on the cultural domain that is under consideration. For example, in England, inactives are found in the domain of visual arts (Chan and Goldthorpe, 2007e), but not in theatre, dance and cinema (Chan and Goldthorpe, 2005) or in music (Chan and Goldthorpe, 2007d). More importantly, the detection of inactives also depends on the indicators that are used in the analysis. For example, Alderson *et al.* point out in note 8 of Chapter 3 that the musical inactives of the US might 'have rich musical lives' outside the highbrow and middlebrow genres that they consider. Conversely, Goldthorpe and I point out that if we restrict our analysis of the consumption of performing arts to live events only (i.e. if cinema is dropped as an indicator), then our performing arts univores would become inactives (Chan and Goldthorpe, 2005). The upshot is that the distinction between inactives and univores is not a hard and fast one.

The other new character that we have introduced, in the context of Chile, England and the US, is the paucivores. Unlike omnivores who consume everything, or univores who consume just one cultural form, paucivores consume a limited range of cultural genres.[5] Paucivores have quite similar profiles in the three countries where they are found. Although they tend to have a slightly lower level of education than omnivores, they are often indistinguishable from the omnivores in terms of social status or income. But when compared to the inactives, paucivores generally have higher social status, income and educational attainment.

Obviously, the existence of this 'in-between' group speaks to the inadequacy, in specific cases, of maintaining a simple dichotomy between omnivores and univores. That this should be the case is perhaps unsurprising, as reality is rarely simple. However, it should be noted that the amount of *substantive detail* that is discernible in quantitative data with statistical models depends, often to a large extent, on sample size. With a sufficiently large sample, one could, in all

---

[5] I thank my colleague Paolo Crivelli, a scholar in ancient philosophy, for suggesting the term 'paucivore'.

likelihood, reject the more parsimonious two latent class model in favour of more complex ones. In other words, some nuance in making inferences from quantitative analyses is warranted.

More importantly, the existence of paucivores does not challenge the basic insight of omnivore–univore arguments, as originally formulated by Peterson and his colleagues (Peterson, 1992; Peterson and Simkus, 1992), namely that in contemporary societies those who are socially advantaged tend to be omnivorous rather than exclusive in their cultural consumption.

The paucivores of Chile deserve a little more discussion because they are comprised of two groups, which Torche calls movie-lovers (22% of the sample) and live-performance aficionados (13%). As members of these two groups consume both highbrow and lowbrow genres, they are neither cultural snobs nor cultural univores. But they also differ from the omnivores, partly because their cultural participation rates are somewhat lower across the board. But more importantly, they have quite specific 'likes' and 'dislikes' (cf. Bryson, 1996). The probability of having been to the cinema in the past 12 months is one for movie-lovers, but zero for live-performance aficionados. At the same time, live-performance aficionados are much more likely to attend dance and other live performances (see Table 5.4).

Torche then points to the intriguing ways in which omnivores, movie-lovers and live-performance aficionados relate to each other. Thus, while there is no statistically significant status difference between them, omnivores tend to be better educated than both movie-lovers and live-performance aficionados. Further, movie-lovers tend to have higher income than the other two groups. These results make a lot of sense in the Chilean context. Specifically, Torche argues that although cinema-going is a 'paradigmatic form of popular culture' in many countries, it is a mark of 'economic advantage' in Chile. So it is not surprising that movie-lovers tend to have higher income, but perhaps also slightly lower social status.[6] In contrast, many live performances in Chile are free or heavily subsidised by the state, and take place in local venues. Thus, live-performance aficionados might be adherents of persisting forms of folk-culture. These are fascinating national

---

[6] Note that in Table 5.6 the status parameter in the contrast between omnivore and movie-lovers is not statistically significant. However, when compared with the inactives, omnivores are of significantly higher social status, while movie-lovers are not.

details, but they do not undermine the basic tenet of omnivore–univore arguments.

9.2 The differentiation/stratification of cultural consumption

Having reviewed evidences on the general form of the relationship between the cultural and social hierarchies, I now turn to consider the way in which cultural consumption is differentiated and stratified.

9.2.1 Socio-demographic variables

In general, women are more active than men in cultural consumption. This can be seen in France, Hungary, the Netherlands and the US, where women have higher odds of being omnivores rather than inactives or univores. In Hungary and the Netherlands, women are more likely than men to be highbrows rather than omnivores, while in England, women are more likely than men to be found at higher levels of cross-domain cultural participation. The only exception here is Chile where there is very little gender difference in cultural participation.

Another finding which is consistent across nations is that geographical accessibility affects cultural consumption. In France, Hungary, the Netherlands and the US, residents of larger towns and cities are more likely to be culturally active. In France, large city dwellers also have higher odds of being omnivores rather than univores. In the Netherlands, living in more urbanised areas is associated with higher odds of being omnivores rather than univores or highbrows.[7]

The results concerning other socio-demographic variables are much less consistent across countries. For example, there are *net* regional differences in cultural consumption pattern in the US, but not in England.

As regards age, older people in England and the US generally report higher levels of cultural consumption. The opposite is true for the Netherlands, where it is younger people who are more likely to be omnivores rather than inactives or highbrows. The pattern is different again for Chile and Hungary, where age is associated with higher

[7] Urban/rural difference in cultural consumption cannot be tested in Chile because the analysis of that chapter is based on an urban sample. In the case of England, the data set analysed does not contain any variable measuring town size.

odds of being culturally inactive. Among the culturally active in Chile, there is no significant age difference between omnivores, movie-lovers and live-performance aficionados. But in Hungary, the odds of being a cultural exclusive rather than a univore or an omnivore increase with age. The pattern in France is most complex, where older respondents are more likely to be univores rather than non-listeners, and non-listeners rather than omnivores. Among listeners, older people are more likely to be highbrow omnivores rather than univores, and more likely to be univores rather than middlebrow omnivores. Finally, it would appear that it is the oldest *and* the youngest age groups that are more likely to be middlebrow omnivores rather than highbrow omnivores.[8]

Coming to marital status, in Chile, Hungary and the US, married or cohabiting respondents are culturally less active than singles. Among those who are culturally active in Hungary, those in marriage or partnership are more likely than singles to be exclusives rather than omnivores or univores. In England, however, marital status makes very little difference to cultural participation.[9]

Some effects of children on cultural consumption are found in England and the Netherlands, but not in Chile, Hungary or the US. However, it should be noted that often it is the presence of young children (say, those who are younger than four) which is associated with lower levels of cultural participation.[10] Since no distinction by child's age is made in the analyses for Chile and Hungary, perhaps some children effects are masked in those two countries.

On the whole, there is a good deal of cross-national variation in the associations between cultural consumption on the one hand and socio-demographic variables on the other. This is perhaps to be expected given various national factors and customs. For example, venues of cultural consumption are probably not child-friendly to the same extent in the six countries. The regions of the US are much larger entities than those of the UK, and so they are not strictly comparable. But for our

---

[8] As many of the contributors of this collection has remarked, the age differences in cultural consumption, whichever form they take, could be the results of (a combination of) age, period and cohort effects. Given the cross-sectional nature of our data, we are agnostic on this question.

[9] Marital status is not included as a predictor in the French chapter. All respondents in the Dutch sample are by design in partnership.

[10] In the Netherlands, children 4 to 12 years of age are also associated with a lower probability of attending concerts, popular or classical.

present purpose, the cross-national variability in the *differentiation* of cultural consumption serves to underline the cross-national similarity in its *social stratification*.

9.2.2 Social stratification variables

Let us begin with education. The association between education and cultural consumption is clear, strong and consistent across the six countries. Better educated respondents are much more likely to be omnivores rather than inactives or univores, and to be omnivores rather than paucivores. The substantive magnitude of these associations is often very large. Thus, for example, in the US, individuals with a post-graduate degree are six times more likely than non-graduates to be omnivores rather than inactives. In England, compared with individuals with no qualifications, those with university degrees are 25 times more likely to be at the highest rather than the lowest level of cross-domain cultural participation.

An association between income and cultural consumption is also observed in all six countries, with omnivores reporting higher levels of income than univores or inactives. There are some cross-national differences, but these concern quite specific contrasts between omnivores and paucivores. For example, in the US, omnivores and paucivores do not differ by income. But in Chile, as mentioned above, movie-lovers report *higher* income than omnivores.

Finally, omnivores invariably have higher social status than univores or inactives. In some cases, there are statistically significant status differences between other groups, e.g. between paucivores and inactives in the US, or between highbrow omnivores or middlebrow omnivores in France. But the key point here is that, with social status and other variables controlled for, there is no, or at best only very patchy, association between social class and cultural consumption. This result supports the Weberian view that cultural consumption, as an aspect of lifestyle, is stratified more by social status than by social class.[11] This result is observed in five of our six countries. Furthermore, the opposite pattern does *not* obtain in the only exceptional case, namely the Netherlands.

---

[11] Of course, the Weberian class–status distinction also implies that the opposite would be true for life-chances or life-choices in other social domains, especially those which concern economic interests, security and prospects. For supporting evidence in the context of the UK, see Chan and Goldthorpe (2007a).

Rather, class and status in the Netherlands are correlated with each other in such a way that there would be a multicollinearity problem if both variables are entered into a regression model as predictors. In other words, the Netherlands is not so much a negative test case as an untested one.

The substantive magnitude of the status effect is quite large. For example, in the US, across the entire range of the social status scale, the odds of being a musical omnivore rather than an inactive change by a factor of four. In England, if social status were to increase by one standard deviation, the odds of being at the highest rather than the lowest level of cross-domain cultural consumption would rise by 84%. In Hungary and the Netherlands, where relevant data is available, we also see that the social status of significant others affects cultural consumption.

9.3 Possible objections

How do our results square with those of other scholars in the field? My reading of the literature is that, generally speaking, they do sit rather comfortably together. Overall, there is very little empirical support for individualisation arguments, and omnivore–univore arguments command much more support than homology arguments (e.g. Coulangeon, 2005; López-Sintas and García-Álvarez, 2002; van Eijck and Knulst, 2005). However, there are three sets of possible objections, coming mainly from defenders of Pierre Bourdieu, that can be made against our findings. The first set of objections concerns the limit of survey data, the second set is about the analytical methods that we use, while the third set pertains to our interpretation of the results. I shall deal with these objections in turn.

9.3.1 *Quantitative vs. qualitative data*

Our results are based on rather standard quantitative analyses of survey data. But is survey data adequate for testing Bourdieu's claims? For example, Holt (1997, p. 102) argues that in contemporary America (and presumably in other societies as well), 'the utility of goods as consensus class markers has weakened substantially', and 'distinction is becoming more and more a matter of practice' (Holt, 1997, p. 103). The implication is that to test Bourdieu's 'theory of taste', we should study *embodied* tastes rather than (or in addition to) *objectified* tastes. In other words, we need to consider not only whether someone has been to the opera, visited a museum, or consumed a particular genre of music, but also the way in which they consume or appreciate such cultural goods, and the meanings they attribute to such experience. As 'quantitative studies using survey data, operationalise tastes only in their objectified form' (Holt, 1997, p. 102), such data are not adequate for a fair test of Bourdieu's theory.

As Goldthorpe and I point out in Chapter 1, qualitative studies do have a very valuable role in cultural consumption research. In particular, they could help determine the subjective meanings that cultural consumption carries for individuals. We have not carried out qualitative research ourselves (although we believe this collection would help create the framework for such research in the future). But a recent UK study has collected both quantitative and qualitative data, and the qualitative evidence of that study suggests that 'those who were culturally engaged did not articulate a clear sense of cultural superiority' (Bennett *et al.*, 2009, p. 66). Indeed, Bennett *et al.* (2009, pp. 70–71) 'find no one remotely corresponding to the figure of the snob...These observations imply cultural dynamics [are] different from those described by Bourdieu.' In other words, the qualitative evidence on consumption practices that is available is, in fact, consistent with the statistical evidence that we present in this collection (see also Halle, 1993; Painter, 2002). Further qualitative research would indeed be helpful. But so far there is no reason to doubt that our survey data are seriously biased against homology arguments.

9.3.2 Analytical methods

A second strand of possible criticism concerns the analytical methods that we use, namely latent class and regression analyses. For example, in his comments on a paper Goldthorpe and I wrote on the visual arts (Chan and Goldthorpe, 2007e), Wuggenig (2007, p. 307) argues that our analyses are flawed because we rely on 'mainstream approaches of Anglo-Saxon quantitative sociology'. Instead, he claims that homology arguments could only be tested with correspondence analysis (CA) or multiple correspondence analysis (MCA), because unlike Anglo-Saxon quantitative methods, they have a special affinity with Bourdieu's 'relational field theoretical approach'. Similar arguments could be levelled against the analyses reported in this collection.

Such arguments are not very convincing. First, as we argue in our reply to Wuggenig (see Chan and Goldthorpe, 2007b), any a priori claim that a particular theoretical position can only be empirically evaluated through the use of one particular technique of data analysis is very dubious. It must surely be open to researchers to use any technique that can produce results that bear on testable hypotheses deriving from a theory. If the results appear negative, defenders of the theory can of course always seek to show that the results themselves are questionable, that their implications for the theory have been misunderstood, and so on. But all such arguments have then to be conducted at the level of specific instances rather than at the level of vague generalities.

Secondly, there is no reason to treat CA or MCA as, in any fundamental way, different from the 'Anglo-Saxon mainstream' of multivariate data analysis in the social sciences. CA and MCA can be regarded as the categorical counterparts of principal component analysis (Gower and Hand, 1996, Chapter 4), while latent class analysis is the categorical counterpart of factor analysis. And of course principal component analysis and factor analysis are closely related to each other. The links between these methods can be seen, for example, in van der Heijden *et al.* (1989) where they discuss how CA and log-linear analysis complement each other in the analysis of contingency tables. More generally, Goodman (1996) brings out the affinities among a whole range of methods for treating the non-independence of cross-classified data, including various forms of correspondence analysis, by showing how they can in fact all be seen as special cases of a single, more general method of analysis.[12] The fact that a close link between these methods exists is sufficient evidence to undermine the claim that CA and MCA alone have some special affinity with a distinctive 'relational' or 'field theoretic' sociology. Instead, CA and MCA should be regarded as a part – valuable but in no sense exceptional – of what would by now best be regarded as an entirely international, or global, corpus of techniques of data analysis.

---

[12] There is a slight difference among statisticians on the relative weights they give to description vis-à-vis inference, or between exploratory and confirmatory analysis. But such difference should not be overdrawn.

Thirdly, it is not clear that MCA would actually lead to a different conclusion regarding homology arguments. Consider again the work of Bennett *et al.* (2009), who are generally sympathetic to Bourdieu's approach and have indeed embraced MCA as their primary analytical tool. They show that the first and most important axis of their MCA differentiates individuals according to levels of social and economic advantages. Thus, going from right to left, we generally go from more advantaged to less advantaged social classes (Bennett *et al.*, 2009, Figure 3.5), or from higher to lower levels of education (Figure 3.8). But their MCA also shows that both 'highbrow' *and* popular cultural activities, such as going to the opera, going to orchestral concerts, and going to rock concerts, are positioned quite close to each other on the right-hand side of this axis (Bennett *et al.*, 2009, Figure 3.1, p. 125, see also Le Roux *et al.*, 2008, Figure 1, p. 1056).[13] Indeed, Bennett *et al.* (2009, pp. 49–50) conclude that their MCA 'does not suggest that the prime cultural division in contemporary Britain lies between "high" and "popular" culture. Rather than opposing "legitimate" cultural forms (e.g. opera going) with "popular" activities (such as urban or heavy metal), it opposes those who are engaged in both with those who participate rarely or never.'[14]

9.3.3 Interpretation of results

The third type of criticism that we might face concerns the interpretation of our main results. To recap, our main results are: (1) that omnivore–univore arguments receive far greater empirical support than do homology or individualisation arguments, and (2) that, in line with Weber's argument, cultural consumption, as an element of lifestyle, is stratified primarily by social status rather than by social class. Both findings are associated with interpretational issues.

Regarding our first finding, it might be argued that omnivorousness is just a new form of social distinction, and thus the contrast between homology and omnivore–univore arguments should not be overdrawn. This criticism does have some force. On the one hand, omnivores may be seen as essentially tolerant individuals (because, say, of their

[13] These activities are more separated on the second axis of the MCA which differentiates individuals by age (see Bennett *et al.*, 2009, Figure 3.6).

[14] See also Chapter 4 of this collection and Coulangeon and Lemel (2007) where MCA is used in a study of musical consumption in contemporary France.

relatively high levels of education and/or their experience of social mobility) who have a general openness to other cultural styles than that into which they were initially socialised and further, perhaps, a desire to experiment with different kinds of cultural consumption. In this case, there is a fairly obvious affinity with the individualisation argument. Omnivores' cultural consumption is concerned more with self-realisation than with setting down status markers and creating social distinction (cf. the discussion of 'the new middle class' in Wynne and O'Connor, 1998).

On the other hand, though, omnivores may be seen as expressing a new aesthetic which, even if more inclusive and 'cosmopolitan' than that of earlier cultural elites, is no less directed towards the demonstration of cultural *and* social superiority – that is, when set against the very restricted cultural styles of univores (López-Sintas and García-Álvarez, 2002). And, in turn, omnivores may still show discrimination, either in the *uses* that they make of mass or popular culture – e.g. often 'ironic' or otherwise condescending uses – or in still rejecting some of its particular forms, such as ones with an especially close association with low-status groups (cf. Bryson, 1996). In this case, then, the omnivore–univore argument could be regarded as taking over a good deal from the homology argument. The mapping of cultural onto social stratification is understood in a more sophisticated way but cultural consumption is still seen as playing a central part in creating symbolic boundaries and in status rivalry and competition.

The two interpretations of cultural omnivores have been noted for some time (e.g. Peterson, 1992, p. 252). But given our state of knowledge, I do not wish to take up any strong position on this issue. As noted in Chapter 1 and Section 9.3.1 above, further research, especially that of a qualitative kind, is needed in order to determine the subjective meanings cultural consumption carries for individuals. Having said that, the limited evidence that is available seems to favour the 'self-realisation' rather than the 'status competition' view. As reported earlier, Bennett *et al.* (2009, p. 70) 'find no one remotely corresponding to the figure of the snob' in their qualitative interviews.

As regards our second finding, recall that in five of the six countries of our sample, both social status and social class can be entered as predictors into a regression model without causing a multicollinearity problem. Moreover, in such a multivariate framework, the parameter measuring social status remains statistically significant, at least insofar as the main contrast between omnivores and univores (or inactives) is concerned. However, the association between social class and cultural consumption, which is evident in bivariate analyses, would disappear when social status and other variables are controlled for.

This is a robust finding and has been reported not just in the chapters of this collection, but also in several related papers on cultural consumption in England (Chan and Goldthorpe, 2005, 2007c,d,e). Those papers have been criticised by Le Roux *et al.* (2008, p. 1051) on the grounds that 'the value of a radical separation between economic properties of class and cultural attributes of lifestyle is contestable. Second, the way in which status is defined and operationalised seems problematic.' More specifically, their view is that since both class and status are occupation-based constructs, these two concepts are not effectively separated. 'What [Chan and Goldthorpe] measure as status, others call class . . . Bourdieu would call the same phenomenon social capital' (Le Roux *et al.*, 2008, p. 1052).

There is an extensive discussion on the construction and properties of the status scale in Chapter 2. Here I wish to highlight three points. First, it is true that both class and status are occupation-based constructs. But different kinds of occupational information are used in quite distinct ways in the construction of these two variables. Social classes are determined on the basis of expert judgment of the employment conditions of occupations, especially in relation to the labour contract–service contract distinction (see Section 2.2.3). By comparison, social status is determined jointly by the occupation of individuals *and* that of their close friend or spouse through an empirical scaling exercise.

Secondly, as I show in Section 2.2.3, although class and status are, as would be expected, correlated with each other, they are, generally speaking, *not* measuring the same thing. There are many instances where the social status of individuals is not congruent with their class position. Further, as Weber points out, class and status can be 'linked in the most varied ways'. We would expect the tightness of the class–status link to vary between countries and over time, and it does.

Finally, although the Weberian class–status distinction is a conceptually cogent one, its utility for advancing our understanding of social inequality in contemporary societies is a matter for empirical investigation. Le Roux *et al.* (2008, p. 1052) argue that my previous work with Goldthorpe 'does not effectively establish that it is *status* which accounts for differential cultural participation'. It is of course entirely up to them and others to judge how persuasive our analysis is. But I believe our case is further strengthened by a paper not cited in Le Roux *et al.* (2008). In that paper (Chan and Goldthorpe, 2007a), we demonstrate the opposite case: that it is class rather than status which predicts economic security, prospects and interest. Further, we show that while social class underlies 'left–right' political attitudes, it is social status which structures 'libertarian–authoritarian' attitudes. Such results are entirely in line with the Weberian class–status distinction.[15]

9.4 The significance of stratification of cultural consumption

In a recent book Dutton (2009, p. 14) cites the survey results of two soviet artists, Vitaly Komar and Alexander Melamid, and notes that 'people in very different cultures around the world gravitate toward the same general type of pictorial representation: a landscape with trees and open areas, water, human figures, and animals', those which are often printed on calendars. Dutton (2009, p. 19) argues that such cross-cultural similarity in artistic tastes is not due to the 'pervasive power of the worldwide calendar industry'. Instead, the more plausible hypothesis is 'that calendars, and the picture preferences they reveal in completely independent cultures – tap into innate inclinations. This fundamental attraction to certain types of landscapes is not socially constructed but is present in human nature as an inheritance from the Pleistocene, the 1.6 million years during which modern human beings evolved.' In other words, the reason why Kenyans and Finns, Ukrainians and Chinese, and people from many other cultures all prefer similar kinds of landscape is that they have much in common with the East African savannah in which our ancestors found nourishment

---

[15] It should also be noted that Le Roux *et al.* (2008, p. 1051) consider the Weberian class–status distinction as an alternative theoretical framework to Bourdieu's. This contrast is, in a sense, quite valid, as on Bourdieu's own account, *Distinction* starts out from 'an endeavour to rethink Max Weber's opposition between class and *Stand*' (Bourdieu, 1984, p. xii). But, in another sense, this contrast is somewhat off the mark. This is because the evidence against Bourdieu's class–culture homology arguments is *independent* of the class–status distinction. One key finding in relation to homology arguments is that those who consume 'highbrow' culture are just as likely as others to consumer popular culture. This finding holds true irrespective of whether it is status or class which underlies the stratification of cultural consumption.

and shelter (see Orians and Heerwagen, 1992, for further discussion of the so-called 'Savannah Hypothesis').

Dutton is advancing a form of evolutionary psychology argument. While intriguing and suggestive, the problems of such arguments are well known (Laland and Brown, 2002). To begin with, very little is known about the environment in which our ancestors evolved: the so-called EEA or Environment of Evolutionary Adaptedness. We simply do not know much about the complex and diverse selection pressure in the Pleistocene which shaped and fashioned the human mind. To equate the EEA with the modern African savannah is a strong assumption. And it would be controversial, to say the least, and probably unjustified to assume that our ancestors lived lives similar to those of modern hunter-gatherers (Laland and Brown, 2002, pp. 178–180). Since the EEA is under-specified, evolutionary psychology arguments often cannot be tested. Also, 'since the range of adaptive stories is as wide as our minds are fertile' (Gould and Lewontin, 1979, p. 587), one can always come up with an adaptive account that fits some aspects of the EEA. This has led to the charge that many evolutionary psychology explanations are no more than 'just-so' stories.

Given these problems, I am agnostic about Dutton's evolutionary account. But if true, his argument would underline the significance of social status in cultural consumption. This can be understood as follows. The status order expresses a hierarchy of perceived, and to some degree accepted, social superiority, equality and inferiority. And individuals' position in the status order constitutes an important part of their social identity. To signal status, often through consumption, is to lay claim to group membership: to whom one has affiliations, and from whom is one different.[16] This interpretation of the link between status and consumption is consistent with evidence from qualitative research, which shows that feeling 'uncomfortable with the scene' or thinking that 'this is not for people like me' are reasons individuals give for not participating in cultural activities (Creative Research, 2007).

Dutton (2009) argues that evolution has led to very similar cultural tastes *between* nations. But it would seem that such a homogenising tendency is counterbalanced *within* nations by the social force of

---

[16] Douglas and Isherwood (1979, p. 12) make a similar claim in relation to material goods: 'goods are neutral, their uses are social; they can be used as fences or bridges'.

status (which might have its own evolutionary roots) in creating large differences in cultural consumption.

9.5 Future research

In what directions should we take research on the social stratification of cultural consumption forward? In Chapter 8, Goldthorpe and I set out some preliminary theoretical ideas. Very briefly, we argue that cultural consumption, as a form of social action, requires individuals to possess sufficient economic resources, relevant cultural capacity, and the motivation to take part; and these constraints and motivational factors are, in turn, captured by income, education and social status in our regression models respectively. Obviously, further theoretical and empirical research are needed in order to develop and test our ideas. It seems to me that the following questions, as yet not fully explored, might provide fruitful testing grounds.

First, cultural omnivores seem to be generally more active than cultural inactives or univores. As we have seen in Chile (Table 5.5), France (Table 4.4) and the US (Table 3.5), omnivores are more likely than others to exercise, to take part in voluntary activity, to engage in home improvement, to go to sport events, to travel, ... And at least in the US, a higher proportion of omnivores work long hours too. The only activity that they seem to spend less time on is watching TV.[17] These results echo what Sullivan and Katz-Gerro (2007), based on their analysis of British time use data, have referred to as voracious consumption. Given that everyone has 24 hours a day, voraciousness obviously bears on the constraints on consumption. It would be illuminating to explore the connection between voraciousness and omnivorousness further.

Related to this, it would be useful to consider in future research the pattern and determinants of *material* as well as cultural consumption. Whilst some individuals might prefer to express their social status through cultural consumption (DiMaggio, 1987), for others, social status might be expressed through material consumption: the car they drive, the watch they wear, where they take their holiday, and so on. Schor (1998, p. 50) argues that 'socially visible products deliver less quality for a given price', and she provides some supportive evidence

---

[17] Bukodi reports in note 8 of Chapter 6 that similar findings are found in Hungary.

for this claim in relation to cosmetic products. Her argument is that while some products might be consumed in public (e.g. lipstick), others are always consumed in private (e.g. facial cleanser). And if social status is an important consideration in consumption, we would expect consumers to be willing to pay more for socially visible products for a given quality. Similarly, Charles *et al.* (2009) show that there are large and persisting differences by race in spending pattern on visible goods (e.g. clothing, jewellery and cars). Again, they interpret their results in terms of status-seeking behaviour. Indeed, conspicuous consumption is just as common and effective in the material arena as in the cultural sphere (Veblen, 1994). So far, research on material consumption and that on cultural consumption have largely proceeded in parallel, but separately. Cultural consumption surveys typically do not include questions on material consumption, and vice versa. But I think much could be learned from the possible complementarity of material and cultural consumption.

Another promising avenue for exploring status motivations is through the status effect of significant others. In this collection, we have already seen some relevant evidence in the Hungarian (Table 6.8) and Dutch (Tables 7.2–7.4) chapters. One difficulty of interpreting the association between social status and cultural consumption is that status is correlated with education, income and other variables. So it is possible that the observed status effect is simply masking some unmeasured effect of, say, a person's information-processing capacity. But since it is unlikely that the social status of an individual's significant others is simply a proxy of his/her information-processing capacity, this allows us to circumvent, at least partly, the unmeasured effect problem. In particular, further research in this area should try and go beyond demonstrating that the social status of one's spouse or father matters in one's cultural consumption. More insights could be gained by looking at cases where there is incongruence between the status of individuals and that of their significant others (see Chan and Goldthorpe, 2007c).

References

Abrams, M. (1958). The mass media and social class in Great Britain. Papers presented at the Fourth World Congress of Sociology, Stresa, Italy.

Adorno, T. W. (1976). *Introduction to the Sociology of Music*. Seabury Press, New York.

Adorno, T. W. (2002). *Essays on Music*. University of California Press, Berkeley, CA.

Alderson, A. S., Heacock, I. and Junisbai, A. (2005). Is there a status order in the contemporary United States? Evidence from the occupational structure of marriage. Paper presented at the 37th World Congress of the International Institute of Sociology, Stockholm, Sweden.

Alderson, A. S., Junisbai, A. and Heacock, I. (2007). Social status and cultural consumption in the United States. *Poetics*, 35(2/3), 191–212.

Allison, P. (2002). *Missing Data*. Sage, Thousand Oaks.

Arum, R. and Müller, W., editors (2004). *The Reemergence of Self-employment: A Comparative Study of Self-employment Dynamics and Social Inequality*. Princeton University Press, Princeton.

Bárdosi, M., Lakatos, G. and Varga, A. (2005). A kultúra helyzete magyarországon (The situation of culture in Hungary). In E. Kuti, editor, *Találkozások a kultúrával (Encounter the culture)*. MTA Szociológiai Intézet, Budapest.

Barros, L. and Vergara, X. (1978). *El Modo de Ser Aristocratico: El Caso de la Oligarquia Chilena hacia 1900. (The Aristocratic Style of Life: The Case of the Chilean Oligarchy Towards 1900)*. Lautaro, Santiago.

Bartholomew, D. J., Steele, F., Moustaki, I. and Galbraith, J. I. (2002). *The Analysis and Interpretation of Multivariate Data for Social Scientists*. Chapman & Hall/CRC, London.

Baudrillard, J. (2000). *The Vital Illusion*. Columbia University Press, New York.

Bauman, Z. (1988). *Freedom*. Open University Press, Milton Keynes.

Bauman, Z. (2002). *Society Under Siege*. Polity, Cambridge.

Beck, U. (1992). *Risk Society: Towards a New Modernity*. Sage, London.

Becker, H. S. (1982). *Arts World*. University of California Press, Berkeley, CA.

Bell, D. (1976). *The Cultural Contradictions of Capitalism*. Heinemann, London.

Benjamin, W. (1936). The work of art in the age of mechanical reproduction. In A. Benjamin, editor, *Walter Benjamin and Art*. Continuum, London.

Bennett, T., Savage, M., Silva, E., Warde, A., Gayo-Cal, M. and Wright, D. (2009). *Culture, Class and Distinction*. Routledge, London.

Berlyne, D., editor (1974). *Studies in the New Experimental Aesthetics: Steps Toward an Objective Psychology of Aesthetic Appreciation*. Hemisphere, Washington.

Bihagen, E. and Katz-Gerro, T. (2000). Culture participation in Sweden: the stability of the gender differences. *Poetics*, 27, 327–349.

Binder, A. (1993). Constructing racial rhetoric: Media depictions of harm in heavy metal and rap music. *American Sociological Review*, 58, 753–767.

Blau, P. M. and Duncan, O. D. (1967). *The American Occupational Structure*. John Wiley and Sons, New York.

Blossfeld, H.-P., Mills, M. and Bernardi, F., editors (2006). *Globalization, Uncertainty and Men's Careers: An International Comparison*. Elgar, Cheltenham.

Bottero, W. and Prandy, K. (2003). Social interaction distance and stratification. *British Journal of Sociology*, 54(2), 177–197.

Bottero, W. and Prandy, K. (2004). Class identities and the identity of class. *Sociology*, 38, 985–1003.

Bourdieu, P. (1984). *Distinction: A Social Critique of the Judgement of Taste*. Routledge & Kegan Paul, London.

Bourdieu, P. (1990). *The Logic of Practice*. Polity Press, Cambridge.

Breen, R., editor (2004). *Social Mobility in Europe*. Oxford University Press, Oxford.

Breen, R. (2005). Foundations of class analysis in the Weberian tradition. In E. O. Wright, editor, *Approaches to Class Analysis*, pages 31–50. Cambridge University Press, Cambridge.

Brunner, J. J. (2005). Chile: ecologia social del cambio cultural (Chile: social ecology of cultural change). In C. Catalan, editor, *Consumo Cultural en Chile: Miradas y Perspectivas*. INE, Santiago.

Bryson, B. (1996). 'Anything but Heavy Metal': symbolic exclusion and musical dislikes. *American Sociological Review*, 61(5), 884–899.

Bryson, B. (1997). What about the univores? Musical dislikes and group-based identity construction among Americans with low level of education. *Poetics*, 25, 141–156.

Bukodi, E. (1999). Educational choices in Hungary. *Hungarian Statistical Review (special English edition)*, 77, 71–94.

Bukodi, E. (2005). Szababdid (Leisure time). Technical report, Office of National Development Plan, Budapest.

Bukodi, E. (2007). Social stratification and cultural consumption in Hungary: book readership. *Poetics*, 35(2/3), 112–131.

Bukodi, E. and Róbert, P. (1999). Historical changes, human capital, and career patterns as class determinants in Hungary. *Review of Sociology*, special issue 42–65.

Bukodi, E., Altorjai, S. and Tallér, A. (2006). A magyar foglalkozási rétegszerkezet az ezredfordul/'o után (The occupational class structure in Hungary after the millennium). *Statisztikai Szemle (Hungarian Statistical Review)*, 84, 733–762.

Chan, T. W. and Goldthorpe, J. H. (2004). Is there a status order in contemporary British society? Evidence from the occupational structure of friendship. *European Sociological Review*, 20(5), 383–401.

Chan, T. W. and Goldthorpe, J. H. (2005). The social stratification of theatre, dance and cinema attendance. *Cultural Trends*, 14(3), 193–212.

Chan, T. W. and Goldthorpe, J. H. (2007a). Class and status: the conceptual distinction and its empirical relevance. *American Sociological Review*, 72(4), 512–532.

Chan, T. W. and Goldthorpe, J. H. (2007b). Data, methods and interpretation in analyses of cultural consumption: a reply to Peterson and Wuggenig. *Poetics*, 35(4), 317–329.

Chan, T. W. and Goldthorpe, J. H. (2007c). Social status and newspaper readership. *American Journal of Sociology*, 112(4), 1095–1134.

Chan, T. W. and Goldthorpe, J. H. (2007d). Social stratification and cultural consumption: Music in England. *European Sociological Review*, 23(1), 1–19.

Chan, T. W. and Goldthorpe, J. H. (2007e). Social stratification and cultural consumption: the visual arts in England. *Poetics*, 35(2/3), 168–190.

Charles, K. K., Hurst, E. and Roussanov, N. (2009). Conspicious consumption and race. *Quarterly Journal of Economics*, 124(2), 425–467.

Clausen, S.-E. (1998). *Applied Correspondence Analysis: An Introduction*. Sage, London.

Compendium of Cultural Policies and Trends in Europe (2007). Changes in consumer prices for goods and services: All items vs. recreation and culture. Technical report, CCPTE. accessed: 29/01/2007.

Connor, W. D. (1988). *Socialism's Dilemmas*. Columbia University Press, New York.

Coulangeon, P. (2003). La stratification sociale des goûts musicaux. *Revue française de sociologie*, 44, 3–33.

Coulangeon, P. (2005). Social stratification of musical tastes: questioning the cultural legitimacy model. *Revue française de sociologie*, 46(supplement), 123–154.

Coulangeon, P. and Lemel, Y. (2007). Is *Distinction* really outdated? Questioning the meaning of the omnivorization of musical taste in contemporary france. *Poetics*, 35(2/3), 93–111.

Coxon, A. and Jones, C. (1978). *The Images of Occupational Prestige.* Macmillan, London.

Creative Research (2007). The arts debate: findings of research among the general public. Technical report, Arts Council England, London.

Davis, J. A., Smith, T. W. and Marsden, P. V. (2003). *General Social Surveys, 1972–2002.* Chicago, IL: National Opinion Research Center, Storrs, CT: Roper Center for Public Opinion Research, University of Connecticut/Ann Arbor, MI: Inter-university Consortium for Political and Social Research, 2nd icpsr version edition.

Davis, K. (1949). *Human Society.* Macmillan, New York.

de Graaf, N. D. (1991). Distinction by consumption in Czechoslovakia, Hungary, and the Netherlands. *European Sociological Review*, 7, 267–290.

de Graaf, N. D. and Ganzeboom, H. (1990). Cultuurdeelname en opleiding: een analyse van statusgroepeffecten met diagonale referentie modellen (Cultural consumption and education: an analysis of status-group effects with diagonal reference models). *Mens en Maatschappij*, 65, 219–244.

Degenne, A., Lebeaux, M. O., and Lemel, Y. (2003). Does social capital offset social and economic inequalities? Social capital in everyday life. In H. Flap and B. Völker, editors, *Creation and Returns of Social Capital: A New Research Program*, pages 51–74. Routledge, London.

DeNora, T. (2000). *Music in Everyday Life.* Cambridge University Press, New York.

DeNora, T. (2003). *After Adorno: Rethinking Music Sociology.* Cambridge University Press, New York.

DiMaggio, P. (1987). Classification in art. *American Sociological Review*, 52, 440–455.

DiMaggio, P. (1994). Lifestyle and social cognition. In D. B. Grusky, editor, *Social Stratification: Class, Race and Gender in Sociological Perspective*, pages 458–465. Westview, Boulder.

DiMaggio, P. and Mukhtar, T. (2004). Arts participation as cultural capital in the United States, 1982-2002: signs of decline? *Poetics*, 32, 169–194.

DiMaggio, P. and Ostrower, F. (1990). Participation in the arts by black and white Americans. *Social Forces*, 63, 753–778.

DiMaggio, P. and Useem, M. (1978). Social class and art consumption: the origins and consequences of class differences in exposure in the arts in America. *Theory and Society*, 5, 141–161.

Domanski, H. (2000). *On the Verge of Convergence. Social Stratification in Eastern Europe.* CEU Press, Budapest.

Douglas, M. and Isherwood, B. (1979). *The World of Goods: Towards an Anthropology of Consumption*. Allen Lane, London.

Dudás, K. and Hunyadi, Z. (2005). A hagyományos és a modern tömegkultúra helye és szerepe a kulturális fogyasztásban (The role of the traditional and the mass culture in cultural consumption). In E. Kuti, editor, *Találkozások a kultúrával (Encounter the culture)*. MTA Szociológiai Intézet, Budapest.

Duncan, O. D. (1961). A socioeconomic index for all occupations. In A. Reiss, editor, *Occupations and Social Status*. Free Press, New York.

Dutton, D. (2009). *The Art Instinct: Beauty, Pleasure and Human Evolution*. Oxford University Press, Oxford.

Eliot, T. S. (1948). *Notes Towards the Definition of Culture*. Faber and Faber, London.

Emmison, M. (2003). Social class and cultural mobility: reconfiguring the cultural omnivore thesis. *Journal of Sociology*, **39**, 211–230.

Erickson, B. H. (1996). Culture, class, and connections. *American Journal of Sociology*, **102**(1), 217–251.

Erikson, R. and Goldthorpe, J. H. (1992). *The Constant Flux: A Study of Class Mobility in Industrial Societies*. Clarendon Press, Oxford.

Erikson, R., Goldthorpe, J. H. and Portocarero, L. (1979). Intergenerational class mobility in three western European countries. *British Journal of Sociology*, **30**(4), 415–441.

Falussy, B. (2004). *Az idő_felhasználás metszetei (The structure of time-use)*. Új Mandátum, Budapest.

Featherman, D. L. and Hauser, R. M. (1976). Prestige or socioeconomic scales in the study of occupational achievement. *Sociological Methods and Research*, **4**(4), 402–422.

Featherstone, M. (1987). Lifestyle and consumer culture. *Theory, Culture and Society*, **4**(1), 55–70.

Featherstone, M. (1991). *Consumer Culture and Postmodernism*. Sage, London.

Ffrench-Davis, R. (1999). *Entre el Neoliberalismo y el Crecimiento con Equidad. Tres Decadas de Politica Economica en Chile (Between Neoliberalism and Growth with Equity: Three Decades of Economic Policy in Chile)*. Dolmen, Santiago.

Filmer, D. and Pritchett, L. (1999). The effect of household wealth on educational attainment: evidence from 35 countries. *Population and Development Review*, **25**, 85–120.

Filmer, D. and Pritchett, L. (2001). Estimating wealth effects without expenditure data or tears: an application to educational enrollments in states of India. *Demography*, **38**(1), 115–132.

Gans, H. J. (1974). *Popular Culture and High Culture: An Analysis and Evaluation of Taste*. Basic Books, New York.

Gans, H. J. (1985). American popular culture and high culture in a changing class structure. In J. Salman, editor, *Prospects: An Annual of American Culture Studies*, volume 10, pages 17–38. Cambridge University Press, New York.

Gans, H. J. (1999). *Popular Culture and High Culture: An Analysis and Evaluation of Taste*. Basic Books, New York, revised edition.

Ganzeboom, H. B. G. (1982). Explaining differential participation in high-cultural activities: a confrontation of information-processing and status-seeking theories. In W. Raub, editor, *Theoretical Models and Empirical Analyses: Contributions to the Explanation of Individual Actions and Collective Phenomena*, pages 186–205. E.S.–Publications, Utrecht.

Ganzeboom, H. B. G. and Treiman, D. J. (2003). Three internationally standardised measures for comparative research on occupational status. In J. H. Hoffmeyer-Zlotnik and C. Wolf, editors, *Advances in Cross-National Comparison: A European Working Book for Demographic and Socio-Economic Variables*, chapter 9, pages 159–193. Kluwer Academic Press, New York.

Ganzeboom, H. B. G., de Graaf, P. M. and Róbert, P. (1990). Cultural reproduction theory on socialist ground: intergenerational transmission of inequalities in Hungary. *Research in Social Stratification and Mobility*, 9, 79–104.

Ganzeboom, H. B. G., de Graaf, P. M. and Treiman, D. J. (1992). A standard international socio-economic index for occupational status. *Social Science Research*, 21, 1–56.

Giddens, A. (1991). *Modernity and Self-identity: Self and Society in the Late Modern Age*. Polity, Cambridge.

Goldthorpe, J. H. (1981). Social standing, class and status. *Survey Methods Newsletter*, 2, 8–11.

Goldthorpe, J. H. (1997). The 'Goldthorpe' class schema. In D. Rose and K. O'Reilly, editors, *Constructing Classes*. Office of National Statistics, London.

Goldthorpe, J. H. (2007a). Cultural capital: some critical observations. In S. Scherer, R. Pollak, G. Otte and M. Gangl, editors, *From Origin to Destination: Trends and Mechanisms in Social Stratification Research*. Campus, Frankfurt.

Goldthorpe, J. H. (2007b). *On Sociology*, volume 2. Stanford University Press, Stanford, second edition.

Goldthorpe, J. H. and Hope, K. (1972). Occupational grading and occupational prestige. In K. Hope, editor, *The Analysis of Social*

Mobility: Methods and Approaches, pages 19–79. Oxford University Press, Oxford.

Goldthorpe, J. H. and Hope, K. (1974). *The Social Grading of Occupations*. Oxford University Press, Oxford.

Goodman, L. A. (1996). A single general method for the analysis of cross-classified data: reconciliation and synthesis of some methods of Pearson, Yule, and Fisher, and also some methods of correspondence analysis and association analysis. *Journal of the American Statistical Association*, 91(433), 408–428.

Gould, S. J. and Lewontin, R. C. (1979). The spandrels of San Marco and the Panglossian paradigm: a critique of the adaptationist programme. *Proceedings of the Royal Society of London, Series B*, 205(1161), 581–598.

Gower, J. C. and Hand, D. J. (1996). *Biplots*. Chapman & Hall, London.

Granovetter, M. S. (1973). The strength of weak ties. *American Journal of Sociology*, 78, 1360–1380.

Greenacre, M. and Blasius, J., editors (1994). *Correspondence Analysis in the Social Sciences: Recent Development and Applications*. Academic Press, London.

Grusky, D. B. (2005). Foundations of a neo-Durkheimian class analysis. In E. O. Wright, editor, *Approaches to Class Analysis*, chapter 3, pages 51–81. Cambridge University Press, Cambridge.

Grusky, D. B. and Sørensen, J. B. (1998). Can class analysis be salvaged? *American Journal of Sociology*, 103(5), 1187–1234.

Grusky, D. B. and Weeden, K. A. (2001). Decomposition without death: a research agenda for the new class analysis. *Acta Sociologica*, 44(3), 203–218.

Halle, D. (1993). *Inside Culture: Art and Class in the American Home*. University of Chicago Press, Chicago.

Hauser, R. M. and Warren, J. R. (1997). Socioeconomic indexes for occupations: a review, update, and critique. *Sociological Methodology*, 27, 177–298.

Hausman, J. and McFadden, D. (1984). Specification tests for the multinomial logit model. *Econometrica*, 52(5), 1219–1240.

Héran, F. (1987). La seconde nature de l'habitus: tradition philosophique et sens commun dans le langage sociologique. *Revue Française de Sociologie*, 28(3), 385–416.

Holt, D. (1997). Distinction in America? Recovering Bourdieu's theory of tastes from its critics. *Poetics*, 25(2–3), 93–120.

Honaker, J. A., King, G., Scheve, K. and Singh, N. (2003). *Amelia, A Program for Missing Data*. Online at http://gking.harvard.edu/stats.shtml.

Horkheimer, M. and Adorno, T. W. (1944/1972). *Dialectic of Enlightenment*. Allen Lane, London.

Hout, M. and DiPrete, T. A. (2006). What have we learned: RC28's contributions to knowledge about social stratification. *Research in Social Stratification and Mobility*, 24(1), 1–20.

Hughes, J. A., Martin, P. J. and Sharrock, W. W. (1995). *Understanding Classical Sociology: Marx, Weber, Durkheim*. Sage, London.

Hugues, M. and Peterson, R. A. (1983). Isolating cultural choice patterns in the US population. *American Behavioral Scientist*, 26(4), 459–478.

Inglehart, R. (1990). *Culture Shift in Advanced Industrial Societies*. Princeton University Press, Princeton.

Jasso, G. (2001). Studying status: an integrated framework. *American Sociological Review*, 66(1), 96–124.

Jenkins, R. (2002). *Pierre Bourdieu*. Routledge, London, revised edition.

Kalmijn, M. and Bernasco, W. (2001). Joint and separated lifestyles in couple relationships. *Journal of Marriage and the Family*, 63, 639–654.

Kant, I. (1790/1986). *The Critique of Judgement*. Oxford University Press, New York.

Kattuman, P. and Redmond, G. (2001). Income inequality in early transition: the case of Hungary 1987–1996. *Journal of Comparative Economics*, 29, 40–65.

Katz-Gerro, T. (2002). Highbrow cultural consumption and class distinction in Italy, Israel, West Germany, Sweden, and the United States. *Social Forces*, 81(1), 207–229.

Kingston, P. W. (2000). *The Classless Society*. Stanford University Press, Stanford.

Kolosi, T. (1984). Status and stratification. In T. Kolosi and R. Andorka, editors, *Stratification and inequalities*. Institute for Social Sciences, Budapest.

Kolosi, T. (2000). *Terhes babapiskóta. A rendszerváltás társadalomszerkezete (Regime transformation and social structure)*. Századvég, Budapest.

Kraaykamp, G. (2002). Cumulative advantages and inequality in lifestyle: a Dutch description of distinction in taste. *The Netherlands' Journal of Social Sciences*, 38, 121–143.

Kraaykamp, G. (2003). Literary socialization and reading preferences: effects of parents, the library, and the school. *Poetics*, 31, 235–257.

Kraaykamp, G. and Niewbeerta, P. (2000). Parental background and lifestyle differentiation in Eastern Europe: social, political, and cultural intergenerational transmission in five former socialist societies. *Social Science Research*, 29, 92–122.

Laland, K. N. and Brown, G. R. (2002). *Sense and Nonsense: Evolutionary Perspectives on Human Behaviour*. Oxford University Press, Oxford.

Lamont, M. (1992). *Money, Morals and Manners: The Culture of the French and American Upper Middle Class*. University of Chicago Press, Chicago.

Lamont, M. and Lareau, A. (1988). Cultural capital: allusions, gaps and glissandos in recent theeoretical developments. *Sociological Theory*, 6, 153–168.

Lash, S. (1988). Discourse or figure? Postmodernism as a regime of signification. *Theory, Culture and Society*, 5, 311–335.

Laumann, E. O. (1966). *Prestige and Association in an Urban Community*. Bobbs-Merrill, Indianapolis.

Laumann, E. O. (1973). *Bonds of Pluralism*. Wiley, New York.

Laumann, E. O. and Guttman, L. (1966). The relative associational contiguity of occupations in an urban setting. *American Sociological Review*, 31, 169–178.

Le Roux, B., Rouanet, H., Savage, M., and Warde, A. (2008). Class and cultural division in the UK. *Sociology*, 42(6), 1049–1071.

Leavis, F. R. (1930). *Mass Civilisation and Minority Culture*. Number 1 in Minority pamphlet. Minority Press, Cambridge.

Leavis, Q. D. (1932). *Fiction and the Reading Public*. Chatto & Windus, London.

Lemel, Y. (2004). *Les classes sociales*. Presses Universitaires de France, Paris.

Lemel, Y. (2006). The social positioning of the French according to the EPCV survey. CREST working paper 14, INSEE, Paris.

Leonard, N. (1962). *Jazz and the White Americans: The Acceptance of a New Art Form*. University of Chicago Press, Chicago.

Levine, L. W. (1988). *Highbrow/Lowbrow: The Emergence of Cultural Hierarchy in America*. Harvard University Press, Cambridge, MA.

Lin, N. and Dumin, M. (1986). Access to occupation through social ties. *Social Networks*, 8, 365–386.

Linder, S. B. (1970). *The Harried Leisure Class*. Columbia University Press, New York.

Lipset, S. M. and Bendix, R. (1959). *Social Mobility in Industrial Society*. Heinemann, London.

Lizardo, O. (2006). How cultural tastes shape personal networks. *American Sociological Review*, 71(5), 778–807.

Long, J. S. and Freese, J. (2006). *Regression Models for Categorical Dependent Variables Using Stata*. Statacorp LP, College Station, TX, 2nd edition.

Looseley, D. (1997). *Politics of Fun: Cultural Policy and Debate in Contemporary France*. Berg, Oxford.

López-Sintas, J. and García-Álvarez, E. (2002). Omnivores show up again: the segmentation of cultural consumers in Spanish social space. *European Sociological Review*, 18(3), 353–368.

López-Sintas, J. and García-Álvarez, E. (2004). Omnivore versus univore consumption and its symbolic properties: evidence from Spaniards performing arts attendance. *Poetics*, 32, 463–484.

López-Sintas, J. and Katz-Gerro, T. (2005). From exclusive to inclusive elitists and further: twenty years of omnivorousness and cultural diversity in arts participation in the USA. *Poetics*, 33, 299–319.

Lynes, R. (1954). *The Tastemakers: The Shaping of American Popular Taste.* Harper, New York.

MacDonald, D. (1957). A theory of mass culture. In B. Rosenberg and D. M. White, editors, *Mass Culture: The Popular Arts in America.* Free Press, New York.

Magidson, J. and Vermunt, J. K. (2001). Latent class factor and cluster models, bi-plots and related graphical displays. *Sociological Methodology*, 31, 223–264.

Marsden, P. V. (1987). Core discussion networks of Americans. *American Sociological Review*, 52, 122–131.

Mauss, M. (1934). Les techniques du corps. *Journal de Psychologie*, 32(3–4).

McCutcheon, A. L. (1987). *Latent Class Analysis.* Sage, Newbury Park, London.

McCutcheon, A. L. and Mills, C. (1998). Categorical data analysis: loglinear and latent class models. In E. Scarbrough and E. Tanenbaum, editors, *Research Strategies in the Social Sciences.* Oxford University Press, Oxford.

McKenzie, D. (2004). Measuring inequality with asset indicators. *Journal of Population Economics*, 18, 229–260.

McKibbin, R. (1998). *Classes and Cultures: England 1918–1951.* Oxford University Press, Oxford.

Mohr, J. and DiMaggio, P. (1995). The intergenerational transmission of cultural capital. *Research in Social Stratification and Mobility*, 14, 167–199.

Moles, A. A. (1971). *Sociodynamique de la culture.* Mouton, Paris.

Morrison, K. (1995). *Marx, Durkheim, Weber: Formations of Modern Social Thought.* Sage, Beverly Hills.

Murphy, R. (1988). *Social Closure: The Theory of Monopolization and Exclusion.* Oxford University Press, New York.

Murray, M. and Ureta, S. (2005). Un país de poetas? Una mirada comparada al consumo de productos mediales y artísticos en la ciudad de Santiago (A country of poets? A comparative approach of media and art product consumption in Santiago). In C. Catalan, editor, *Consumo Cultural en Chile: Miradas y Perspectivas.* INE, Santiago.

Nagel, I. and Ganzeboom, H. B. G. (2002). Participation in legitimate culture: family and school effects from adolescence to adulthood. *The Netherlands' Journal of Social Sciences*, 38, 102–120.

Nakao, K. and Treas, J. (1994). Updating occupational prestige and socioeconomic scores: how the new measures measure up. *Sociological Methodology*, 24, 1–72.

National Council for Culture and the Arts and National Institute for Statistics (2004/2005). First survey of cultural consumption and time use. Computer file.

National Institute for Statistics (1989). *IV Encuesta de Presupuestos Familiares (IV Family Budget Survey)*. INE, Santiago.

National Institute for Statistics (1999). *V Encuesta de Presupuestos Familiares (V Family Budget Survey)*. INE, Santiago.

National Institute for Statistics (2004). *Anuario de Cultura y Tiempo Libre (Culture and Leisure Yearbook)*. INE, Santiago.

Nylund, K., Asparouhov, T. and Muthen, B. (2006). Deciding on the number of classes in latent class analysis and growth mixture modeling: a Monte Carlo simulation study. Mimeo, Graduate School of Education and Information Studies, UCLA.

OECD (2000). *Literacy in the Information Age. Final Report of the International Adult Literacy Survey*. OECD, Paris.

Offe, C. (1985). *Disorganized Capitalism: Contemporary Transformations of Work and Politics*. Polity Press, Cambridge.

Office for National Statistics (2005). *The National Statistics Socio-Economic Classification: User Manual*. Palgrave Macmillan, Basingstoke.

O'Hagan, J. (1996). Access to and participation in the arts: the case of those with low incomes/educational attainment. *Journal of Cultural Economics*, 20, 269–282.

Orians, G. H. and Heerwagen, J. H. (1992). Evolved responses to landscapes. In J. H. Barkow, L. Cosmides and J. Tooby, editors, *The Adapted Mind: Evolutionary Psychology and the Generation of Culture*, chapter 15, pages 555–579. Oxford University Press, New York.

Painter, C. (2002). Images, contemporary art and the home. In C. Painter, editor, *Contemporary Art and the Home*, chapter 11, pages 195–237. Berg, Oxford.

Pakulski, J. and Waters, M. (1996). *The Death of Class*. Sage, London.

Parkin, F. (1971). *Class Inequality and Political Order*. MacGibbon and Kee, London.

Peterson, R. A. (1972). A process model of the folk, pop and fine arts phases of jazz. In C. Nanry, editor, *American Music: From Storyville to Woodstock*, pages 135–151. Transaction, New Brunswick.

Peterson, R. A. (1976). *The Production of Culture*. Sage, Thousand Oaks, CA.

Peterson, R. A. (1990). Why 1955? Explaining the advent of rock music. *Popular Music*, 9, 97–116.

Peterson, R. A. (1992). Understanding audience segmentation: from elite and mass to omnivore and univore. *Poetics*, 21(4), 243–258.

Peterson, R. A. (1997). The rise and fall of highbrow snobbery as a status marker. *Poetics*, 25, 75–92.

Peterson, R. A. (2004). Le passage á des goûts omnivores: notions, faits et perspectives. *Sociologies et sociétés*, 36(1), 145–164.

Peterson, R. A. (2005). Problems in comparative research: the example of omnivorousness. *Poetics*, 33, 257–282.

Peterson, R. A. (2007). Comment on Chan and Goldthorpe: omnivore, what's in a name, what's in a measure. *Poetics*, 35(4), 301–305.

Peterson, R. A. and Anand, N. (1994). The production of culture perspective. *Annual Review of Sociology*, 30, 311–334.

Peterson, R. A. and Berger, D. G. (1975). Cycles in symbol production: The case of popular music. *American Sociological Review*, 40, 158–173.

Peterson, R. A. and Kern, R. M. (1996). Changing highbrow taste: from snob to omnivore. *American Sociological Review*, 61(5), 900–907.

Peterson, R. A. and Rossman, G. (2007). Changing arts audiences: capitalizing on omnivorousness. In B. Ivey and S. Tepper, editors, *Engaging Art: The Next Great Transformation of America's Cultural Life*. Routledge, New York.

Peterson, R. A. and Simkus, A. (1992). How musical tastes mark occupational status groups. In M. Lamont and M. Fournier, editors, *Cultivating Differences: Symbolic Boundaries and the Making of Inequality*, chapter 7, pages 152–186. University of Chicago Press, Chicago.

Piña, J. A. (2006). Teatro: fundacion, renovacion, y compromiso en la escena nacional (Theater: foundations, renovation and commitment in the national stage). In C. Gazmuri, editor, *100 Años de Cultura Chilena 1905-2005*. Zig-Zag, Santiago.

Portes, A. and Hoffman, K. (2003). Latin American class structures: their composition and change during the neoliberal era. *Latin-American Research Review*, 38, 41–82.

Prandy, K. (2002). Ideal types, stereotypes and classes. *British Journal of Sociology*, 53(4), 583–602.

Prandy, K. and Lambert, P. S. (2003). Marriage, social distance and the social space: an alternative derivation and validation of the Cambridge scale. *Sociology*, 37(3), 397–411.

Reiss, A., editor (1961). *Occupations and Social Status*. Free Press, New York.

Relish, M. (1997). It's not all education: network measures as sources of cultural competency. *Poetics*, 25, 121–139.

Róbert, P. (1997). Social determination of living conditions in post-communist societies. *Czech Sociological Review*, 5, 197–216.

Róbert, P. and Bukodi, E. (2004). Changes in intergenerational class mobility in Hungary, 1973–2000. In R. Breen, editor, *Social Mobility in Europe*. Oxford University Press, Oxford.

Rose, D., Pevalin, D. J., and O'Reilly, K. (2005). *The NS-SEC: Origins, Development and Use*. Palgrave Macmillan, Basingstoke.

Runciman, W. G. (1997). *Applied Social Theory*, volume III of *A Treatise on Social Theory*. Cambridge University Press, Cambridge.

Santerre, L. (2000). De la démocratisation de la culture à la démocratie culturelle. In G. Bellavance, editor, *Démocratisation de la culture ou démocratie culturelle? Deux logiques d'action publique*. Presses de l'université de Laval, Sainte-Foy.

Schor, J. B. (1998). *The Overspent American: Why We Want What We Don't Need*. Harper Collins, New York.

Schuessler, K. F. (1948). Social background and musical taste. *American Sociological Review*, 13(3), 330–335.

Schuessler, K. F. (1981). *Musical Taste and Socio-economic Background*. Ayer, Manchester, NH.

Scopp, T. S. (2003). The relationship between the 1990 census and 2000 census industry and occupation classification systems. Technical Paper 65, US Census Bureau, Washington, DC.

Scott, J. (1996). *Stratification and Power: Structures of Class, Status and Command*. Polity Press, Cambridge.

Shavit, Y. and Blossfeld, H.-P., editors (1993). *Persistent Inequality: Changing Educational Attainment in Thirteen Countries*. Westview Press, Boulder, CO.

Shavit, Y. and Müller, W., editors (1998). *From School to Work: A Comparative Study of Educational Qualifications and Occupational Destinations*. Clarendon Press, Oxford.

Shavit, Y., Arum, R., and Gamoran, A., editors (2007). *Expansion, Differentiation and Inequality of Access in Higher Education: A Comparative Study*. Stanford University Press, Stanford.

Shils, E. (1962/1975). Class. In E. Shils, editor, *Center and Periphery: Essays in Macrosociology*, chapter 14, pages 249–255. University of Chicago Press, Chicago.

Shils, E. (1972). *The Intellectuals and the Powers: And Other Essays*. University of Chicago Press, Chicago.

Silva, E. B. (2006). Distinction through visual art. *Cultural Trends*, 15(2/3), 141–158.

Skelton, A., Bridgwood, A., Duckworth, K., Hutton, L., Fenn, C., Creaser, C., and Babbidge, A. (2002). Arts in England: attendance, participation and attitudes in 2001. Research report 27, Arts Council England, London.

Social and Cultural Planning Bureau (2001). *Trends in de tijd (Trends in Time)*. SCP, Den Haag.

Sontag, S. (1966). *Against Interpretation and Other Essays*. Farrar, Strauss and Giroux, New York.

Sørensen, A. B. (2001). The basic concepts of stratification research. In D. B. Grusky, editor, *Social Stratification: Class, Race and Gender in Sociological Perspective*, pages 287–300. Westview, Oxford, second edition.

Stabili, M. R. (2003). *El Sentimiento Aristocratico (The Aristocratic Spirit)*. Andres Bello, Santiago.

Statistical Innovations Inc (2003). *LatentGold 3.0*. Belmont MA.

Stewart, A., Prandy, K., and Blackburn, R. M. (1973). Measuring the class structure. *Nature*, 245, 415–417.

Stewart, A., Prandy, K., and Blackburn, R. M. (1980). *Social Structure and Occupations*. Macmillan, London.

Stigler, G. J. and Becker, G. S. (1977). De gustibus non est disputandum. *American Economic Review*, 67(2), 76–90.

Sullivan, O. and Katz-Gerro, T. (2007). The omnivore thesis revisited: voracious cultural consumers. *European Sociological Review*, 23(2), 123–137.

Tironi, E. (1999). *La Irrupcion de las Masas y el Malestar de las Elites: Chile en el Cambio de Siglo (The irruption of the masses and the elite malaise: Chile at the Turn of the Century)*. Grijalbo, Santiago.

Torche, F. (2005a). Status stratification in a highly unequal country: The case of Chile. Mimeo.

Torche, F. (2005b). Unequal but fluid: social mobility in Chile in comparative perspective. *American Sociological Review*, 70(3), 422–450.

Torche, F. (2007). Social status and cultural consumption: the case of reading in Chile. *Poetics*, 35(2/3), 70–92.

Tóth, I. G. (2003). Jövedelem-egyenl_tlenségek· rényleg növekszenek vagy csak úgy látjuk? (Inequalities of income: are they increasing or do they just seem to be increasing?). *Közgazdasági Szemle (Review of Economics)*, L, 209–234.

Treiman, D. J. (1977). *Occupational Prestige in Comparative Perspective*. Academic Press, New York.

Tuijnman, A. (2001). Benchmarking adult literacy in North America: an international comparative study. Technical Report 89-572-XPE, Statistics Canada.

Ultee, C. W., Batenburg, R. and Ganzeboom, H. B. G. (1993). Cultural inequalities in cross-national perspective. A secondary analysis of survey data for the 1980s. In A. Rigney and D. Fokkema, editors, *Cultural participation. Trends since the Middle Ages*, number 31 in Utrecht Publications in General and Comparative Literature. John Benjamins Publishing Company, Amsterdam/Philadelphia.

Ultee, W., Arts, W. and Flap, H. (1992). *Sociologie: Vragen, Uitspraken, Bevindingen (Sociology: Questions, Propositions, Findings)*. Wolters-Noordhoff, Groningen.

United Nations (2005). *Human Development Report*. Oxford University Press, New York.

Upright, C. B. (2004). Social capital and cultural participation: spousal influences on attendance at arts events. *Poetics*, 32, 129–143.

US Department of Commerce, Bureau of the Census (2004). Current population survey, August 2002: Public participation in the arts supplement. Technical report, US Department of Commerce, Bureau of the Census, 2003. Ann Arbor, MI: Inter-University Consortium for Political and Social Research, Washington DC.

van Berkel, M. and de Graaf, N. D. (1995). Husband's and wife's culture participation and their levels of education: a case of male dominance? *Acta Sociologica*, 38, 131–149.

van de Werfhorst, H. G. and Kraaykamp, G. (2001). Four field-related educational resources and their impact on labor, consumption and sociopolitical orientation. *Sociology of Education*, 74(4), 296–317.

van der Heijden, P. G. M., de Falguerolles, A. and de Leeuw, J. (1989). A combined approach to contingency table analysis using correspondence analysis and log-linear analysis. *Journal of the Royal Statistical Society, Series C, Applied statistics*, 38(2), 249–292.

van der Meulen, R., Ruiter, S. and Ultee, W. (2005). 'Bowling apart'? Vier vragen over nederlandse sportclubs en omgang tussen arm en rijk. (Bowling apart? Four questions on Dutch sports clubs and the mixing of the poor and rich). *Mens en Maatschappij*, 80, 197–219.

van Eijck, K. (1997). The impact of family background and educational attainment on cultural consumption: a sibling analysis. *Poetics*, 25, 195–224.

van Eijck, K. (1999). Socialization, education, and lifestyle: how social mobility increases the cultural heterogeneity of status groups. *Poetics*, 26, 309–328.

van Eijck, K. (2001). Social differentiation in musical taste patterns. *Social Forces*, 79(3), 1163–1184.

van Eijck, K. and Knulst, W. (2005). No more need for snobbism: highbrow cultural participation in a taste democracy. *European Sociological Review*, 21(5), 513–528.

van Eijck, K. and Mommaas, H. (2004). Leisure, lifestyle, and the new middle class. *Leisure Sciences*, **26**, 373–392.

van Rees, K., Vermunt, J. and Verboord, M. (1999). Cultural classifications under discussion: latent class analysis of highbrow and lowbrow reading. *Poetics*, **26**, 349–365.

vander Stichele, A. and Laermans, R. (2006). Cultural participation in Flanders: testing the cultural omnivore thesis with population data. *Poetics*, **34**, 45–64.

Veblen, T. (1899/1994). *The Theory of the Leisure Class*. Macmillan, New York.

Warde, A. (1997). *Consumption, Food and Taste*. Sage, London.

Warde, A. and Tampubolon, G. (2002). Social capital, networks and leisure consumption. *Sociological Review*, **50**(2), 155–180.

Warde, A., Tomlinson, M. and McMeekin, A. (2000). Expanding tastes? Cultural omnivorousness and cultural change in the UK. The University of Manchester CRIC Discussion Paper No. 37.

Warner, W., Meeker, M., and Eells, K. (1949). *Social Class in America*. Science Research Associates, Chicago.

Weber, M. (1922/1968). *Economy and Society*. University of California Press, Berkeley and Los Angeles.

Weber, M. (1930/1985). *The Protestant Ethic and the Spirit of Capitalism*. Allen & Unwin, London.

Weber, M. (1946). *From Max Weber: Essays in Sociology*. Oxford University Press, New York.

Weeden, K. A. and Grusky, D. B. (2005). The case of a new class map. *American Journal of Sociology*, **111**(1), 141–212.

Weininger, E. B. (2005). Pierre Bourdieu on social class and symbolic violence. In E. O. Wright, editor, *Approaches to Class Analysis*, chapter 4, pages 116–165. Cambridge University Press, Cambridge.

Weinstein, J. (2005). *Chile quiere mas cultura. Definiciones de Politica Cultural (Chile wants more culture: Definitions of Cultural Policy)*. CNCA, Santiago.

Wesolowski, W. (1976). The notions of strata and class in socialist society. In B. L. Faber, editor, *The Social Structure of Eastern Europe*. Praeger Publishers, New York.

Wilensky, H. L. (1964). Mass society and mass culture: interdependence or independence? *American Sociological Review*, **29**(2), 173–197.

Wnuk-Lipinski, E. (1983). Patterns of leisure. In T. Kolosi and E. Wnuk-Lipinski, editors, *Equality and Inequality under Socialism: Poland and Hungary Compared*. Sage, London.

World Bank (2006). *World Development Indicators*. The World Bank, Washington D.C.

Wuggenig, U. (2007). Comment on Chan and Goldthorpe: pitfalls in testing Bourdieu's homology assumptions using mainstream social science methodology. *Poetics*, 35(4), 306–316.

Wynne, D. and O'Connor, J. (1998). Consumption and the postmodern city. *Urban Studies*, 35, 841–864.

Yang, C. (2006). Evaluating latent class analyses in qualitative phenotype identification. *Computational Statistics and Data Analysis*, 50, 1090–1104.

Index